telep
barc
T'
R
F
in
b

Le

IN A TIME OF WAR

Some nineteen German planes they say,
You had brought down before you died.
We called it a good death. Today
Can ghost or man be satisfied?

W.B. YEATS

JOHN DENNEHY

IN A TIME OF WAR

OF WAR

TIPPERARY 1914–1918

MERRION

First published in 2013 by Merrion
an imprint of Irish Academic Press

8 Chapel Lane
Sallins
Co. Kildare

© 2013 John Dennehy

British Library Cataloguing in Publication Data
An entry can be found on request
978-1-908928-20-7 (cloth)
978-1-908928-21-4 (paper)
978-1-908928-22-1 (e-book)

Library of Congress Cataloging in Publication Data
An entry can be found on request

Typeset by www.sinedesign.net

Printed in Ireland by SPRINT-print Ltd

Contents

Tables and Figures

List of Abbreviations

ASC	Army Service Corps
CCORI	Central Council for the Organization of Recruiting in Ireland
CR	Connaught Rangers
DORA	Defence of the Realm Act
DRI	Department of Recruiting in Ireland
INV	Irish National Volunteers
IPP	Irish Parliamentary Party
IRB	Irish Republican Brotherhood
IRC	Irish Recruiting Council
IV	Irish Volunteers
LGB	Local Government Board
RAMC	Royal Army Medical Corps
RDF	Reserve Defence Forces
RE	Royal Engineers
RFA	Royal Field Artillery
RGA	Royal Garrison Artillery
RIC	Royal Irish Constabulary
RIRegt	Royal Irish Regiment
RIR	Royal Irish Rifles
RM	Resident Magistrate
RMF	Royal Munster Fusiliers
UIL	United Irish League
VAD	Voluntary Aid Detachment
UDC	Urban District Council

Acknowledgements

This book began as a doctoral thesis under the supervision of Gabriel Doherty at University College Cork and would not have been completed without his advice, encouragement and support. Professor Dermot Keogh, Dr Andrew McCarthy, Dr David Ryan, Charlotte Holland and Geraldine McAllister all provided help at various stages and made the Department of History an enriching place to study.

The department also provided a part-McEnery scholarship and a postgraduate travel grant, which allowed me to undertake archive research and I'm very grateful for this. Fellow postgraduate students Liam O'Callaghan, Laurence Fenton, John Fitzgerald-Kelly and Richard McElligott, among others, provided invaluable companionship and debate.

Thanks also to the international education office for the chance to study at Washington College in the United States and to Professors Michael Harvey, Richard Striner and Richard Gillin at the college who all made my time there a stimulating one.

The staff of the following libraries, archives and councils were incredibly helpful in guiding me through the sometimes labyrinthine nature of primary source collections: the staff of UCC's Boole Library; the Public Record Office in Belfast; British National Archives, Kew; British Library; Royal Artillery Museum in Woolwich; Imperial War Museum; National Library of Ireland; National Archives, Dublin; South Tipperary County Council; North Tipperary County Council; St Mary's Church, Clonmel; Ken Bergin for access to the Bolton Library in Cashel; Clonmel Corporation; Templemore Town Council; staff at Mary Immaculate College, Limerick; and Tipperary County Museum.

I would also like to send a special note of thanks to Mary Guinan-Darmody and John O'Gorman (both of whom went far beyond the call of duty) at Tipperary Local Studies in Thurles. I would especially like to thank Elaine FitzPatrick of FitzPatrick Printers in Tipperary for kind permission to use several photos in her possession, including the jacket image.

Other thanks go to Des Marnane, Rita Larkin, Philip Lecane, Myles Dungan, Catriona Pennell, Timothy Moloney, Michael Ahern, Proinsias Ó Drisceoil, John Morrissey, Maureen Annetts at the Commonwealth War Graves Commission, R.J. Mickleson, Michael Pegum of the Irish War Memorials Project, Patrick Bracken, Gavin Sheridan, Mark McCarthy, Philippa Mansergh-Wallace, Simon O'Duffy, Quartermaster Mick Dolan, Walter O'Shea, Martyn Pring, Diarmuid Breathnach, Fred Daly, Patrick Leamy, Tony Butler and Dan MacCarthy.

At the *Irish Examiner*, I owe a great debt to my editor Tim Vaughan for granting me leave that provided vital writing-up time in 2009.

Many thanks must also go to Lisa Hyde of Irish Academic Press for taking a chance on the book.

My family have given me constant help and support over the last number of years. For everything, much more than thanks.

J.D. Cork - Dublin - Abu Dhabi, 2005 to 2013

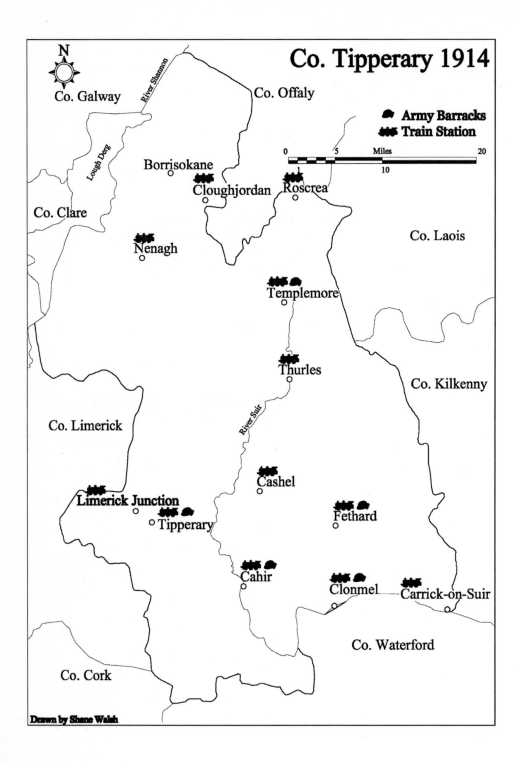

Co. Tipperary 1914

N

Co. Galway

River Shannon

Co. Offaly

🐖 Army Barracks
🚂 Train Station

0   5   Miles   20
              10

Lough Derg

Borrisokane

Cloughjordan

Roscrea

Co. Clare

Co. Laois

Nenagh

Templemore

Thurles

Co. Kilkenny

Co. Limerick

River Suir

Cashel

Limerick Junction

Tipperary

Fethard

Cahir

Clonmel

Carrick-on-Suir

Co. Waterford

Co. Cork

Drawn by Shane Walsh

x

INTRODUCTION

A SENIOR BRITISH official visited Tipperary in January 1916. Ivor Wimborne, the Lord Lieutenant, took in a coursing meeting at Kilsheelan, inspected a lace factory in Clonmel and met recruiting officials in the town to discuss the war effort. More than 3,500 people attended the coursing and the police reported that at one spot 130 cars passed by on the way to the grounds.[1] Wimborne was given a warm welcome and the Royal Irish Constabulary (RIC) reported that the vast majority of the people were loyal to the British Empire.[2] No Lord Lieutenant had visited in decades and Wimborne brought some of the pomp and glamour of the Empire to the area. This should have been the high point of the war effort in the locality, an expression of warmth and respect between both countries over the joint response to the conflict. But by this stage, the battle for hearts and minds had been lost.

The war, of course, was not expected to have lasted for so long — it should have been over by Christmas.[3] In local newspaper reports, however, one finds evidence for the view that this was going to be a long war. The editorial of the *Nenagh News* on 26 September 1914, for example, predicted a long, difficult conflict,[4] and Kitchener's belief that the war would last three years was widely circulated.[5]

This work explores the impact, both immediate and long term, of the First World War on Tipperary. The response to the outbreak of war is explored in Chapter One. This is intended to give an impression of what life was like on the ground and how politically, militarily, economically and socially, the county was deeply affected by the outbreak of the conflict. In particular, the claim that mobs of people were baying for German blood in a burst of 'war enthusiasm' is deconstructed.

In Chapter Two, I examine how nationalist leader John Redmond's call for recruits from the Irish Volunteers, 'wherever the firing line extends', was received in Tipperary. How active were Irish Party MPs in spreading this message? Did they believe in the policy? Was it successful? Trying to infer the motivations of anyone, especially soldiers, is fraught with difficulty, if not impossible. It is unlikely that one single factor proved decisive in the decision to enlist, and most recruitment decisions would have been the result of several different, and often competing, sources of motivation. The first recruiting meetings were held at this time – how successful were they and how did they set the tone for the campaigns to follow? This chapter also looks at the bias of the press in reporting the immediate impact of soldiers' letters, and how, from the outset, people were well aware of what was happening at the front.

The first attempt by the British government at a coherent recruiting campaign came in the shape of the Central Council for the Organization of Recruiting in Ireland (CCORI), which is the subject of Chapter Three. The CCORI was established to tap areas that had previously supplied few recruits. An important point to note here is that I do not wish to sympathize, empathize, criticize or identify with soldiers who enlisted. I have simply sought to set out the recruiting campaigns and examine why a person may have taken the decision to enlist. This chapter also explores two areas that were frequently mentioned on the recruiting platform: conscription and atrocity reports. The fear of conscription existed in Tipperary from the outset, as was noted in police and military reports. As the war went on, calls for the introduction of conscription increased in frequency and many speakers began to threaten the audience with compulsion if more men did not enlist. This, in turn, worked against the recruiters and was acknowledged by the recruiting bodies as doing so. Recruiters also frequently used reports of atrocities in their appeals and suggested that the Germans had scant regard for human rights. These reports featured prominently, and it is instructive to examine how often exaggerated atrocity reports stimulated recruitment and set the image of Germans as barbaric or somehow inhuman. This chapter also examines the influence of the Roman Catholic church on recruiting in the country.

Chapter Four carries this recruiting theme forward into the subsequent Department of Recruiting in Ireland, another body established in late 1915 by the government to spur recruitment. This coincided with a significant rise in the fear of conscription amongst people in the county. Irish Parliamentary Party (IPP) politicians were forced to deny the imminent coming of compulsory military service when recruiting officials made frequent threats regarding the coming of conscription on what they perceived as a recalcitrant population. Britain was at this time also moving away from the voluntary system to compulsion, which only intensified the concerns. This was a long war and there was a continual fear of being forced to enlist.

Chapter Five pulls back from the recruiting campaigns in Tipperary and examines the patterns and motivations of recruiting: how many joined, who and why. It is not enough just to ask how many enlisted in the forces, but it is also necessary to ask why these men took arguably 'irrational' decisions to enlist and how their social and economic make-up played a role, if any, in influencing them.

The devastation and killing of the First World War was reported from the start. People in Tipperary were not shielded from the casualties and unique brutality faced by soldiers and civilians. Father Michael Maher, a priest based in Thurles, kept a diary during these years and recorded his astonishment at how the authorities were able to secure recruits: 'It is really astonishing how many they are able to get considering the tales told by soldiers invalided home of hardships which the troops have to endure in the fighting line.'[6]

This was accentuated in Tipperary when, in 1916, the town was chosen as a depot for recuperating soldiers. Thousands of injured and disabled soldiers were based there recovering from their experiences at the front and that added to a sense of a unique wartime experience. This is something I examine further in Chapter Six, which is a thematic chapter on the home front and everyday life, and explores this sense of a community at war. As a local newspaper described: 'Ireland has never been ungrateful. She will not be unmindful now of the men who have come back to her stricken in their heroic efforts to keep her sacred shores inviolate and to save her women and children, her churches and her convents from the horrors that have desolated Belgium and Poland.'[7]

Soldiers also appeared in court on various charges ranging from abuse of alcohol to low-level violence. Many suffered from psychological problems and were unable to cope with civilian life after the trauma of the front. The expression 'my head is gone' was often used by soldiers in court cases at this time. Belgian refugees materialized in the towns of Tipperary and made the issue of Prussian militarism very real.[8] The war was not shielded from people and they were made aware of the bloody, brutal toll.

While men were moved to fight, women were mobilized to help them, playing a central role in fund-raising for charity organisations, training in first aid and sending 'comforts' to troops in the field. Women also became involved in the various soldiers' and sailors' help societies that sprang up, and their role was crucial, given the increase in social problems resulting from the new currents of 'separation allowance' that spread into the homes of servicemen. In addition, the First World War, as it did in every other European country, played a significant role in the emergence of women's freedoms in Ireland.[9]

For the combatant nations, the war developed into a bitter endurance test and here economic resources were of huge importance. The war brought economic gains to the county, which is the subject of Chapter Seven, and those gains were mainly felt by farmers who enjoyed significant price rises for their stock. This gave them a solid economic stake in the war and also a reason not to enlist,[10] much to the annoyance of the authorities who accused them of being content to 'live off the blood' of their neighbours. Given that land reform was mainly resolved in Ireland, their recruiting appeals focused on defending what farmers already had, or against potential German attack. On several occasions, farmers in Tipperary were warned that their lands were already mapped out in Berlin. The unskilled working class, however, did not fare as well, and their story remained one of grinding poverty. Food shortages and the failure of wages to keep up with price increases meant that for them the war would be a tough one.

The conflict did not lead to a suspension of politics. John Redmond banked on full participation in the war in return for passing Home Rule. While the bill was suspended, Redmond still believed that strategy was the correct one and the vast majority of the Volunteer movement backed him. This group, which later became the Irish National Volunteers (INV), then began a slow but steady decline and effectively ceased to exist past the 1916 Rising, while on the other hand, the militant minority Irish Volunteers (IV) that did not support Redmond in 1914 flourished. Redmond's own fate, and that of the IPP, was tied to this strategy. While the country pulled back from the brink of civil war, competing visions of Irish identity were played out through participation in conflict, and this is explored in Chapter Eight.

Germany's offensive on the Western Front restored mobility to the battlefield, something that had not been seen since the early days of 1914, and this, in turn, put huge pressure on British manpower — so much so that the government announced it was extending conscription to Ireland. The reaction and mass protests that followed are the subject of Chapter Nine. The county was gripped by the crisis, and protests were held in every town and village. This is a continuation of the conscription theme that runs throughout this account. The Conscription Crisis was so serious in 1918 because it confirmed the suspicions people had for so many years; it built on deep-rooted fears. The crisis resulted in a unified protest, with the Roman Catholic church joining the resistance effort, which gave a huge boost to Sinn Féin and laid the groundwork for the eventual Sinn Féin rout of the IPP in the December election, which arguably legitimized the Dáil Éireann declaration of independence the following January.

There has been a surge of interest in Ireland's role in the war over the past thirty years.[11] This started with the work during the 1980s and 1990s by Pat Callan, Martin Staunton and David Fitzpatrick.[12] This resurgence was not always without controversy. Professor George Boyce's 1993 article in *History Ireland* entitled 'Ireland and the First World War' drew a critical response from some quarters.[13] Keith Jeffery, writing in 2000, noted that enough had been done on Ireland and the war to 'look intelligently and with a more informed perspective than hitherto on the period'.[14] Almost ten years later, enough has certainly been done — helped by works such as John Horne's (Ed) *Our War: Ireland and the Great War* and Catriona Pennell's recent work on responses to the outbreak of the war[15] — to move First World War studies forward from acknowledging the previously neglected nature of this history to an interrogation of the war that is free of that context. This is something I attempt to do. I have tried to examine not only the political but also civilian responses to and experiences of the war. Military aspects are only mentioned when they impact in some way on the county. Other areas, like the fate of returning servicemen and commemoration of the war, both extremely rich topics for research, must remain outside the scope of this book, which focuses on the war years from 1914–1918. One important point to note is the use of newspapers as a primary source. Newspapers are an important source for any study on the period, particularly for a local one. While there is a heavy reliance on newspapers in parts, I have tried to balance this with use of police and military reports, private papers, council, local authority and religious primary sources.[16]

1 VISTA

Members of the Harris family, Tipperary 1914. An Anglo-Irish family, they had three sons serving and a daughter nursing overseas during the war. Tipperary People Publications.

THE EDITORIAL OF the *Nenagh News* on 2 January 1915 reviewed the events of the preceding year thus:

> The year 1914 which closed yesterday, will go down to history as the year in which the recognition of the rights of small nations was acknowledged as a duty by great states… From the Irish political point of view, the year 1914 will stand out as the time when the old feuds between this country and Great Britain were buried, and the struggle for Irish liberty which lasted over a century, ended in the triumph of the popular cause.[1]

The outbreak of war on 4 August 1914 made an editorial like this seem plausible. The conflict would bring huge changes to Tipperary and its soldiers would play a small, but notable, role. Clonmel was the regimental depot of the Royal Irish Regiment (RIRegt) and the Bachelors Walk shootings on 26 July, where three civilians were killed by British troops following the Howth gunrunning by Irish Volunteers, made a deep impression on this heavily garrisoned town — so much so that the Royal Field Artillery (RFA) were confined to their barracks for a number of days. Rumours also spread that the reserves of the RIRegt would not report, but these proved to be unfounded, and moderate nationalists were inclined to 'blame Redmond for not coming to some terms of settlement [over Home Rule] lately when he had the chance'.[2] Clonmel had a personal connection to the events at Bachelors Walk, as the father of Captain Hugh Cobden (of the King's Own Scottish Borderers, the regiment involved in the confrontation) resided in Raheen house. The police acknowledged strong feeling on the matter and arranged protection for Cobden.[3] Their fears, however, also proved unfounded.

Bachelors Walk reinvigorated the Volunteers, and local branches organized commemorative parades.[4] The funeral procession for the victims was about a mile long and watched by 200,000 people. This was filmed and screened at cinemas across Ireland.[5] Father Michael Maher, a priest at Thurles, gave this assessment: 'This event gave a great impetus to the National Volunteer Movement.[6] There was a noted increase in the attendance at our own drills in Thurles and I have reason to know that the same was the case in all parts of Ireland.'[7]

Most of the rank and file of the Volunteers had no weapons, and were limited to drilling with hurleys and forming fours. Those who did get their hands on some of the archaic models available noted their misfortune:

> I happened to be one of the half dozen Volunteers who were selected to carry these Russian rifles, and I felt very proud indeed when I was shouldering that rifle through the streets on the way to the railway station in Nenagh. By the time we reached there I had learned my lesson. I was lathered with sweat from the weight and clumsiness of the gun, and by pretending to a pal of mine that I was conferring a favour on him induced him to take the weapon from me. By the time we got back from Castleconnell

that night the company nearly lost all its Russian rifles for the want of Volunteers who were prepared to carry them.[8]

Funds were a persistent problem, and the money that was collected went to former British Army drill instructors. In the north of the county — Nenagh and Roscrea for example—the situation was not viewed with as much anxiety: 'The most energetic men are the ex-army and militia instructors who are making money by it. No really prominent men of means or standing are actively supporting the movement.'[9] The police also claimed 'little real interest is taken in politics'.[10]

THE DECLARATION OF WAR

As late as 31 July, Bachelors Walk had still not been overshadowed by events on the continent, but over the bank holiday weekend the tension was rising. On Sunday 2 August 1914, prayers for peace were made at most services across the county. The declaration of war was not unexpected in Tipperary,[11] and the postponement of the Clonmel horse show and horse races, at which Lord Carbery, Ireland's famous airman, was to have performed his feat of looping the loop, was the biggest inconvenience.[12]

Politically, the *Nationalist* considered John Redmond's call for the union of both Volunteer corps in the House of Commons on 3 August to be a masterstroke.[13] The paper's editorial of 5 August lauded Redmond, but made it clear that the Irish Volunteers would 'protect Ireland against invasion by Germany', thus enabling the regular troops to be deployed elsewhere'. The Chairman of the East Tipperary United Irish League asserted that the 'blood of many Irishmen had been shed in cementing and building the empire… knowing this they would stand against any foreign foe but would demand and demand in no uncertain voice that Ireland would get management of Irish affairs'.[14] The war deflected people's attention to personal concerns: 'Hundreds of people in and about Thurles whose sons, brothers, relatives, and friends are away at the front are, of course most anxious about them, and eagerly watch for the smallest bit of news.'[15]

The first troops left Clonmel on Wednesday 5 August by the 2p.m. and 3.45p.m. trains. They were local men (reservists, mostly Catholic) departing to their various regiments (the majority serving in Irish units) such as the RIRegt, Connaught Rangers (CR) and Royal Munster Fusiliers (RMF). Reserve men had already left Carrick-on-Suir (Carrick) and Cahir.

'Nothing at all approaching it has ever been witnessed by anyone living. The local newspaper offices have been constantly besieged by crowds anxiously asking for the latest details of the crisis and all day long the bulletins issued outside the *Nationalist* are scanned by hundreds.'[16]

On 5 August, a large number of reservists along with Colonel Kellet from Clonacody, Fethard, who had been appointed to Lord Kitchener's staff, left for the front.[17] At about 9:00p.m., 500 Irish Volunteers drilled at Clonmel station before a crowd of 1,500.[18] The train was already crowded with soldiers upon arrival at Clonmel, and as it steamed into the station fog signals were exploded and there was a great volley of cheers. The reserve men — many Irish Volunteers — repeatedly called for cheers for John Redmond, and cheers for the Irish Volunteers, calls which were 'lustily responded to'.[19] The Volunteers, under Commandant Frank Drohan, were then inspected by Kellet who 'with deep emotion' gave a short speech:[20]

> Men, this is indeed a fine sight, and it does my heart good to see you in such numbers and so well drilled here tonight. I must answer to the call of duty and go to the war [cheers]. I am going out foreign [*sic*] to take my place in the fight that is being waged against the enemy by these islands. I know that here at home you will do your duty, and I hope to do mine [cheers]. Thank God, the day has come when Northerns and Southerns in this country have joined hands. In a very little time all those silly dissensions and party feelings will have been forgotten. Thank God, today we stand for a United Nation [great cheering].[21]

Colonel Kellet then entered the train as the crowd sang 'A Nation Once Again', and a reservist shouted 'the first volley we fire will be a volley for Ireland'. As the train pulled out a 'thunderous roar of cheering went up' that, according to the *Nationalist,* sounded like a 'salvo of artillery for the men who had gone to war'.[22]

At 8:30p.m. the following evening, 330 men of the 2nd Battalion RIRegt marched from the regimental depot to the station escorted by 500 Volunteers, the People's Prize Band and a large crowd. At the station, the Volunteers formed single files near the platform creating an impromptu guard of honour. About 5,000 people were present. As the soldiers boarded the train, several exchanges took place:

> Numbers of the soldiers called for three cheers for John Redmond, to which there was a ringing response by the men on the train. This was followed by calls for cheers for the Volunteers, which were also heartily responded to. Both people and soldiers sang 'Let Me Like a Soldier Fall', 'It's a Long Way to Tipperary', and 'Auld Lang Syne' and as the voices rang out on the quiet night air one could not [but] be struck with the pathos of it all.[23]

So moved were the military authorities that they wrote to the secretary of the Clonmel Irish Volunteers: 'On behalf of the officers, non-commissioned officers, and men of the Royal Irish, I should like to express my sincere thanks to the Clonmel Volunteers for the splendid send-off they gave the party of reservists,' wrote Major Welch at the depot. 'The farewell given them will ever be treasured in the annals of the regiment'.[24] None of the RIRegt men would volunteer to remain in charge of the depot, as they were all 'anxious to go to the front'.[25] Further departures from Clonmel continued into the weekend, 600 drafts from the 3rd Battalion left for the North Wall in Dublin on Saturday, and 120 likewise on Sunday.[26] Father Maher recorded the events:

> I went to the station with them [the reservists] and gave them my blessing saying a few words of encouragement to them. I was the

only priest to do so in Thurles… The scenes at the station were heartrending. The wives, sisters, fathers, brothers and friends of the reserve men were there in force and gave expression to their grief, but the men were cool and faced the ordeal with manly self-restraint. A crowd of townspeople came to the station too and gave the fellows a hearty send-off. Many of us who were aware of the German forces felt that a good number of these young men would never come back or at least that they may return maimed for life. I was touched to the heart a few times when a young fellow after his confession would say "Give me your blessing Father, I'm going to the war."[27]

Similar scenes took place in Tipperary town, Thurles, Nenagh, Carrick, Cahir, and throughout the county.[28] Two thousand soldiers were encamped at the racecourse in Thurles controlling and guarding sections of the rail line. Public transport was effectively under military control and trainloads of soldiers were passing through many parts of the county. The outbreak of war controlled and dominated events. For example, the Royal Dublin Fusiliers passed through Thurles on 8 August heading towards Queenstown (Cobh); Thomas Connors, a Volunteer instructor who had been in charge of training the Thurles Corps, departed on 5 August, giving a speech at the station; and at Tipperary barracks, the Shropshire Light Infantry had dispatched their regimental colours to their depot at Shrewsbury and were preparing to leave.

Local government bodies were also affected: Carrick Urban District Council passed a resolution condemning the 'aggressively militant party in Germany in embroiling Europe in a terrible war' and the monthly meeting of Clonmel Corporation summoned for Thursday evening was cancelled as all the members were at the station seeing off the soldiers. The *Clonmel Chronicle* and the *Nationalist* published pages of war telegrams in each edition.[29] During a debate on the Bachelors Walk shootings among the Tipperary Guardians, it was stated that 'the soldiers have enough to do now besides shooting down women and children'.[30]

A more sinister development was the case of Gunner Larred, RFA. It was alleged that he had spread false reports of injuries received by men who were serving in the war and who had relatives in Clonmel. It was also believed that 'alarming reports entirely devoid of foundation have been circulated in Clonmel with regard to the fate of Irish regiments at the front'.[31] Larred was remanded for court martial as the military authorities were taking 'active measures to deal with parties who go about spreading false reports of fatalities and injuries to British troops'.[32]

The British troops were also leaving. On Friday 15 August, a thunderstorm swept through Tipperary, torrential rain, thunder and lightning persisted into the early hours of Saturday morning. During the storm, the 86th Battery RFA left Clonmel for Belgium. Howitzers, commandeered horses, officers and men left on three special trains. Despite the hour, and the weather, the people of Clonmel turned out 'in their thousands' to send them off.[33] The 86th was composed mainly of Englishmen, so the nature of the send-off was of some interest. Clonmel's townspeople clearly felt an affinity for the gunners: 'The scene on the platform all through the night and far into the morning was a remarkable one, soldiers and civilians fraternizing pleasantly, and joining together in snatches of song.'[34]

When a large group left at about 3:30a.m., in answer to the cheers that were reverberating around the station, Major Hardman, commanding the battery, 'stood at the salute at the carriage window' and the battery moved 'out in the dark of the morning, followed by the plaudits of a stranger people who had learned to like them'.[35] In Fethard, the 43rd Battery enjoyed a similar reception. The Volunteers paraded at 5a.m. and the town band played the troops to the station where two special trains sent them off. The 2nd Brigade RFA made their delayed exit from Cahir on 18 and 19 August. On the latter, St Mary's Brass and Reed Band 'headed a large number of soldiers on their way to the train station'.[36] There they played 'Let Erin Remember', 'A Nation Once Again' and 'Auld Land Syne' and about 1,000 people converged at the tracks. Each soldier was given something to eat and dispatched with a parcel of food—'the gift of a number of local ladies'. Eleven trains were required to convey the batteries from Cahir, and the station was guarded by the police under District Inspector (DI) Potter, and a large number of military.[37]

These reports convey some of the chaotic and vibrant nature of army mobilization. Coming so rapidly after the crisis over Home Rule, unionist officers were applauded and Irish soldiers in the Crown forces were given enthusiastic send-offs. The war had made its mark.

One interesting consequence of the outbreak was the commandeering of horses by the War Office, which lent a 'wholly new and novel aspect to the fair'.[38] Once mobilization orders were dispatched, most horse owners in the locality received government notices of the War Office's intention to commandeer animals. The fifth of August was fair day in Clonmel. The influx of traders, dealers and low-level merchants accentuated the tension and nervous excitement regarding the war. Business continued in the town despite the closure of the banks. A 'sensation' was caused when a number of artillerymen marched to the Thomas Murphy & Son brewery where twelve horses were taken.[39] Throughout the day, officers and detachments of men visited several establishments in the town, including W. Phelan and Sons, Messrs Cleeves, from where eleven horses were taken, and Clonmel Corporation. These animals were paraded outside their workplaces, and veterinary surgeons and military officers made selections. About 200 horses were taken by the authorities during that day.[40]

Private owners also had their animals requisitioned. Richard Burke (Master of the Tipperary Foxhounds) for example, was requested to supply fifteen hunters.[41] In Tipperary town, posters stated that the government was purchasing 11,000 horses in total. War Office buyers requisitioned a large number of animals at double what they might command in ordinary time.[42] The work was continued at Clonmel and Fethard — a veterinary surgeon and Sergeant Booth RIC commandeering horses in both towns. One hundred horses were taken in Fethard.

Friday and Saturday saw further 'extensive purchases of horses in Clonmel'.[43] In Nenagh, the town presented 'the appearance of a horse fair so numerous were the animals exhibited for sale to the government representatives'. The

RFA, however, believed that 'the class of horse arriving is considered very bad on the whole and unlikely to last any length of time on service'.[44] This commandeering not only affected businesses, but also the Volunteers. At a Fethard Volunteer tournament at the end of August, a small party of the Fethard Cavalry turned out under Instructor Higgins. They would have made a 'bigger show' but for the fact a great many horses in the district had been taken for 'army purposes'.[45] The commandeering continued for a time; 157 horses, for example, were purchased as remounts and stabled in Clonmel artillery barracks on 10 October.[46]

WAR ENTHUSIASM

A popular perception of August 1914 is of mobs of people baying for German blood, full of excitement for war.[47] This has been construed as 'war enthusiasm' as reportedly the onset of war was 'greeted with rapture' in Tipperary.[48] Were people across the county really excited and enthusiastic about the conflict? One basis for this claim has been through the send-offs given to local troops, particularly the RIRegt, in towns and villages. Cheering crowds saw those soldiers off and this was reinforced by John Redmond's offer in the House of Commons on 3 August to unite the Irish Volunteers and Ulster Volunteers in a home defence unit to guard against German invasion. This offer and the European developments had seen the prospect of civil war, which had hung over Ireland that summer, recede. These send-offs had also led unionist and nationalist, Catholic and Protestant, to express hopes for a new understanding in Irish politics, and a British general even reviewed Irish Volunteers at Clonmel rail station before leaving for the Western Front. This was a new dynamic and was replicated at rail stations in towns and villages across the country. It is not hard, therefore, to see why this had been construed as enthusiasm. But it is possible to dig a little deeper. Who were these reserves? Many were local lads. Some were married to local women, had children and lived in the community. They were part of the local fabric. Many at the station were the wives and children and relatives of these men and they knew there was a very good chance they would never see each other again.

The farewell afforded to the troops, therefore, should not be viewed as unique or as evidence of 'war enthusiasm'. Clonmel was a major garrison town, the depot of the RIRegt and a centre of military power for hundreds of years, and send-offs were nothing new. Two examples — from the Boer War in 1899, a conflict that was deeply unpopular in Ireland, and the Crimean War in 1855 — illustrate that these send-offs were not unique. And while the political situation had given them more resonance in August 1914, it did not represent enthusiasm for bloodshed. The Boer campaign was opposed by most Irish national parties, but politics were eschewed when it was a case of supporting the troops:

> Shortly before three o'clock the detachment of reservists with their arms and full equipment left the barracks, and proceeded to the railway station, headed by the band of the 4th Battalion, and followed by an immense crowd of townspeople of all classes, including the immediate friends and relatives of the men themselves. Amongst the airs played by the band were 'Soldiers of the Queen', 'Garryowen' etc… About a quarter past three, after the men were entrained, the train took its departure amidst waving of handkerchiefs and considerable cheering from the assembled crowd, in which the soldiers seemed full of enthusiasm, after they had taken farewell of their relatives and friends… The train moved off slowly, several fog signals being exploded in honour of the men leaving for the front.[49]

That could easily have come from a report in 1914, while the accounts from the Crimea are also quite similar:

> At ten minutes to four o'clock, p.m., the barrack gate, which had been closed during the day, was reopened, and the gallant 13th marched out amidst the vociferous cheering of the immense

concourse of people congregated outside to accompany them on their way to the train, and give them a farewell cheer when parting. The men seemed in the best possible spirits, and re-echoed the shouts of the assembled throng with a redoubled vigour, but amidst their enthusiastic plaudits might be heard the miserable heart-rending cries of the soldiers' wives as they bade farewell to their husbands who, in all probability, were about to be separated from them forever. With difficulty the poor creatures were dragged away from the afflicting scene... All the arrangements being complete, the engine whistled, and away went the train with its living cargo, amidst the loudest cheering of both soldiers and bystanders. So long as the train remained in sight, we could perceive several of the gallant fellows hanging out of the windows of the carriages, and cheering most lustily.[50]

The singular difference between 1914 and previous campaigns was the belief that Home Rule was within grasp. During these two weeks of August 1914, county volunteer instructors donned khaki, future IRA supremos were reviewed by British colonels, Crown force regulars were cheered, and Tipperary's garrison towns witnessed jubilant scenes of departure. Many of the soldiers were local men, and there is no doubt that the townspeople were excited and indeed emotional, given the reality that many soldiers might not return. But it could not be described as 'war enthusiasm'.

The newspapers of August 1914 are filled with exuberant reports on the Irish Volunteers and the shifting continental landscape. August 1914 was not, however, a unique or isolated occurrence. People were certainly interested, as is confirmed by the police:

The war is naturally the absorbing topic of interest in this Riding. A strong feeling of loyalty to the Crown has been espoused, with the exception of a few people (and those mostly ignorant) who have adopted the position of 'we have no quarrel with Germany'.

> This feeling of loyalty has been intensified by the atrocities
> perpetrated by the German army, specifically in the burning of
> Louvain and other towns and the assassination of women and
> children.[51]

The report illustrates the bias of the police, but it still provides a useful spotlight on public feeling at the time. The southern parts of the county were sketchier, as the police believed that the Volunteers desired to be armed and trained by the government: 'From some parts [of the region] come reports of genuine loyalty and readiness so to act. From other parts reports of dissatisfaction… but there is a growing lack of enthusiasm pending the government's decision and a suspicion is entertained that the government may intend that they should forego the HR [Home Rule] bill.'[52] In the garrison town of Templemore, a local priest described these opening weeks:

> The outbreak in August 1914 was full of local importance. The
> English regiment, stationed in the barracks, was ordered to the
> front, and the whole town was out to see them off. Our brass band
> led the march to the railway station playing all the sentimental
> tunes it knew. The people were on the side of the soldiers. They
> had little time for Germany and did not know much about it.
> Vaguely, it was the place where toys were made. Somewhere out
> there it had loomed across the border of Belgium and its shadow
> was falling as far as Karrigeen.[53]

But the dizzying effects of August 1914 had obscured the nuances that divided nationalists and unionists.[54] These would become more pronounced as the war developed. There is some truth to Colonel Maurice Moore's opinion that if the war had lasted six months then Redmond's policy might have indeed paid off.[55]

IMMEDIATE EFFECT ON THE ECONOMY

A ruptured economic fabric in the county was an immediate consequence of the outbreak of war.[56] On 9 August, the parish priest of St Peter and Paul's church in Clonmel said at mass:

> Our brave men have gone abroad to do their duty… but we here at home have other duties… There is the duty of defending our own country, and that will be done by our own grand Volunteers. There is the duty of the merchant and the trader — not in a sordid and selfish way to be trying to make immense profits out of the terrible crisis.[57]

Likewise in Thurles, Father Maher painted a stark picture of life for those the reservists had left behind: 'In many poor families the main support of the family — the father or one of the sons — was gone, perhaps never to return… their main supports were gone, and to add to their misery the price of food was raised on them. The result would be that they and their little children would go hungry.'[58]

Father Maher went on to echo his colleague's call for retailers to refrain from raising prices of goods, and in Nenagh, Reverend Gunning appealed to the shopkeepers and others 'not to raise unduly the prices of provisions as there was no necessity for so doing. It would inflict a hardship on the poor.'[59] Rising costs were an increasing concern, as it was widely believed that such action was undertaken for profit.[60] Local officials criticized traders for increasing prices. During a discussion at Clonmel Corporation, Councillor O'Connell said the 'merchants in Clonmel are far worse than the Germans to raise the price of foodstuffs without any necessity'. Councillor Farrell said 'butter, eggs, potatoes and bacon were raised in price and he could not understand this in the face of the statements made by ministers of the Crown and the department that there was a plentiful supply in the country'.[61] Retailers in Thurles were accused of keeping supplies of sugar in stock, but trebling the price once they got the chance. Certain creameries increased the price of butter: 'that the price of a native product like butter should be raised 4.5*d* per lb in a few days seems extraordinary'.[62]

At Clonmel Asylum, three contractors wrote informing the committee that they could no longer supply bread, butter and sugar at the contract price.[63] Harriet Bagwell,[64] in a letter to the *Clonmel Chronicle*, announced the intention of reopening the Shamrock Rooms (a quasi soup kitchen) because of the distress owing to the war. She pointed out that as a result of the sharp increase in prices, it will be 'impossible to carry on the work without help, not only from those who have given in the past, but from others'.[65] Sugar was now selling at 6*d* per lb, butter had gone up to 1*s* 6*d* per lb, bacon was up 1*d* per lb in Clonmel. Flour had risen 4*d* per stone and a 4 lb loaf had risen one penny. Indian meal had gone to £1 4*s* per sack and coal had been increased by 3*s* 6*d* a ton.[66]

On 12 August prices had stabilized. Butter had reduced 1*d* per lb and sugar 1*d* per lb while coal was unchanged. A retailer on Clonmel's Gladstone Street wrote to one of the local papers to answer some of the criticisms:

> As some misapprehension appears to exist in reference to the prices charged for groceries in Clonmel since the outbreak of the war, I wish to state that I have been only charging normal prices for the goods I had in stock at the outbreak of hostilities and will continue to do so as long as these goods last. It is only in the case of goods which were purchased at increased rates that the prices have been advanced.[67]

This is borne out by the mayor of Clonmel, Thomas Fitzgibbon, also a retailer, who confirmed that when he had tried to buy sugar the price quoted was '51*s* 3*d* per cwt, so you will see that when it is delivered in Clonmel it could not be sold for less than 61. The stores are full of sugar but we cannot get it from them.'[68]

At the asylum, Alderman Peters said that traders in Clonmel did not raise the prices as they had 'already been raised on them by those from whom they purchased'.[69] In addition, some firms took the initiative in sating the taste for profiteering. The Going and Smith firm in Cahir, for example, announced that they would supply heads of families in their employment with flour at 1s 6d per stone while the war lasted.[70] Also, the Murphy Brewery in Clonmel issued a supply of sugar to their workers at 3d per lb.[71]

Similar concerns were expressed in the north of the county. Nenagh Town Council called a special meeting where the clerk stated that wholesale traders had caused the increase and not retailers. Sugar, which was selling at 18s before the war, was now trading at 45s per cwt or 5s 7.5d per stone by 8 August.

Of course all were aware that since the outbreak of war no sugar came from Austria or Germany — the two large producing centres. Yet some of the big wholesale houses had a very large stock in hand, and were taking advantage of the war to put up the price. A certain gentleman near Newport, who offered to take charge of the National Volunteers, was charging 6s per stone for sugar. Still, that same gentleman considered himself a patriot.[72]

The clerk outlined that everything from potted meats to cornflour had increased from 10 per cent to 20 per cent and that everyone could acknowledge it was the retail trader and consumer that suffered. The wholesalers were making '200 per cent profit', while other council members expressed their surprise that milk and butter had risen, especially butter, which was now on a par with London prices.[73] In November, a meeting was held to protest against increases in the price of milk: 'Fellow townsmen, we are here tonight when the whole empire is at war, at which our sons, brothers and even our very sisters are fighting for their country. It is not a time at which heavy money should be levied on the people and poor of the town.'[74]

The instability continued into late autumn. The Local Government Board (LGB) informed the Clogheen Guardians that they could not agree to price increases for their contractors as 'prices fluctuate from day to day'.[75] The Carrick Guardians saw the tender for sugar shoot from 16s per cwt to 36s per cwt.[76] The Clonmel Asylum board criticized buyers for raising prices and the government for doing nothing. The *Clonmel Chronicle* published an article warning of the possibility of a German blockade, and urged farmers to put 'as much as may be possible of their land under tillage immediately' as food could rise to 'famine prices'.[77] Carrick Urban District Council struck a dissonant note, however, when they widely agreed that no distress existed in the town, and there was 'more employment and more of a circulation of money than before the war'.[78]

The Charles J. Kickham branch of the Irish National Foresters criticized the 'houselords of Clonmel' who had raised the rent from 2s 6d to 3s per week, at a time when 'trade and labour are at their lowest ebb… times when the purchasing power of £1 is only worth 14s'. The Foresters believed that the most affected were the 'fathers and mothers, the grandfathers and grandmothers of the brave boys who were defending this country from invasion'.[79] In opposition to Carrick Urban District Council, they held that 'very little money was in circulation' and the 'necessities of life were costing abnormal prices'.[80]

Economic unrest was endemic during the autumn and winter of 1914, particularly among publicans. They also were forced to deal with an influx of soldiers into a number of local towns. Tipperary publicans met in Tipperary town on 26 November. They discussed the new taxes on beer, and organized a local vintners association as they were like a 'flock of sheep without a shepherd… bearing every loss'.[81] In December they held a series of meetings to protest against the taxes on alcohol imposed, as they viewed it, by an overly vindictive chancellor of the exchequer.[82] Prices of beer and stout rose 1d per pint and bottle. A rumour swept Murphy's brewery in Clonmel that fifty employees were to be laid off because of this new duty.[83] This was later denied.

At a meeting in Clonmel's Town Hall the brewery's employees called on the people of Clonmel to choose Murphy's over Guinness in order to boost its sales, and ensure its survival in these 'serious times'.[84]

In Tipperary town, vintners were also anxious about the early closing order resulting from the presence of so many military. They agreed to send a deputation to the barracks, as they believed they could guarantee no soldiers would be supplied if they were allowed an extension to 9:00p.m.[85] About 1,500 troops were based in Tipperary training for the front. The police there were forced to increase their presence by one sergeant and six men as they believed that a 'great deal of drunkenness prevailed'.[86] The following month there was a decrease, but drunkenness still existed to an 'undesirable extent'.

In Templemore, the police went to court in order to ensure publicans ceased trading at 8p.m as there were 2,000 prisoners and military in the town, and, according to District Inspector Wilson, the increase in drunkenness and disorderly conduct had been tangible.[87] With similar restrictions in place in all of the garrison towns in Tipperary, infractions were a certainty. Moloney's in Tipperary town, for example, was fined 10s for serving men after 8:00p.m.[88]

IMPROVED ECONOMIC PROSPECTS

Despite the reports of a severe hit to the local economy, business was good at Clonmel fair in November. Prices increased for three-year-old bullocks from 10s to 20s per head, and only a 'very small proportion' of the animals brought to market remained unsold. Exporters faced difficulties in transporting cattle across the channel: 'Brisk as business was, it would have been more so were it not for the dislocation in shipping arrangements caused by the war'.[89] At Fethard, there was also a significantly higher level of activity as the number of rail waggons 'laden with cattle leaving Fethard today was largely in excess of the number at the corresponding fair twelve months ago'.[90]

In Ardfinnan the large woollen mills were working at full tilt — they had secured a government contract to make khaki serge for military uniforms. These mills at Ardfinnan were held as a shining light: 'The Ardfinnan woollen mills have had to refuse another big War Office contract, as their resources are taxed to the utmost, and it will take them a long time to work off the orders on hands'.[91] A *Nationalist* editorial called for investment in boot making and leather-based goods seeing as Clonmel 'is the centre of the biggest cattle district in the country'. Such investment, it was believed, would push more financially lucrative war contracts Tipperary's way. [92]

The market fluctuated wildly in August and September and there were condemnations of alleged profiteering. Some local councillors said that when Irish soldiers were fighting in Europe it would be immoral to raise prices. Police reports did acknowledge that labourers found the price of fuel and food costly. However, police reports in October also acknowledged that 'no distress exists and employment is plentiful, wages showing a tendency to rise'. In November, they felt farmers were benefiting greatly from the war as 'farmers are prosperous and work is fairly procurable' while 'prices for agricultural produce are good but the supply is scarce'.[93]

The instability that existed in the opening months was inevitable. Some were hit harder than others such as closure restrictions on publicans and horse owners who had their animals requisitioned. But also inevitable would be an increase in the prices paid to farmers and an increase in government contracts to companies like Ardfinnan woollen mills. In general, the war cannot have been said to have brought any great hardship in these months. On the contrary, it seemed that the county was showing signs of economic growth.

CHARITY AND COMFORT DRIVES

The outbreak of the First World War opened up a vista of bazaars, collections and fêtes. The local gentry figured prominently in these campaigns, chairing meetings, establishing committees and organizing charity events. Comfort societies and civil aid organizations such as the National Relief Fund, Soldiers Families Relief Fund, Soldiers and Sailors Help Society and the St John's Ambulance Association were established.[94] These efforts sought to create a quasi home front, alleviate financial problems among soldiers' dependents, mail parcels to soldiers in the field (aimed mainly at the local RIRegt), and also to train local people — particularly women — in the basics of first aid. Advertisements appeared in all of the local papers requesting help and donations.[95]

At a meeting called by the mayor of Clonmel to establish a branch of the St John's Ambulance Association, a Dr Blackeney said there was a possibility that wounded soldiers from the British and German armies might be sent to Clonmel. 'German prisoners of war might also be sent and he was sure that if there were any sick or wounded amongst these prisoners the members of the association would do all that was necessary for them.' The chairman, Richard Bagwell, agreed, replying to applause that 'if I know anything of Great Britain or Ireland, I know this, that wounded German prisoners will be treated as well as our own'.[96] The lineage of the provisional committee — the Hon. Mrs de la Poer elected as Chair and Lady Emily Humphreys as Vice-President — is a typical example of such a society's organizational make-up.[97]

A typical example of how the gentry dominated the organizational make-up of these societies can be found at a meeting of the Clonmel Soldiers and Sailors Families Association on 11 August. The president, Mrs Church, pointed out that she was sorry to know that 'already some of the soldiers' wives in Clonmel were feeling the pinch. The men's pay was some ten days in arrears, and Mrs Welsh and Colonel Cooke were doing all they possibly could to tide the women along'. Mrs Welsh said that those who called to her for assistance were the wives of the 'poorest' of the reservists. She was also 'proud' to say of the RIRegt that the women who could at all pull along by 'getting credits in the shops or otherwise were not applying for, and would not accept assistance'. She added that she had already paid '£2 to the very poor people' and it would take 'about £5 a week to keep such going until the men's back pay came from Cork'.

A Reverend Patten amplified this concern as a 'great many men' had gone to the front from the rural portion of the country, whose families were 'unprovided for'. He said 'two reservists had left Fethard leaving behind them their wives and ten children without a penny coming into their houses'.

Informing the committee that the war might 'last months', Reverend W.H. Smith advised 'caution in the distribution of the funds', while the press were notified that the soldiers' pay was in arrears as it would show them (shop owners and traders) that they ran 'no risk in giving the women credit'. Mrs Welsh said that she was very glad to be able to say that the traders of Clonmel were 'standing by the women in this respect'.[98]

By 3 October, Lady Emily Humphreys was collecting for the 12th Brigade RFA, of which her husband was commander.[99] Similar appeals were made for the 43rd Battery RFA that had been based in Fethard.[100] Harriet Bagwell and Mrs Kellet of Marlfield and Clonacody respectively canvassed for the 2nd Battalion RIRegt.[101] Socks, tobacco, bootlaces, vests, towels and chocolate were requested. The people of Guernsey mailed a cheque for £25 to Mrs Kellet — the battalion (RIRegt) was stationed there from 1910 to 1913 — after seeing the appeal in their local papers. 'It is terrible to think how they have suffered. The regiment was so popular here, and the tradespeople were so fond of them all.'[102]

These appeals continued in the run up to Christmas. In November, an appeal was made to the 'friends' of the 43rd Battery RFA, recently stationed at Fethard, for tobacco. Major St Leger, commanding 2nd Battalion RIRegt, wrote to Colonel Kellet's wife in Clonacody thanking her for parcels already sent and asking for under-drawers, capes and socks. In Cahir, comfort drives for the 2nd Brigade RFA were started.

Not just for those at the front, Miss Clarkson of the Soldiers Home, Clonmel, appealed for cakes, mince pies, tea and money for the soldiers at home wounded or on leave on Christmas day. Mrs Hardy at the rectory in Cashel was receiving subscriptions for the Indian troop fund,[103] and on 21 December, Clonmel's 'share' of the cargo of the American Santa Claus ship arrived at the town hall, consisting of gifts from 'beyond the Atlantic for the children of wounded soldiers'. These gifts were believed to bring 'joy and excitement' into thousands of 'humble' homes in Ireland, of which many are 'bereaved and darkened by the toll of war'.[104]

Lady Dunalley was appointed secretary of the Tipperary branch of Queen Mary's 'Work for Women' Fund.[105] This sought to provide employment for women who found themselves out of work on account of the war. Alice Fitzgibbon (the daughter of Clonmel's Mayor) had joined, and had 'already received a fair amount of subscriptions'. On 9 December, the Carroll's of Rocklow organized a sale of work in aid of the Soldiers and Sailors Families Association and the Belgian refugees. Many of the items on sale were made by the wives of 43rd Battery RFA, residents of Fethard, and women in Dublin and London who had been 'thrown out of work' owing to the war.[106]

A letter in the *Irish Times* stating that something should be done for the soldiers prompted an immediate response from Harriet Bagwell of Marlfield. She appealed for help in establishing surplus entertainment rooms for the newly arrived men of the Army Service Corps (ASC) — about 600 in total. Also requested were goods and material to furnish recreation rooms.[107]

The comfort drive continued into Christmas. Letters were a continual presence in the papers requesting donations for toys, food and money for the numerous soldiers' homes, and charity for the RIRegt and other prisoners of war in Germany.[108] A practical relief scheme was devised by Mrs Dease (wife of Major Dease, a local resident magistrate) who had shirts made for the army by women of the town who had suffered most from 'want of employment through the war'.[109]

On 13 August, 1914, a branch of the Nenagh Red Cross Society was established. Lady Dunalley presided over the meeting. 'Their soldiers were at present out fighting for the nation, and all present, she was sure, were ready to do their share so far as providing clothes and other necessary articles and hospital requisites for the wounded.'[110]

A Voluntary Aid Detachment was also provisionally established. In a letter to the *Nenagh News* on 3 October, they had sent '75 flannel shirts, 20 bed jackets, 200 pairs of socks and 10 "helpless case" shirts'. Male and female first aid classes had also been organized.[111]

In conjunction with these efforts, the Nenagh distress society dealt with some of the problems the war had brought. They believed that the government warning to retailers over profiteering had 'done all the good in the world'. Concerns regarding the wives of soldiers and alcohol were also raised. It was mooted that lists from all societies offering help (including the LGB) be sent to the distress society to ensure that there would be no repeat or double payments, thus preventing abuse of the system or fraud. Re-employment schemes were considered for people out of work. Mrs Dease believed, however, that there was 'a great call for men for the front, and I think we should not encourage giving employment'. The idea of a labour bureau was also put forward, and if those who applied for assistance turned down work, then no assistance would be given. One justice of the peace at the meeting said that he had 'refused to sign papers in connection with the soldiers and sailors societies on the grounds that the parties could get work'.[112]

In November, the Nenagh Relief Committee outlined that the War Office would 'support any allotment made by a soldier to his father, mother or other relation by an additional sum equal to twice the soldier's weekly contribution'.[113] This was graded and tied to the soldier's contribution, but the War Office pointed out that a soldier could not be forced to make these payments. In December, the committee received five boxes of cheese, sent as a gift to Nenagh from the 'people of Quebec'. Clothing sent by children in America to the 'children of Irish soldiers serving with their regiments' was also received. The committee felt that children of killed or wounded soldiers should have first priority.[114] But Dan Breen, IRA guerrilla supremo-in-the-making, saw it thus: 'The landed gentry, the well-to-do merchants and most of the 'strong' farmers supported the drives that were organized to provide comforts for British soldiers. We did our best to frustrate such activities'.[115]

These comfort drives have much been located within the 'war enthusiasm' argument. It was not unlikely that such initiatives would spring up, coalescing as they did around Tipperary's garrison towns. Aside from the Belgian Refugee collections, the aid societies for regular soldiers were already established and those that benefitted tended to be the wives of reservists. The regular soldiers of the reserve that had been seen off in August were local boys. And the emotional context of their departure guaranteed that interest in their welfare would be maintained, at least initially. Certainly, the scale of the comfort drives was more comprehensive then hitherto. But those involved—whether organizer or recipient—usually came from the top or bottom of the social strata.[116]

BELGIAN REFUGEES

Another more targeted comfort drive was for Belgian refugees who had fled in the face of the German advance. On 28 October, a public meeting was held in Nenagh regarding the Belgian refugees. The Bishop of Killaloe and a number of lesser clergy, the County Surveyor, Lord Dunalley, and county and local officials wrote letters in absentia but affirming their support.[117] Another subscription list was passed and the 'barbarous' Germans were condemned while horror was expressed that Belgian 'homes had been demolished and their women and children outraged'.[118]

Led by the gentry, the Belgian refugee meetings provided a tidy platform for anti-German propaganda stories. The *Nenagh News* was satisfied that the people of north Tipperary would take on the 'burden of maintaining them [Belgian Refugees], of assuaging their sufferings, and making their stay as pleasant as possible' until the 'allied armies have driven the barbarian invader from their territories'.[119]

Parallels were drawn to the Catholicism of both countries and the debt that Ireland owed to Belgium for their accommodation of Irish priests at Louvain. At a Nenagh Relief Committee meeting, the military agreed that the local barracks could be used to accommodate Belgians. A further twenty-five refugees were requested, added to the twelve already invited. Concerts were held at Borrisokane and Roscrea; allied flags and bunting were flown and the Belgian national anthem was sung.[120]

The Belgian refugee drives owed a debt to the press that faithfully reported these German atrocity stories.[121] A letter to the *Nenagh Guardian*'s editor sought to confirm the stories, saying that authorities in Britain had Belgian girls that 'had their eyes put out', one had 'half her tongue cut off' and that they only had maimed children there.[122] At Roscrea council, some reports of the Belgian atrocity stories were doubted with several council members expressing disbelief that Germans or 'civilized' people could be guilty of cutting off the hands and legs of Belgian children to prevent them from seeing service.[123]

Robert Brownlow, a trooper with a cavalry regiment, the South Irish Horse, wrote letters that represent a typical illustration of what was being published. Brownlow had been a correspondent with the *Nenagh Guardian* prior to the war, and each of his letters was reported in the paper: 'The stories of the refugees are something awful — too awful to be described in words, or at least my vocabulary is not extensive enough to attempt it. I will leave it to your own imagination. All I can say is that the German is a barbarian to the very core.'[124]

In a second letter:

> Dear father, you talk about your blood boiling when you read
> about the cruelty of the Germans, but if you saw the sights that
> are to be witnessed here… I saw one middle-aged man wheeling
> his bed-ridden mother on a wheelbarrow… Another was three
> very old women, cripples and three children being drawn in a
> small truck by a couple of dogs.[125]

On 12 December, the *Nenagh Guardian* published Brownlow's final letter as
he had been killed in action. Brownlow thought enlistments would be easily
secured if people in Tipperary could see what was happening in Belgium: 'I
think if only all the young men at home were only to see what Belgium has
suffered by this war they would immediately enlist so as to prevent Ireland
from suffering a similar fate if it were invaded.'[126] And he again reinforced
what he saw as the horror of the refugee situation in Belgium:

> I was very glad to see by the dear old 'Guardian' [*Nenagh Guardian*]
> that Nenagh was putting up a good number of refugees. I believe
> if the inhabitants of the town actually saw the sufferings of these
> unfortunate people they would willingly put up a whole Belgian
> family each. What the poor people are suffering is undescribable.
> I have seen orphanages turned out on the roads and the poor
> children trudging along on the cold and wet under the charge of
> nuns. The German spares no one in order to get his own ends.[127]

When refugees arrived in Nenagh, in spite of all sentiments, it was felt that
Belgians should not displace local labour or take local jobs.[128] It was mooted
that several of the uninhabited 'castles, mansions and other buildings' could
be used instead of the workhouse, and the land on these houses could be
used by the Belgians 'without interfering in any way with local labour'. In
Clonmel, the workhouse was opened (despite objections that it was socially

and symbolically unacceptable) to the refugees should it be required.[129] The *Nenagh News'* editorial was clear: 'So far as possible we should facilitate the Belgians to engage upon work for which they are adapted. We do not mean that they should be brought into factories or business houses to displace Irish workers, but that they should be employed in some independent enterprise.'[130]

SOCIETY AND SPORT

Some unfortunate consequences accompanied the maelstrom that characterized those opening months. In the courts, cases regarding theft of military clothing, illegal drinking, and instances of low-level abuse towards uniformed servicemen were common.[131] Sports were also affected but serious displacement was felt only in areas that had been patronized by British officers, and those connected with the Crown. The problems faced by the Tipperary Hounds in November 1914 represent a typical illustration of this. Based in Fethard — a village with a minor but substantial garrison — the opening meet of the hounds' season was vastly down on its attendances. Many of those who usually rode had gone to the front, and the melodramatic newspaper report that a 'heavy and unpleasant fog hung over the countryside, symbolizing the war cloud' added further gravitas to their difficulties. The departure of the military in August had also greatly depreciated the visual grandeur of the ceremony: 'Now the barrack is empty, and on Tuesday the large entrance which usually furnished a setting for a brilliant and light hearted company was closed, and the whole place was cheerless.'[132] The organizers of the hunt had debated about whether to go ahead with the programme, but ultimately it was decided to press on as unemployment would result from its abandonment.

The prolonged absence of the military also accelerated the demise of cricket as a popular sport in Tipperary. From 1900, the game had been retreating from the countryside to the garrison towns, but the war proved a powerful cementing factor in this.[133]

Another social consequence of the war, extensively covered in the media, was the issue of separation allowances.[134] Separation payments sent currents of money through the homes of soldiers in Tipperary. A fiscal remuneration was vital for dependents and families of Irish servicemen. But some were unable to cope with such substantial increases. A case in Thurles heard how one woman 'cruelly neglected her five children' aged between eight and a half years and two months, despite the fact that she had received in a month an allowance of £6 19s. 10d. Her husband, a RIRegt soldier, had been based in Kilworth, County Cork, since August 1914. The National Society for the Prevention of Cruelty to Children (NSPCC) inspector visited her house on 17 September and found her drunk and her children in an 'indescribable state of dirt, and were almost naked. There was no furniture in the house, and the family bed consisted of a wisp of soaked dirty straw.'[135] The children were sent to the workhouse, and she was sentenced to three months' imprisonment. Murray Hornibrooke, Resident Magistrate (RM), said it was a 'shockingly bad case'. [136]

More abuses of the separation allowance system were detailed at Thurles Petty Sessions when two women — wives of soldiers — were censured for neglecting their children and keeping them from school. The school attendance officer pointedly explained that there were some cases where women were getting substantial allowances but the children were badly treated, and sometimes in rags.[137] In cases such as these, the magistrates had power to compel parents to bring their children before the courts so prosecutions by the NSPCC could be initiated. In Carrick, a woman with five sons at the front was sentenced to three months' imprisonment for repeated drunk and disorderly offences.[138] In Clonmel, however, charges were dropped against a woman who was 'riotous', as her son had recently died of wounds in Germany.[139]

By 12 December, about 300 separation allowances were being paid in Clonmel weekly.[140] There were exceptions to this of course, and many cases highlighted genuine experiences of hardship and underlined the British government's sometimes casual regard for the welfare of dependents. A widowed woman in Clogheen with five sons in the army (three of whom in hospital) had not received any separation allowance by mid-November.[141]

CONCLUSION

In garrison towns, the movement of troops was nothing new and, as has been illustrated in the examples from the Boer and Crimea, send-offs to local reservists were nothing truly unusual. The departures and speeches of August certainly had an edge, but it was not unprecedented.

Socially, the war had resulted in unfortunate cases of theft and alcohol abuse in the courts, and had put some sporting events in the county on hold. Economically, there had been market fluctuations and uncertainties — not unusual for the outbreak of a major conflict — but by November and December, these uncertainties had evened out, prices were starting to rise and sections of the local economy were starting to do well. Politically, there had been a positive response to the war, with police reporting most of the population, if not fanatically for Britain, then at least on the side of the Allies and against Germany. The Volunteers supported the reservists leaving for the front. Now the county would wait for John Redmond's next move regarding Home Rule, the Volunteers, and his position regarding recruitment and the British Army. It is to this that we now turn.

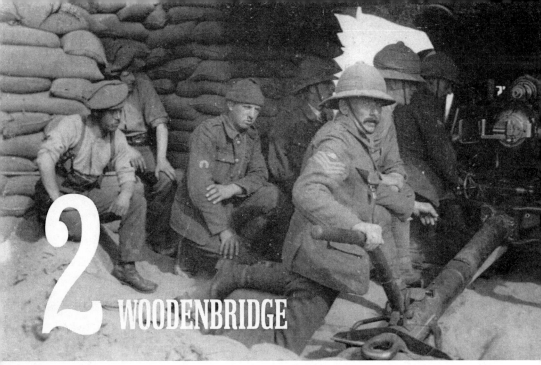

2 WOODENBRIDGE

Bleu Harris, a member of an Anglo-Irish Tipperary family, serving in Egypt during the war. Tipperary People Publications.

YOU ARE NOT doing your work for your country standing there with your hands in your pockets and your pipe in your mouth... There are some hundreds of fine strong able men of military age in this crowd and out of their number at least fifty ought to come forward and volunteer right away.[1]

On 3 August 1914, John Redmond made a dramatic intervention in the House of Commons, declaring that the British could withdraw their forces from Ireland as the Volunteers would defend Irish shores from foreign invasion with the Ulster Volunteers. British Foreign Secretary Edward Grey described this apparent truce in Ireland as the one 'bright spot' in the situation.[2] Troops for home defence needed equipment and training, however, and the Volunteers had neither in the quantities or quality needed.

The Irish Volunteers were not a conventional army, but a largely unarmed citizen militia. In Tipperary, the RIC considered that a large number of them were lukewarm and many had joined 'without knowing what it is for'.[3] The police felt that most had hoped for a political settlement to the Home Rule crisis, but 'certain local leaders who were interested in the movement' were 'much perturbed' by Redmond seizing control.[4] They also believed that southern parts of the county would take on a 'critical and dangerous' aspect if the situation in the north deteriorated. As William Langhorne, Tipperary County Inspector of the RIC, said: 'There are those who see ulterior objects and my own opinion is that there will eventually be a struggle to capture the tail'.[5]

The local press lauded Redmond for his speech. The offer was seen as a sincere gesture to reach out that was made in the hope that the crisis would lead to a new understanding between unionism and nationalism. Initially, there was a positive response from Protestant and gentry figures. Colonel R.J. Cooke, Kiltinane Castle, Fethard, for example, noted his appreciation of Redmond's pronouncement: 'I am at present called up for duty with the regular forces, so cannot enroll [sic] myself in the National Volunteers, as I would otherwise have done, but will co-operate with them in every way I possibly can.'[6]

Captain R.M. Minchin joined in Cloughjordan, becoming a County Inspector and Colonel H.S. Massy of Grantstown Hall, Kilfeacle, wrote to Redmond citing his military record and stating 'I might perhaps be useful to you',[7] as did Colonel Wyndham-Quinn.[8] Villiers Morton Jackson, a retired lieutenant colonel, handed them £50 'for the defence of Ireland' and offered them use of Clonmel racecourse for training.[9] Lord Donoughmore, Knocklofty, wrote to the Clonmel president of the Irish Volunteers explaining that he could not give active help owing to his work in parliament, but he enclosed a cheque for £50: 'I welcome, with profound thankfulness, Mr John Redmond's recent speech in the House of Commons, which has united all Irishmen in assisting to do whatever they can on behalf of their country in the present crisis.'[10] Donoughmore, who became president of the Irish National Volunteers in Clonmel, rejected pressure from the southern unionist agitation body, the Irish Unionist Alliance (IUA), to refrain from involvement with the

Volunteers: 'In the crisis, the whole of our Imperial existence is at stake. The National Volunteers have offered to take their part; I have already subscribed to them; I intend to assist them in every way in my power'.[11]

After 4 August, Redmond and John Dillon spoke at the United Irish League's (UIL) convention at St Patrick's College in Thurles. Dillon was the deputy IPP leader and Redmond's chief lieutenant. Redmond said that the critical issue facing Ireland was ending the war 'not alone by our courage upon the battlefield but by scrupulously maintaining the political truce and promoting and inculcating wisdom, toleration and unity amongst all classes of our people'.[12] Dillon felt that the Volunteers, such as reservists and ex-soldiers who had rejoined the British Army, would prove useful.[13] If the 'final struggle' were forced on them, a Volunteer force, 'stiffened by the soldiers that had returned from the front' would prove decisive. Dillon saw the war as an opportunity that would be beneficial to any future war of independence.

At an Irish Volunteer demonstration in Ballina, MP for Tipperary North, Dr John Esmonde, was ambiguous on the war. He said it was not the Irish people's duty to 'go out of their way to defend the Empire unless the British government was true to Ireland'. Kitchener was asking for recruits, he said, but compared with Britain, Ireland was sending 'three times as many men in proportion to any other country in the British Empire'.[14] Esmonde said he could not understand how the government would go to war to protect one small nationality and leave another small nationality within its own Empire in bondage and degrade its people as slaves. But he felt sympathy with the Allies, as they had made an 'honourable alliance' with England. On recruitment, Esmonde said: 'His [Esmonde's] answer to Lord Kitchener's appeal for recruits was if they got the Home Rule Bill on the Statute Book and they were free men in their own country, and there was danger to the Empire they would do as they always did [applause]'.[15]

Esmonde gave a politically evasive speech. His sympathy was with the Allies, but Ireland did not have to do anything for the Empire or Britain as they were degrading Ireland. Nonetheless, he felt that if Home Rule was attained, the situation would change once more. Esmonde, therefore, was articulating several positions.

PASSING OF THE HOME RULE BILL

On 18 September, the Home Rule Bill was passed by the House of Commons. No official celebrations occurred in Clonmel, but the Board of Guardians sent a message congratulating Redmond, Asquith and the Liberals.[16] Some people 'illuminated' their houses and the Volunteers marched through the streets accompanied by bands.[17] In other parts of the town, people started bonfires. In Thurles, the *Nenagh Guardian* also reported lighting of bonfires, bands playing national airs and people parading the streets: the scene was 'most enthusiastic'.

Dr John Harty, the Archbishop of Cashel and Emly, said that they had won a 'great victory' and 'the old order of things was being swept away'.[18] In Carrick, the Volunteers led a torchlight procession, which concluded with 'cheers for Redmond and the IPP'.[19] The county, borough and district councils, the guardians and Ancient Order of Hibernians passed resolutions praising Redmond.[20] In Cashel, the Dean made a speech:

> To the people of England, Ireland is grateful. This gratitude Ireland is prepared to show at all times, in war as well as in peace. We are prepared to share our fair proportion of the burdens of the Empire, and proportionately to our population to fill the ranks of the British Army... We thank the Irish Party with John Redmond at their head; we thank the people of England and their fearless and brilliant leader — the immortal Asquith. We thank the King of England, and we pray God to bless that royal hand that has just signed the charter of Irish freedom.[21]

On 20 September, a review was held in Eglish in north Tipperary, at which about seven companies of Volunteers were present including those from Terryglass, Ballingarry and Borrisokane. Esmonde made mention of the passing of the bill but focused instead on rumours of conscription and said that they were not to take any notice of reports the Volunteers were to fight for Britain as they were 'Irishmen first and Britishers afterwards [cheers]'.[22]

REDMOND ADVOCATES BRITISH ARMY RECRUITMENT

If there are tipping points in Irish history, then 20 September 1914 is one. On that date, John Redmond told Volunteers assembled at Woodenbridge in Co Wicklow:

> It would be a disgrace forever to our country and a reproach to her manhood and a denial of the lessons of history if [the] young [men of] Ireland confined their efforts to remaining at home to defend the shores of Ireland from an unlikely invasion and shrinking from the duty of proving in the field of battle that gallantry and courage which has distinguished our race all through its history. I say to you therefore, your duty is twofold... account yourselves as men, not only in Ireland itself, but wherever the firing line extends, in defence of right, of freedom and religion in this war.[23]

It had been Redmond's intention to deliver a major speech on the new approach at a larger review, but on that date while en route to Aughavanagh, his country home, he was asked to inspect the Volunteers.[24] This speech at Woodenbridge went much further than his 3 August House of Commons intervention, when he committed the INV to home defence only.[25]

Redmond felt that the war offered an opportunity to mend the relationship between unionists and nationalists and that, with the mutual shared sacrifice on the battlefield, could lead to a renegotiation of the Home Rule Bill, one without the need for partition. Redmond believed that there was a growing antipathy towards partition in Ireland and he felt the presence of southern unionists in the ranks of the INV confirmed this.[26] Redmond had pointed out that nationalists always maintained that there was no strategic risk to Britain in conceding Home Rule and here, he argued, was the opportunity to prove it.[27] There was also a strong tactical argument for Redmond's move, as any other would have played into the hands of Ulster.[28] Nothing could have induced Ulster unionists into a Home Rule state: Home Rule remained Rome

Rule. But it could be argued that no one genuinely committed to Irish unity could have acted differently from Redmond in 1914.[29]

After the speech, the extreme elements of the Provisional Committee repudiated him. The resulting schism in the Volunteer body, however, appeared to solidify Redmond's base, and in Tipperary the 'factionalism' of Redmond's Woodenbridge dissentients was criticized:

> The spectacle of a small and irresponsible Dublin group dictating terms of high policy to the National leaders was, however, too much for the people... Our county parliament at their sitting on Wednesday spoke vigorously and to the point, reiterating their confidence in the party under Mr Redmond's leadership, approving of their policy and congratulating them on their glorious Home Rule victory.[30]

Extreme elements in the Volunteers — the Provisional Committee — had always resented Redmond's takeover, and Woodenbridge provided the perfect opportunity to splinter from the body. The breakaway group retained the title of the Irish Volunteers while Redmond's majority repositioned as the Irish National Volunteers. The Irish Volunteers were to provide the nucleus for the Easter Rising. IRB and Irish Volunteer organizer Eamon O'Duibhir put it like this:

> I remember, at one of the IRB meetings somewhere about this period — certainly after the commencement of the world war — being told of the Supreme Council [IRB] decision to work for a revolt now that war had begun. There was a chaotic situation by this time in the Irish Volunteers and it remained until Redmond declared himself for aiding Britain on September 20, 1914. Now we knew where we were.[31]

The Volunteer area of O'Duibhir (Knockavilla) was an extremist stronghold, and the vote they carried — very much the exception in the county — was: 'We are for Sinn Féin, we are not going to be recruits for Britain or to aid the Empire in its dirty work.'[32] In comparison, the Thurles Corps was 'amazed' by the extremist line from the Provisional Committee. The Tipperary Volunteer Board felt it in their 'best interests' to endorse Redmond's leadership.[33] A new board was elected, and the bulk of the movement in the county followed their lead.[34]

In Nenagh, battalion organizers met to endorse or reject Redmond's leadership over the Woodenbridge crisis. R.P. Gill, the County Engineer, chaired the meeting, and said that he had been studying Redmond's line since the beginning and found no fault with it:

> He [Redmond] did not intend going about calling on the Volunteers to join the army and go to the front, as the orders were for the Volunteers of Ireland to keep together in defence of their own country. Mr Redmond said he would like to see some men going out as an Irish brigade, and it was yet open to any young man to join if he wished to go across the water; but it is no disgrace for any young man to say, 'I will remain at home, and defend my country against any invader — Carson or the Kaiser.' In doing that he was doing a right and noble work.[35]

John Esmonde then spoke, and dismissed suggestions that Redmond should have attempted to secure further concessions from Britain. Redmond was a 'diplomat', and as such was not able to accomplish this. Any attempt to do so would run the risk that we 'might have done or said something which would be misunderstood by the great democracy of England'. At this Nenagh meeting was future vice commandant of the First Tipperary Brigade, Liam Hoolan:

> The matter [allegiance to either MacNeill or Redmond] was subsequently put before the general body of the Nenagh

Volunteers and there was only one loud voiced dissentient, a painter named Hegarty. It afterwards became clear that there were several others who dissented from Redmondite control, but at the meeting they were overawed by the big guns of the Irish Political Party, including Dr Esmonde MP, who were present. Thus, the control of the Volunteers fell into the hands of followers of John E. Redmond.[36]

Overawed or not, Esmonde's comments were met with cheers. Buttressed by patronizing descriptions of Ireland,[37] Esmonde was largely sympathetic to Redmond's call for recruits. Across the county, support veered towards Redmond. The County Tipperary Board of the Irish Volunteers reaffirmed their allegiance to Redmond and the IPP.[38] South Tipperary County Council applauded Redmond and condemned 'factionism and Carsonism'. Clonmel Corporation also praised Redmond, while politicians also made efforts to keep the Volunteers united. The fact that the Corporation's statement made no reference to the split was probably due to the local MP Tom Condon, who did not wish to alienate the Irish Volunteers.[39] At an Irish National Volunteer review in Newport, for example, Esmonde pleaded for cohesion:

> They all knew the Volunteer movement had gone through a crisis. If there was any man in the ranks who could not see eye to eye with his brothers let him remain in the ranks, but as a volunteer he was... duty bound to go with the majority... when the war is over we will have 20,000 reserve men back, and then I see no fear from the Ulster volunteers.[40]

Politicians and local officials also tried to clarify Redmond's position. In Nenagh, Gill told a group of Volunteers:

> Mr Redmond never intended that the Volunteers should go fight for England. His intention was that they should protect the

shores of Ireland, but he did say he would be glad to see young men go into the fighting line, as many good Irishmen have done before [cheers]. It was no disgrace to say that they would fight against the Kaiser or Sir Edward Carson.[41]

Some weeks later Esmonde again tried to clarify Redmond's Woodenbridge statement: 'Mr Redmond never pledged himself to send out the Volunteers, and the pronouncement he made on that historic occasion was, as they were aware, that the Volunteers would defend the shores of Ireland (cheers). If there was any man who wanted to go to the front let him go of his own free will and choice.'[42]

In Clonmel, local MP Tom Condon canvassed the Volunteers for Redmond, while Frank Drohan 'tried to keep them together' but Drohan sympathized with the radical element and they split, leaving Drohan in command of about forty young and inexperienced Volunteers.[43] Drohan's group, however, was well armed as it acquired thirty-two rifles that Drohan had earlier ordered for the Clonmel Corps before the split. This was the source of much bitterness between the sides.[44] Drohan felt that the Redmondite Volunteers had been shaken by Woodenbridge: 'A lot of the Redmondite Volunteers were by this time becoming shaken in their allegiance as they saw that the only outlook for that organization was to provide recruits for the British Army and so the organization began to dwindle away.'[45]

The split, then, had become 'more accentuated'.[46] The ranks of the Irish Volunteers were ambiguous about enlisting in the British Army. The police felt there was a 'slackness and apathy' about enlisting and 'in parts of the Riding [south] Sinn Féin opinions prevail, but it is too early to say yet if they will succeed in preventing enlisting'. They believed that most of the Volunteers were 'Redmondites', but that unless pressure was brought to bear on them by their own leaders, then 'recruiting will be a failure'.[47] Despite these assessments, Irish Party MPs in Tipperary were prepared to follow the party line. At a Volunteer event in Ballyporeen on 27 September, John Cullinan, MP for Tipperary South, tacitly espoused this new direction:

They had heard a lot of nonsense in Ireland to the effect that the manhood of Ireland would not march under Kitchener's flag, but any Irishman who went to the war did not go under Kitchener's flag but under the flag of all the allies. He went to fight for nationalities dear to every Irish heart — he went to fight for France and for the brave people of Belgium… It should be an honour to every Irishman to throw in his lot with such a gallant people. This war was a war for civilization and freedom. He asked them to consider what the position would be in the near future if through any mishap the Germans were successful. Ireland would be turned into the same scene of devastation and ruin and disaster as Belgium had been. Her beautiful churches, her monasteries and convents would be destroyed, the honour of the people of Ireland would be torn down over their heads, and their women and children butchered.[48]

Condon took a similar line. Addressing the Clonmel Volunteers on 6 October, he said that conscription was not on the agenda, but any man who decided to enlist would be 'discharging as patriotic a duty to Ireland in helping to keep back the onward rush of the Prussian Hun as he would be in the fair valley of the Suir'.[49] Condon's appeals could be at best described as very sympathetic to advocating recruiting, at worst recruiting-sergeant mode. He supported the recruiting policy, considered the war 'just and holy', and said that if he was a young man, he would 'volunteer to go the front to save my country and people'.[50] In March, Condon, in his capacity as mayor of Clonmel, visited Cashel. Five hundred INV turned out for him and the priest at Cashel, Reverend T. Dunne, introduced Driver James O'Brien (who won the French Legion of Honour), Private (Pte) Daniel McCarthy of the Irish Guards (whose leg was amputated), and Pte Christopher Cullen RIRegt, who had been wounded twice. Condon congratulated them on what they had done 'for their country'. Condon also said that he was 'proud of the doings of the Cashel soldiers at the front and was glad to see that they were upholding their country's traditions for courage'.[51]

At a prize-giving ceremony on 28 October for students in Tipperary town, T.P. Gill, Secretary of the Department of Agriculture and Technical Instruction, said that the 'interests of Tipperary were being fought for and defended on the fields and valleys of France, the dykes of Flanders and the ditches of Belgium'. Gill called on them not to 'leave it to others to defend the homes of Tipperary'.[52] It was very clear, then, that a determined effort was being made to put forward the case for recruiting. Britain's war was Ireland's, the front was where one fought for freedom, and Tipperary's interests were at stake. The war, therefore, was presented as a place where Tipperary men could do noble deeds, gain valour in the field and defend their homes. Colonel Maurice Moore addressed the issue of recruitment on 13 October in Cashel:

> He had one warning to give the volunteers of Tipperary, and that was not to believe the stories that were in circulation that men were to be taken away because they were volunteers and sent to other parts of the world to fight for other people. The Irish Volunteers would maintain their own organization in their own country and would not leave it.[53]

Dr Esmonde reinforced this, and told the Volunteers in English that they would not be 'sent to fight England's battles on the Continent…They were Irishmen first and Britishers afterwards'.[54] But Esmonde followed with a baffling *non sequitur*:

> You belong to a county which produced one of the finest regiments in the civilized world, the 18th Royal Irish [Regiment]. Many of your fathers fought in it. I had an uncle myself who fought for the British Empire in days gone by, when we were persecuted and branded as outcasts because we believed in our solid faith… The men of the 18th Royal Irish fought for a cause in which they did not believe, but which they had pledged themselves to defend, and they showed everyone the fighting spirit of the

Tipperary people. Your duty, Irish Volunteers, is to stand by each other as comrades. I do not think there is a man in the room who disagrees with the manifesto of Mr Redmond, but if there is such a man present let him be welcomed into the ranks… He [Redmond] has never asked the Volunteers as a body to go forth and fight for the Empire. What he has pledged himself to do is to see that Ireland takes her place in the defence of the British Empire, but he is not asking the Volunteers as a body to do it. He says if any young Irishman wishes to go forth, as his father and grandfather has done before him to fight in the Irish regiment in the cause of the British Empire, he can do so, and shall not be looked upon as an outcast by any Irishman.[55]

Esmonde made a passionate case for enlisting. He justified recruiting by explaining that allegiances are interchangeable and amorphous. Many who had fought for Britain in past campaigns had not believed in the cause, but that did not matter as a man could be a Volunteer and a soldier of the Empire. In addition, Esmonde eulogized family tradition. For him, there is a responsibility to at least consider going to the front. At many meetings across the county, the IPP drew on images of Tipperary's perceived martial spirit and historical images of military tradition. These usually went hand-in-hand with condemnation of German 'aggression' and support for Belgium. At a meeting in Nenagh to organize help for the Belgian Refugees, he said:

They had people in Ireland who had relations out fighting the Germans and doing their duty to Ireland in helping the Allies towards victory… they were all looking back at the great deeds done by the Irish soldier, and in the future they would look on them as men ready to do the same. They had seen them fighting before as Irishmen, and now they were fighting as Irishmen helping little Belgium.[56]

An engaging exchange in the *Nenagh Guardian* outlined the position of the Toomevara Volunteers.[57] One of the paper's correspondents asked if the Volunteers had decided to go to the front. The secretary of the Volunteers sourly responded that they were not going to the front and would go there 'for Ireland only'. He said it was nonsense to call Irish National Volunteers 'pro-German because they are not in sympathy with the unnatural idea of sending yet more Irishmen to the German slaughterhouse where already Ireland has far excelled her quota'.[58] The correspondent said that if he went to the front he would find 'many a gallant Tipperyman [*sic*]', who has secured the 'fertile plains of Tipperary from the "black marias [*sic*]"'.

> About 5,000 Tipperarymen are in the fighting line for the liberties of Europe. With them, I should be in valiant company...
> I know that the Toom [Toomevara] Volunteers are proud of the achievement of their countrymen and I believe if the time came that they believed it was their duty to enter the firing line in defence of a noble cause they would not shrink from the ordeal. Those who have gone or may go carry with them the good wishes of their countrymen. They may be going to a German slaughterhouse on the Continent, to again repeat the quotation from Moran's Leader, but they are helping to save Ireland from being a slaughterhouse.[59]

A Toomevara volunteer and future active service member of the North Tipperary Brigade simply put it that the majority of the Toomevara Volunteers 'disagreed with John Redmond' and the movement then collapsed.[60] As Thomas Ryan, future war of independence commander with the 5/6th Battalion 3rd Tipperary Brigade of the Irish Republican Army, saw it:

> The people of the garrison towns and the villages in my area [Cahir] were 100% pro-British and some 85% of the country people had similar leanings. My best pal at the time, who was

also my 2nd in charge of the Volunteer Company, a lad named O'Brien, fell for the propaganda of the period and decided to join the British Army... He was killed at the battle of Mons and I often regretted his passing when later we were fighting the British, knowing that he would have been foremost in the fight for Ireland on the hills of Tipperary. False propaganda had brought him to his doom.[61]

IPP members made the recruiting pitch at meetings across the county, and they attempted a delicate balancing act. They insisted that Redmond had simply said that anyone who wanted to join was welcome, but the Volunteers as a unit would not be asked to do so: there was no compulsion, and anyone who did not go to the front was doing a similarly important duty in Ireland. They emphasized the moral importance of the war, condemned the brutality and inhumanity of the German war machine, constantly invoked the fate of Belgium, and some alluded to the military tradition of Tipperary families. They undoubtedly encouraged recruitment.

Unionist involvement continued, for a time, with the INV. For example, Edward Lysaght placed Raheen Manor in Tomgraney at the disposal of Maurice Moore as a temporary barracks.[62] And one unionist, a Justice of the Peace, addressed a Volunteer meeting in Ballina, having been swayed by the sight of Irish reservists departing from the North Wall in Dublin. He perhaps naively considered that all Irishmen could now put up their hands and say 'God save Ireland' and 'God save the King'.[63] But inevitably, southern unionist co-operation melted away when it was clear the Volunteers would not transfer en masse to the British Army or establish as proxy for the Crown forces. Unionists felt there needed to be some form of oath to the king, at the very least. E.G. Stewart-Croswait, rector of Littletown in Thurles, proposed a corps of 'sharpshooters' for 'gentlemen of leisure' who had not seen their way to joining a corps that had in its foundation a 'political bias'. Such a corps, by his definition, would be 'non-sectarian and non-political', for the only oath to be taken would be to King and Empire.[64] Some of the advanced nationalists in the ranks of the Volunteers before the split were also wary of their involvement. When the Clonmel Corps of Volunteers were reviewed by Powerstown Park owner Morton Jackson on 20 September 1914 and asked to enlist, Seamus O'Neill, one of the IRB leaders, protested and was ordered to leave. A number of others followed him.[65] When a company of Volunteers was reviewed by Major Cooper at Killenure, near Knockavilla, some reportedly walked off the field:

> When Major Cooper had reviewed the men he turned on the propaganda and he asked them all to help and any of them that could should volunteer to fight for King and Country. I immediately called on the volunteers to march off the field and they did so, leaving him standing astounded and speechless and with only about half a dozen of the Irish Party followers and some other toadies with him.[66]

Underlining the reality of unionist disengagement was a letter of resignation from Captain R.M. Minchin of Cloughjordan as an inspecting officer of the volunteers in Tipperary. In the letter, he said he would like to see the volunteers recruiting for the army and pledged to come over from the army to help Maurice Moore if he decided to attempt to establish a Tipperary brigade for the new army as men are 'badly needed and I know better men than Tipperary men cannot be got'.[67]

THE FIRST FLUSH OF THE RECRUITING CAMPAIGN

Recruiting meetings were not organized in Tipperary until the spring of 1915. This coincided with the appearance of route marches by local military units. These marches were designed to harden troops and raise their profile.[68] For example, the 16th Royal Engineers marched through Clonmel to Mallow. Any march, the *Chronicle* reported, 'created a bit of a stir in the town, but the coming of the 16th Company of the Engineers was quite an event in Clonmel'.[69] The *Chronicle* supported the recruitment drive and said that the campaigns in Kilkenny and Waterford had showed what a success it could be, particularly in Kilkenny, where farmers and their sons — men who had a real stake in the country — had enlisted.[70] Managed by Captain C.R. Jorgensen of the RIRegt, it had reportedly attracted 350 men in Waterford.[71] The *Nationalist* also supported the upcoming campaign, and felt that although Clonmel 'had contributed a large body of men, including a considerable proportion of our Volunteers to the army, Captain Jorgenson's visit is sure to have further satisfactory results'.[72] The *Nationalist* also published a letter from the Roman Catholic (RC) Bishop of Waterford and Lismore, Revd Dr R.A. Sheehan, who sent a message of support to a recruiting meeting in Waterford town:

> I regret that I will not be able to attend, but you may rest assured that you have my best wishes for your success. The object of your gathering appeals and appeals powerfully to every man in the land. This war is not an English war alone, or a French or Belgian war — it is an Irish war to save our country and people from ruin and misery.[73]

What was an early recruiting effort like? On 26 April 1915, a campaign opened in Clonmel. Posters urging enlistment covered the boardings and walls of the town. A RIRegt band marched through Clonmel to the recruiting office in the courthouse. They played some 'national airs' and then went to the RIRegt depot and were met by the commanding officer, Colonel Cooke. Here, a 'couple of men' offered themselves for recruits, and during the evening men enlisted in 'twos and threes'. That evening, at about 8p.m, the band played through the town again. The media reported that crowds followed the band and joined in with the songs. At the courthouse, young men were urged to enlist, with twenty joining on the first day of the campaign and about thirty-six by Wednesday, it was reported.[74] There were economic incentives. A £2 prize went to Richard Anderson, a brewery worker of the Old Bridge area, in Clonmel for securing the most recruits — fifteen.[75] Some firms offered incentives to enlist. Murphy's Brewery, for example, offered to keep a job open for any man who enlisted and also said they would pay 7*s*. to a man with dependants for every week he was away.[76]

At the end of the week, a major recruiting meeting was held in Clonmel. Chairing the meeting was the Marquis of Ormonde. A letter was read from the wife of Colonel Watson (a prominent member of the local gentry): 'As you know, all our sons are doing their duty… We would be ashamed to have them at home and it is the duty of every parent at this grave juncture to urge the lads to join the army.'[77] A second letter, from Father Edmund Kelly, the curate at Mullinahone who was now a chaplain to 49th Brigade, was then read:

> The freedom of the world is at stake… Of course the idea of an arrogant Prussian imposing his will on Europe is simply intolerable. But who is to prevent him? Our soldiers; and never did soldiers fight in a more holier or patriotic cause. Irish soldiers at the present crisis are our truest patriots… Some say that they will shed the last drop of their blood if the Germans dare invade Ireland. When, say, Clonmel is being shelled from outside Dungarvan Bay they will begin to bestir themselves.[78]

Two letters then, from both ends of the spectrum, one from the Protestant gentry perspective and another from a Catholic priest, each appealing for recruits. For the Marquis of Ormonde, the war was a question of Prussia and its visceral desire to project power in Europe. The Marquis appealed to what he perceived as Tipperary's martial spirit and military tradition. He lauded the fighting qualities of Tipperary soldiers and said that he was sure that the men 'who enlist now will nobly sustain the traditions that have been handed down to them'.[79] Politically, he felt an end to sectarianism was possible through a joint effort in the conflict.[80]

Archdeacon Flavin said that the crisis had never been equalled since the beginning of the world, and he also emphasized that Tipperary had a unique martial spirit. Flavin too believed in military tradition and continuity with Tipperary men who had fought in previous conflicts. 'Every man had now to do his duty and he was sure that the nationalist sons of Tipperary, always remarkable for their fighting spirit, would step forward to guard and defend the green shores of Ireland.'[81] The priest criticized the Kaiser, saying: 'If the brutal emperor had his way he would come over and destroy their schools and their universities, and butcher their priests and nuns.' He also said that he would enlist as a chaplain if he were thirty years younger.[82]

The rector at St Mary's Church, Canon Leslie, had said previously that he and the Catholic priest might have had to apologize for sharing the platform, but not any more, because of what had happened to Belgium. The Canon then launched an attack on the farmers and their sons for not joining the army. He praised the gentry and labourers for enlisting:

> But in between those two — the gentry on one hand and the workers on the other — there was a class which had not done splendidly. He referred especially to the class who were doing women's work behind the counters [applause]. There were plenty of women able and willing to do the work that those men were doing [A voice: "The farmers' sons"].[83]

The Canon mocked the farmers' sons as men who, to him, were acting as women. Clonmel's Sub-Sheriff, Arnold Power, went further and said that he only came to the meeting to say that farmers' sons should be enlisting. He credited Cahir, Carrick and parts of Clonmel for their contribution to the war effort, but was unreservedly critical about those whom he saw as slackers or shirkers. 'There were two classes which would not go to the front — the sons of farmers and the boys behind the counters, most of whom were the sons of farmers [cheers]. In the town of Clonmel they had big, able farmers' sons measuring out yards of ribbon when they should be pouring bullets out of machine-guns [loud applause].'[84] Power said that the farmers who would not let their sons enlist were hurting themselves because the longer the war continued, the heavier the taxation the government would inflict on them. 'What about the gallant officer behind the counter with his yard stick by his side and his hair done in the latest style? [laughter]. A decent girl should be ashamed to recognize such men on the street… [the] Mammy's son that stopped at home should be looked upon with contempt.'[85]

The final speaker was Lieutenant Piggott of the RIRegt. He said that many men were hanging back until conscription came: 'Did such fellows expect that they would be treated like voluntary soldiers?' He declared that the sight of Belgium would make the blood of Irish soldiers boil. He also claimed that conscripts would not get the separation allowance, would be treated as slackers and objects of ridicule by men who had volunteered and girls would point the 'finger of scorn at them as men who let others go and defend them'.[86] Piggott appealed to women to send their men to enlist, as this was their 'female duty'.

In Nenagh, a recruiting meeting was held with a similar cast on the recruiting platform: Lord Dunalley, local solicitors, a resident magistrate, and two army captains. Captain Dease spoke about how many more men were needed in Flanders because of the body count. He also gave what the *Nationalist* described as a 'thrilling' account of the Germans' use of poison gas.[87] In Templemore, the Town Clerk presided over a recruiting meeting that witnessed a gunner, Michael Heffernan, speak about German atrocities and emphasize their callous disregard for life, particularly the sinking of the *Lusitania*. The report claimed that all eligible men in the town enlisted after the meeting.[88]

The *Chronicle* reported that from Saturday 24 April to the following Friday, 109 joined the army in Clonmel.[89] This figure from the *Chronicle* was only two off the actual recruiting total for that week, which stood at 107.[90] The official figures showed a sharp increase in enlistment during the week, which proved the effectiveness of recruiting campaigns.[91] Of the total number of recruits, sixty-eight were brought in by the recruiting campaign, which it considered 'very creditable in [a] town which has sent away so many men since the beginning of the war' since thirty-five had joined the previous week, while the 'average for the previous six weeks was between forty-five and fifty'.[92] The police assessment of the meeting, however, was more sober:

A special recruiting office has been... opened in Clonmel during the last week and it is aided by the band of the RIRegt. Though a number of men have already gone from the town, some 50 recruits have been obtained. A recruiting meeting was held on the 30 April presided over by the Marquis of Ormonde, which was very well attended. The farmers' sons and the shop boys, however, still fail to come in.[93]

The main themes of the Magner's meeting were Prussian militarism, the threat of invasion, martial spirit, military tradition, the plight of Belgium and how the European War was an Irish one. These should be enough to motivate any man, claimed the speakers, and if not, then there were others such as the threat and shame of conscription (go now or risk being humiliated by force) and how women look with contempt upon slackers. Both Piggott and Power criticized farmers' sons and shop assistants for their apparent unwillingness to enlist. They mocked them as cowards. They emphasized gender roles in encouraging enlistment, and there was a clear attempt to emasculate men who did not enlist, i.e. 'real' men joined whereas men fit for 'cutting ribbon' stayed at home. Women in Tipperary were told to have no respect for these shirkers who left the fighting to others. A 'female's duty' was to send her men to enlist, as the soldier at the front was a man's man and obviously more desirable and more worthy of respect and adulation; the slacker who stayed at home was pathetic.[94] The recruiters also used the prospect of heavy tax increases as a weapon of fear in trying to get men to enlist. In Nenagh, the heavy death toll of the war was accepted and one of the speakers even spoke about the Germans' use of poison gas. From the outset, people were not spared any detail regarding the high human cost of the conflict.

THE PRESS

The *Chronicle* and the *Nationalist* were two of the main newspapers in Tipperary; both were based in Clonmel and both were published twice a week. The *Nationalist* in particular was the leading paper of south Tipperary during the First World War with a distinct nationalist slant. Brandon J. Long had edited the paper since 1909. The *Chronicle* traditionally had been the paper of the Conservative Party, but had developed a reputation for accurate and reliable reporting during the nineteenth century. The paper repositioned itself in the years prior to the war as independent of all parties and began to adopt a more national flavour as the war progressed.[95] The local newspapers supported the official reports of the conflict. In some ways, they could even be described as pro-war, and caution must be exercised when using their reports and editorials. On 28 April, for example, the *Nationalist* made clear that it supported Jorgenson's recruiting efforts. The summer of 1915, it felt, would see fresh offensives that would 'shatter forever the infamous Prussian military spirit'. The paper accused Prussia of plunging Europe 'into the horrors of the most devastating conflict in the world's history'. The editorial read like a War Office press statement:

> Many gaps have been made in the ranks of our gallant fighters who gave up everything for the defence of their country and these gaps must be filled and more men must be sent to the assistance of the fighting lines. The more soldiers and munitions we can send to the front, the sooner the goal [of an offensive] can be reached.[96]

The *Nationalist*, echoing the recruiters, emphasized that Irish soldiers possessed a martial spirit and were a 'fighting race'. With Home Rule now secured, Irish soldiers fought for their 'own county, the Empire [of] which they are now willing and vigorous partners...'. The paper praised the RIRegt as an extension of Tipperary's pedigree and commitment to the war, and lauded soldiers who had been decorated:

Our great county regiment, the Royal Irish [RIRegt], helped to stem the first German rush to Paris, and to drive the Huns back to the borders of France. The regiment lost heavily, but Tipperary helped generously to fill the gaps and make up the fresh battalions in training for the field. The honours of war were shared by brave Tipperarymen like O'Brien of Cashel, who won the French Legion of Honour, Ussher of Slievenamon who won the DCM, while Cooper, long resident in Clonmel, won the Military Cross. Tipperary also gave Admiral Carden, who successfully opened the naval operations to force the Dardanelles.[97]

The intersection between the editorial and the recruiting campaign is informative in gauging the extent to which the media supported the official line. The paper's roll of honour glamorized the war. The battlefield was a place to prove your masculinity, and Jorgensen's campaign provided the opportunity to do so. This was an Irish war, it argued. The country had become an enthusiastic member of the Empire and needed more recruits.[98] The editorial certainly offered the strongest case for enlisting on the British side. The *Nationalist* supported the recruiting efforts as the war progressed, and was represented at a conference hosted by Wimborne at the Viceregal Lodge in October 1915, where the paper's support was pledged for the new recruiting campaign.[99] It is important, therefore, to be mindful of the fact that papers of the time had their own agenda. In the *Nenagh Guardian*, the main newspaper for north Tipperary, pro-recruiting pieces also appeared:

If every town and district like Falvey's Lane, Nenagh, furnished as many boys — indeed they are but boys — there would be no lack of soldiers at the front. There are in all 11 boys from the lane in question gone to face the Kaiser's cut-throats. Only thirteen houses are inhabited, so the population of Falvey's Lane cannot be said to be congested. Considering such a number of soldiers being present from the one small lane named, the parents of some of the families should be entitled to a pension. Many of the London illustrated papers have been giving photographs of soldiers at the front. Can any of them beat Falvey's Lane?[100]

The correspondent added: 'I have just heard there are nearly a score of men, both married and single, from the Birr Road, now also at the front. If other parts of the country can show as well as those two thoroughfares, Nenagh can well hold its own against other towns, and she will take some beating.'[101]

Recruiting speeches made regular reference to the 'barbarism of the Hun'. These comments did not make specific reference to the progress of the war, which, in turn, correlated with government policy in restricting information, which irritated the press. The *Freeman's Journal* expressed its resentment that the feats of Irish troops were being 'officially ignored'.[102] But they also published letters of soldiers that offered a different slant on the war's progress. These letters appeared frequently in the opening months of the war; less so as it progressed.

Some letters amplified the remarks on German barbarism — particularly an alleged German delight in attacking civilians and religious orders. Stories of German atrocities in Belgium tended to fuel outrage in Ireland. Although discredited after the war as Allied propaganda, it is clear that invading German troops were guilty of extreme brutality.[103] Corporal Kavanagh of the RIRegt, for example, was the first wounded man to return to Clonmel from France. He said that his regiment and other Irish regiments were enraged at the German murder of priests, Sisters of Charity nuns and English nuns. Kavanagh also said that some Red Cross men had had their hands cut off.[104] Another Clonmel soldier claimed:

I have seen it done over and over again. They fired on the ambulance cars and also on the hospitals. We were not a mile out of St Quentin when we saw the big hospital in flames. The Germans burned all the villages also as they came to them... The burnings of the poor villagers' houses was bad enough to see, but the sight of the poor women and children fleeing before the Germans would break a man's heart.[105]

South Tipperary's medical advisor, Lieutenant A.P. Kennedy of the Royal Army Medical Corps, declared that he had interviewed many people who had told him of their personal experiences of German brutality, and in one house he saw the body of a young girl ripped up to the chest bone, apparently by a bayonet.[106]

A Lieutenant Kennefick returned to Clonmel in November. An interview with him in the *Nationalist* detailed what 'murderous savages' the Germans were, 'stealing, looting, and killing whilst destroying opulent French houses and turning them into pigsties'.[107] Many interviews and letters expressed the same sentiments, lauding the Belgian army, damning the Germans, and detailing the harsh conditions regular soldiers faced at the front.[108] Other letters, however, showed the lax attitude taken by some newspapers in printing material that could be seen as beneficial to the enemy. Sergeant John O'Dwyer of the Irish Guards had his leg blown off and was taken prisoner during the retreat from Mons. He had praise for the Germans:

> I lay there for a time in the forest with no one but my friends, the Germans, who were not at all unkind to me. They gave me water and wine to drink, and two of their Red Cross bandaged my leg temporarily… I shall soon see you, please God. Let me know how the old city [Cashel] is looking or if there is any change there.[109]

Hugh Donnolly had been a Volunteer instructor. He wrote to his family in Borrisokane from France. A reserveman, Donnolly was a private in the Connaught Rangers:

> Don't mind what you see in the papers about the Germans being no good. They are great fighting men… The Irish Guards got it

hot… Some regiments got killed right out. I am not thinking of home, wife or children. My rifle and God is all I have to think of now. Don't think I am afraid. There is no fear in a soldier. I feel as if I was going to a hurling match. Shot and shell bursting over our heads every day. The Boer War was only child's play to this.[110]

John Lynam,writing to his mother in Pound Street, Nenagh, from a hospital in London said:

It is not war, it is worse; it is murder pure and simple. The German trenches are only about 100 yards away from ours, and to see the poor fellows getting shot carrying rations to us in the trenches is awful. There are German snipers everywhere. Excellent shots they are. They get up trees or sneak along in hollow ground, shooting sentries and listening for patrols. They risk their lives for the Kaiser's Iron Cross. The papers will never publish a complete list of the dead; it is kept hidden from the public.[111]

Such reports were not likely to encourage recruiting or engender hopes of a swift war.

EXPOSURE AND REACTION TO WAR

Men in Tipperary were exposed to a wide variety of conditions that helped create a sense of a community at war. An interesting point to note is that the many casualties and industrialized killing of the war were reported from the start. Father Maher bluntly told his Thurles congregation that: 'already it was acknowledged that the Germans had lost 25,000 men — more people than were ever collected together at Thurles races, lying dead — and yet that was only a small incident of the mighty contest, only a small skirmish. The real war hadn't started yet.'[112] High casualties reported in the British media were circulated in Ireland along with Kitchener's prediction that the war would last three years.[113]

The press reported on Volunteers who enlisted, received commissions or who rejoined the army. For example, in March, a Carrick Volunteer and manager of the local cycle and motor works, Edward Orange, joined the army as part of the Despatch Riders Corps. A local battalion of INV and the Irish National Foresters saw him off at the station.[114] Cahir Volunteers turned out to send-off their instructor, Jas Lonergan, who rejoined the RIRegt. The Boytonrath Fife and Drum Band marched with the Volunteers in the rain to the station.[115] In Clonmel, three local postmen enlisted in the Post Office Rifles. All three had also been Volunteers. The postmaster, local staff and a 'large number of townspeople' saw them off at the station.[116] A Volunteer instructor joined the Royal Engineers (RE) in early February. The station was 'crowded with hundreds of his friends, who ranged from the youngest of his club mates [he was a football man] to the first magistrate of the town, the Mayor of Clonmel, Alderman T.J. Condon MP'. As the train steamed out he was 'given a rousing cheer and there was a regular salvo of fog signals exploded'.[117]

Increasing numbers of former non-commissioned officers (NCOs) in Clonmel were re-enlisting. This denuded the Irish Volunteers of their most competent men, but added steel to the new army formations. The establishment of the 5th Battalion RIRegt, for example, resulted in considerable numbers of former soldiers signing up.[118] These were seasoned campaigners. For example, two Clonmel sergeants — ex-Colour Sergeant Michael McGrath and ex-Sergeant James Wallace — who had fought in the Boer War re-enlisted.[119] G.H. Scott, manager of the Suir Vale Hotel, left Clonmel on 10 September to rejoin the 20th Hussars: he had retired with the rank of Squadron Sergeant-Major in 1905 with twenty-two years' experience and the Egyptian medal and star. Thomas Higgins from Fethard, local instructor to the squadron of mounted Volunteers, left to take up a post as sergeant in the 18th Hussars.

Others, such as Bobbie Burns, instructor of the Clonmel Volunteers, John Manly of the Borstal service, and James Wallace, who also had two sons fighting in the artillery, all chose to rejoin.[120] The level of commitment and military tradition was underlined by a report regarding Mary Dillon of 18 College Street, Clonmel, whose husband had just rejoined as a sergeant. Aside from him, she had six brothers and one uncle all serving in the Crown forces.[121]

The newspapers added to these reports by printing regular recruiting numbers. At the start of December, the local press claimed that 400 Carrick men were in the army. The breakdown they offer is instructive: '100 were already soldiers at the outbreak of hostilities, 200 were in the reserve, rejoining when mobilization took place, and almost 100 have since joined, including many time-expired soldiers, some of whom had served in India and elsewhere'.[122] About 75 per cent of these enlistments were either soldiers, reserve men or ex-army. In January, it was reported that Tipperary had contributed thousands of soldiers for the front, 'nearly every district being represented. Clonmel has sent many hundreds and we learn that more than 300 men from Carrick are at present either serving with the army abroad or at home stations. Four men from the town have been killed in action and more than forty wounded.'[123] At the weekly meeting of the Nenagh Health Society, it was claimed that about 300 members of the society from the town were serving at the front.[124] The national press also seemed to reinforce this perception. In March, the *Irish Times* claimed that 'notwithstanding the hundreds of Clonmel men who have already joined the colours, recruiting continues pretty briskly in Clonmel and old soldiers and young men — shop assistants, tradesmen and others — are enlisting every week. The Clonmel Volunteers have supplied quite a large number and this week some more joined. The Post Office staff has been depleted by the number of postmen and telegraph boys who have joined.'[125]

From the perspective of London, however, the gushing praise of the local papers seemed misguided. Reports in the *Times* and the *Daily Mail* did not consider that Ireland had given a good account of itself in recruiting terms. Cashel Urban District Council took issue with this. Chairman of the Council, Reverend Dunne, referred to these reports, particularly in the *Times*,[126] which suggested an 'alleged' paucity of recruits from Ireland. Dunne said that it was quite impossible that any more men could be spared to enlist as the government had advised farmers to till more land, yet the farm-hands had all volunteered for service. Dunne said that he had noticed that the same papers had excuses for English agricultural districts, as they said that the country could not afford to have its agriculture hampered by scarcity of labour: 'But when they came to deal with Ireland they changed their tune and said that even more men should come forward. Cashel could send no more; she had sent her full quota. If the same proportion went from the English districts they would be crying out against the taking away of all their labourers...'[127] Similarly, at the Clonmel Rural Council, the Assistant Clerk read out a letter from the LGB regarding recruitment. The Chairman interrupted:

> Damned nonsense, we have enough of this sort of thing... he saw in the press that the landlords of Ireland were complaining very much about scarcity of men willing to go to the front. According to the conditions prevailing in Ireland, it made very little difference whether England was victorious in the war or not. The people in Glenahiery were enslaved from one end of the year to the other making money for the landlords. He noticed that very few of the landlords went to the front. When the soldiers were asked to make a charge against the Germans, they could not move because their feet were stuck in the mud, but it would be a very good thing if they got some of the landlords and put them in the trenches for the soldiers to walk on. The people of Ireland were walked on long enough.[128]

The presence of landlords and men perceived as locally unpopular on recruiting platforms was an issue that would reappear in a larger form later on. Despite this, the police claimed a slight improvement in recruiting during February, this being due to the fact that senior members of the IPP had joined the army. John Redmond's brother, William, and son, William Archer, joined. The Irish Party MP for Tipperary North, Dr Esmonde, received a commission as captain in the RAMC and was posted to Tipperary barracks. Esmonde's son, John Lymbrick, was already a lieutenant and Stephen Gwynn, MP for Galway, was also in the army.[129] In the north of the county, the police felt that the recruits who were coming in were primarily from the towns, and were concerned that people from less urban areas did not understand the importance of the war.[130] In the south, the RIC felt that 'a number of recruits from the towns were of a better class than hitherto had been joining, especially in Clonmel'.[131] The police continually stressed that people somehow did not understand or appreciate the significance of the war. Father Maher, writing in his diary at Thurles, claimed, however, that it was 'astonishing' how many men they were able to get, given 'the tales told by soldiers invalided home of hardships which the troops have to endure in the firing lines'. He agreed with police assessment on the war: 'We are quite used to it now and although we read the papers with interest, the clash of arms has made very little difference in this country. The people are as light-hearted and are ready to amuse themselves as at any previous time as they go about their... daily lives, as if the whole of Europe was at peace.'[132]

There was vibrant discussion of the recruiting issue locally. The Chairman of the Clonmel Guardians said the sub-sheriff had cast a 'great slur' on the farmers at the Magner's recruiting meeting, 'but it was not forgotten that he and his battering-ram had carried out evictions in the past and had driven the people out of the country'. Another board member said that 'it looked like a very scratch crowd that was got together excepting our Reverend Archdeacon [Flavin]. We never saw Lord Ormonde in Clonmel before last night.'[133] Another asked why Ormonde did not go to the front: 'Why does he not go to the front himself — him and the likes of him? The landlords and their backers drove the people out of the country and sent them to America in coffin ships and now they are crying because the men are not there to go and fight the Germans.'[134] A solitary dissenter said: 'Our leaders have advocated recruiting and support of the Allies' cause. It is ridiculous to talk of a man of Lord Ormonde's age going to the front... it should be said that he is the best landlord in the whole country.'

The drapers' assistants also chastised the sub-sheriff for singling them out when many other clerks such as 'solicitors' clerks, grocers' assistants and pawnbrokers' clerks' were 'far more numerous' than drapers. They claimed that more drapers' assistants had joined than from other of those mentioned and 'no male assistant in Clonmel ever sells yards of ribbon'. They also took aim at the landlord system, saying that they had stayed at home to make a living rather than take an 'emigrant ship' like those who had been forced to under 'one of the worst systems of landlordism that ever cursed a fair and Christian land'.[135]

CONCLUSION

August 1914 to the spring of 1915 had seen a haphazard recruiting campaign. There was no centralized control and little evidence of any clear strategy by the authorities. Redmond had the approval of the Irish Party for advocating recruitment, but MPs told the INV, and indeed any prospective recruit, that there was no question of compulsion, i.e. the call at Woodenbridge was merely a suggestion. The war was portrayed in idealistic terms — this was a fight for freedom and civilization against German aggression; Ireland owed a debt to Britain for granting Home Rule; and Ireland also owed it to Catholic Belgium, which had provided a safe haven for Irish priests in the seventeenth century. War news was faithfully reported in the media and the recruiting campaign was supported by the Irish Party MPs. But some discussions, at the boards of guardians, rural, district and county councils, underlined the unease some felt at the campaign, and some of the methods used by recruiters had clearly not endeared them to locals. The choice of speakers in this regard also had not been helpful. In Britain, recruiting activity had been monitored by the Parliamentary Recruiting Committee during the same period. The recruiting committee acted in an advisory role, helping local groups with their work, and this produced a consistency that was lacking in Ireland and in Tipperary.[136] The military conceded the principle of a central civilian body at the end of this period, but did not attempt to analyse the methods. It is to this that we now turn.

3 THE CAMPAIGN BEGINS

Lady helpers of the Soldiers' and Sailors' Buffet provide free refreshments to soldiers at Limerick Junction railway station, Co. Tipperary, during the latter years of the war. Tipperary People Publications.

IF IN A short time men won't come forward and have got to be fetched whether they like it or not, there will be no credit due to them then. A voice questioned: What about the farms?
The farms will have to look after themselves then.[1]

James Somers arrived in Cloughjordan, Co. Tipperary, on Saturday evening, 28 August 1915.[2] He had just been given leave from the army where he was serving as a sergeant in the 1st Inniskilling Fusiliers. At Cloughjordan railway station, he was greeted by the Lord Lieutenant for Tipperary, Lord Dunalley; the recruiting officer Captain Lefroy; the Irish National Volunteer Brass Band; a number of military officers and other members of the local gentry. This reception was not afforded to every soldier who returned on leave, but James Somers had just won the Victoria Cross.[3] In a letter to his father, he described how he won it:

I beat Turks out of our trench single handed and had four awful hours at night… It is certain sure we are beating the Turks alright. In the trench I came out of it was shocking to see the dead. There lay about 3,000 Turks in front of our trench and the smell was absolutely chronic. You know when the sun has been shining on those bodies for three or four days it makes a horrible smell. A person would not mind if it was possible to bury them. But no, you dare not put your nose outside the trench, for if you did you would be a dead man.[4]

A meeting to honour Somers in Cloughjordan House served as a potent propaganda tool. The RIRegt band played beforehand, and on the platform were Major General Lovick Friend, commander of the forces in Ireland, the RIC County Inspector, the editor of the *Nenagh Guardian*, Dunalley, deputy lieutenants, colonels, reverends, church curates and local officials. Somers was presented with a cheque and war loan stock worth £240.[5] Speeches were made lauding the VC winner, how through his action he had won glory for the county and justified hope that a new Ireland would evolve from the war. The same speeches also called for more recruits to follow in Somers' footsteps.

This spectacle marked the apex of the Central Council for the Organization of Recruiting in Ireland's (CCORI) campaign in Tipperary during 1915. But it glossed over the numerous divisions, such as the recruiters' belief that many more men could be spared, the resentment from local bodies over their methods, and further tension over perceived snubs to deeds of valour by Irish soldiers.

The CCORI was formally established on 23 April 1915[6] and Henry MacLaughlin was appointed honorary director.[7] The council was established to extend the recruiting programme and more specifically to tap areas in Ireland that had previously provided few recruits. A key part of this was encouraging civilian effort in support of the voluntary recruiting campaign. But the organization was not particularly effective, and was set up without serious consideration being given to its functions. It only offered a narrow range of activities, and its work was marked by a lack of imaginative revision of accepted recruiting modes.[8] The central problem with the council was its traditional approach: it focused on poster campaigns, recruiting meetings, speeches from 'prominent' men and regimental tours.[9]

STAR SPEAKER

The council used large-scale recruiting tours to spread its message. Hedley le Bas (an advisor to the authorities on recruiting during the opening months of the war) had bombarded specific areas with propaganda advertisements and meetings for short periods during the first flush of the campaign, and these tours were an attempt to apply this principle to a wider canvas. MacLaughlin saw potential in these tours and thought that they might galvanize support at a local level.[10] The CCORI's tours largely relied on star speakers such as Thomas Kettle[11] and Stephen Gwynn[12].

Clonmel played host to Mike O'Leary, the first Irishman to win the Victoria Cross in the war.[13] On 17 July 1915, O'Leary was met by the mayor of Clonmel, Thomas Condon MP, and also by the RIRegt area commander, Lt-Col R.J. Cooke. The band of the Inniskilling Fusiliers was brought in and all available men of the ASC and RIRegt in town were on duty. A number of men wounded in the war were also given seats on the balcony of Hearns Hotel, opposite the town hall. The mayor presided and 'practically every member of the Corporation' was on the platform. He said that:

> He knew that the heart of Tipperary went out to Michael O'Leary.
> Nowhere was Sergeant O'Leary more honoured than in this
> great old town, the capital of Tipperary. O'Leary was an honour
> to the Irish race… Today, he and his comrades at the front were
> guarding our Irish homes and our women and children and
> saving us and saving them from the fate of the homes and the
> women and children of the fair plains of Belgium. To him and
> his comrades they tendered their heartfelt thanks and, speaking
> for himself, he [the mayor], would say this: that if he were young

enough and able, and fit to join O'Leary in the fighting line he should be the first to go [applause].[14]

Condon maintained that Irish and Tipperary soldiers had a military tradition — fighting was in their blood — and men would be inspired to enlist because of O'Leary:

On Flanders, the Wild Geese in the old days fought as bravely as O'Leary and his comrades… He hoped and trusted that this war which had been forced upon the world by the Kaiser and the militarists of Potsdam would have only one ending, that it would result in wiping out the appalling spectacle of militarism and the rearing aloft of the banner of human liberty and human freedom the world over. Sergeant O'Leary is of our own flesh and blood, we know him and love him and I hope our young men will strive to emulate him and his comrades who are doing such honour to our country at the front.[15]

O'Leary made a short recruiting statement: 'I am proud of having done some little service for my King and country. I call on men of all military age to respond to that noble call… We want men and more men, and when we get them we will put down the German hordes.' MacLaughlin joined the meeting and paid tribute to the men from Clonmel who had enlisted:

He was delighted some weeks ago when he read of how many young men had come forward from that district and he always liked to address an audience who seemed…to realize the position of affairs as to do so well as Clonmel had done. But Clonmel cannot have done its best when there remains in the town one man between 18 and 40 years fit and able to fight for his country.[16]

MacLaughlin said that 'if he was half the man he [the speaker] took him to be, [he]would also tell them how desperately ashamed he was of those who might have borne their share of the struggle and yet remained in Clonmel'.[17] At the close of the meeting, Col Cooke thanked the mayor, and in particular for the trouble Condon had taken in bringing O'Leary to Clonmel. The mayor echoed the call made by MacLaughlin, and said that the best thanks he could get would be to see men responding to the call, because in fighting against the Huns in Flanders and France, they would be fighting for the best interests of their own land.[18]

The comments by Condon underline how strongly he, an Irish Party MP, supported the recruiting campaign. The town clerk also acknowledged this, telling J.M. Wilson: 'The mayor is in favour of it strongly and this reflects both town and county'.[19] It is unlikely that this meeting could have inspired half as many recruits as the CCORI hoped given the antagonistic posture adopted by MacLaughlin. But during his address, he went much further than just stating that he was ashamed. This was something that he would repeat time and time again over the course of the CCORI's tenure. The honorary director was known as a blunt man, and in an interview carried in *Irish Life* he was described by a listener at one of his meetings in Belfast as a 'bulldog in spats'.[20] MacLaughlin said that 'no eligible man could make an excuse for not taking his place in the army'. He said that there were no distinctions when it came to soldiers:

> Now, I say, you can enlist, I don't care whether you come from the peer's castle — and I know peers' sons have enlisted — from the millionaire's house, from the bank or the shop, or the farm, or the peasant's cottage. You must enlist and protect your womenfolk. I am glad to talk to you because you have done so well and if you had not done well I would be ashamed to talk to you... Well Clonmel has done well, but there are a few farmers sons left still. [A voice: And a few clerks in the brewery too.]

He followed this, however, with a baffling contradiction, and offered to establish a battalion for farmers so they wouldn't have to enlist with 'common townsfolk'. He said that he had received special permission from Sir Lawrence Parsons, commander of the 16th Irish Division, to announce a special farmers' company of 200 or 250 in the 7th Inniskilling Fusiliers. 'They would train together and fight together, as part of the 16th Irish Division. So there was no excuse now', he said, 'and harvest excuses?'

MacLaughlin said that men from the 16th Division would be made available for hire, the number from any one battalion working on farms not to exceed 100. Pay would be 3s to 4s a day, and the military would feed the men. Army horses and waggons would be made available for farm work at 15s per day, and single horses if the farmers provided the waggons at 5s per day. MacLaughlin now felt that nothing should stand in their way and that he had given the farmers' sons a 'rattle'.[21] MacLaughlin then turned his fire on shop assistants.

> He was serious when he said that no man had a right to do anything but a man's job, and if he was doing a woman's job for God's sake let him put on a woman's skirt [laughter and applause]. He would not like to say that those men who were doing women's jobs behind the counters were cowards, but they were damned near it. In France, there were no men doing a woman's job... There, women act as tram drivers, ticket collectors, make boots for the army, and make the shells for the "75" guns... There were no men left at home in France, except the old men and the effeminate men.[22]

He then called for 150 within a fortnight. This hostile and critical attempt to secure recruits would arguably have had the opposite result.[23] A list of rules for recruiters that appeared in *Irish Life* at the time refuted these tactics: 'Don't, if you have unsuccessfully endeavoured to enlist a man, call him a shirker and a coward. One reason is, you have no right to do so. I have met scores of young men who, by being rated as cowards, have been driven into a dogged, sullen and resentful determination never to come in unless compelled.'[24]

Hectoring and condescending, his appeals would be criticized by many local officials and bodies in Tipperary a few months later. O'Leary made a number of other stops through Tipperary. Earlier, passing through Cahir en route to Clonmel, O'Leary was cheered and in Carrick after the Clonmel meeting, Michael Power, Justice of the Peace (JP), and members of the Urban council, two companies of the INV and the local band escorted him through the town. MacLaughlin was also there, and said that 'Carrick sent men to the front as few other towns had done and had not alone sent men, but sent women also and a Carrick nurse was mentioned in dispatches'. O'Leary passed through Cahir without stopping, though a large crowd watched him pass and a local musician played some tunes. In Tipperary town, however, there were complaints that no reception had been organized for him: 'Perhaps the time-table didn't permit it, but it does seem strange that the famous Irishman should have slipped like a stranger unnoticed through Tipperary — the very name of which is a trumpet call and an inspiration in this great war... With the recruiting campaign, which has been in progress in Tipperary for the past few weeks, in full swing, it certainly was a unique opportunity lost.'[25]

This lack of organization was endemic throughout the CCORI. The meeting at Clonmel had been organized at short notice, and sometimes the distinction between the CCORI and the military recruiting systems was unclear. The military had not yet ceded control to civilian groups, and continued to utilize route marches for recruiting purposes. For example, a company of the 6th RIRegt left its depot at Clonmel to visit surrounding districts with the band.[26] However, damage caused by recruiters had a lasting effect on attitudes towards enlisting.

ATROCITY AND CONSCRIPTION SCARE TACTICS

It is useful here to examine two key recruiting topics used by recruiters under the aegis of the CCORI. Many of the recruiters used the same style of arguments during the time of the council. The idea that Ireland could be united; its military tradition; unique martial spirit; and virtues of masculinity in soldiering, figured on recruiting platforms. While Pat Callan has asserted that atrocity reports did not figure prominently in Ireland when compared with Britain,[27] I have found multiple examples of such reports in the Tipperary press. We have seen some in Chapter 1, and also during the council's tenure. The stories were of the lurid type of impaled babies, decapitated toddlers and mutilated members of religious orders and were exaggerated.[28] But did the Germans commit atrocities? Leaving aside non-combatants killed in bombardments and crossfire, a generous interpretation given the unprovoked nature of the German attack, about 4,000 Belgian civilians were killed deliberately by the German army. The majority of these were men of military age, some women, some children and clergy. For example, on 8 August 1914, the German 165th Infantry Regiment took seventy-two inhabitants, including women and girls, of the village of Meten out into a meadow and executed them.[29] The rationale for these killings was that they were in retaliation for activities of the *Franc-Tireurs* — supposed Belgian guerrillas who had taken up a resistance-type movement against the invading Germans. There is scant evidence for any movement like this. In any case, the idea of collective responsibility of civilians was outlawed under the Hague Convention, as was the taking and shooting of hostages.[30]

Henry MacLaughlin told a recruiting meeting in Clonmel three graphic atrocity stories:

> A German regiment entered a small village and as they came along the street the villagers heard the jeers and the laughter of the soldiery and they came out to see what was happening. What did they find? They found that all this merriment and all this sport was caused by a three-months-old baby kicking its life's blood out on the point of a German bayonet. That was their fun and I say if we are men at all in the name of God Almighty we must protect the innocents. The evening vespers bell was ringing, the peasantry came into the small churchyard for evening prayer.

They found no priest, their priest, a man of 80 years, and after hunting to see where he was, they found him pulling the bell for vespers, tied by the heels to his own belfry with his brains dashed out against the side of his own steeple... one more incident... a father and mother with their hands tied behind their backs and their legs tied together, proper against the wall of their own kitchen while three butchers cut off the hands and feet of their three innocent children under five years of age... Are we going to stand at home in luxury and ease and allow these things to occur in Belgium? You say "I am not going to enlist; I am not going in as a common soldier". There is no common soldier today. The only common men I find are civilians and I am, unfortunately, one of them.[31]

A Captain Deane told a recruiting meeting in April at Nenagh's courthouse that he had seen their dirty tricks. He 'could smell the terrible gas. This dirty trick was absolutely contrary to the Hague Convention, the rules of which the Germans had signed'. For Deane, the Germans were 'inhuman' and 'dirty', they 'killed children' and 'innocent, inoffensive men', and 'hated English, Irish and the whole British empire'. In essence they 'didn't play fair' and were not 'good sports'.[32] James O'Brien, a solicitor, declared to the same recruiting meeting that it was the Germans' use of poison gas and the sinking of the *Lusitania* that changed the game.

The use of these gases, which is contrary to the law of civilized warfare, is sufficient to stir genuine anger in Irish hearts, but that in itself was bad enough. What have we had last Friday within eight miles of our own Irish coast? You had fifteen-hundred non-combatants — many of them women and children, some of them going home to see the land they had left many years before — sent without warning to an early and watery grave...'

O'Brien told the crowd that any Tipperary man who wanted to avenge the 'sack of Louvain, havoc of Antwerp and the scandal of the wreck of the *Lusitania*' would be doing 'high and holy work'.[33]

Major Dease, the resident magistrate, railed against the German war machine, the use of poison gas and what he perceived as their scant regard for human rights.

> The soldiers lie for one or two or three days in awful agony until death claims them as a relief, and the doctors say that those who recover will be incapacitated for life and that life will be a short one. We in this country do not realize what war is. We do not hear the sound of the guns; we do not see the sights on the battlefield and it is therefore, very hard for people to realize what they are up against. But when you come to think that the enemy we are fighting has foully murdered four hundred people in sight of the silent shores of Ireland — that brings the matter home to us. Picture to yourselves those forms lying on the cold ground in Queenstown [Cobh], with their lifeless bodies calling to heaven for vengeance. Anybody who read the story of the wreck of the *Lusitania* and does not feel stunned is not fit to live in this country.[34]

There is some evidence that this outrage over the *Lusitania* is borne out, as Father Maher wrote in his diary at Thurles:

> The only thing in connection with the war that moved people to the heart was the sinking of the *Lusitania* with its freight of civilians, made up of men and women and children, none of whom had any part in the war nor had anything to say to it. That dastardly act aroused the indignation of the Irish people as it did of all civilized peoples except those in league with the central powers.[35]

Captain Lefroy said he heard of one case where '78 Belgium priests had been shot... Churches had been desecrated and obscene language used before the crucifix'.[36] At Moneygall, a meeting was held in the grounds of an army major's pile. Here the crowd was 'treated to the novelty of a female speaker who proved herself to be equally adept as the male speakers'. She told the crowd of the 'awful crimes against women and girls which had disgraced the advance of the savage huns and asked were the chaste and lovely womanhood of Ireland to fall by the same foe for want of men to defend them'.[37] At Borrisokane, M.J. McKenna, the commander of the Tipperary INV, presided over a public meeting in the town's square. W.G. Lloyd, a former president of the Young Ireland branch of the UIL, said he had been a National Volunteer and a United Irish Leaguer. He said the reports of Belgium's 'priests [being] fired upon, her women insulted and the sanctity of her churches violated... should be an incentive to Irishmen to don the khaki and have revenge for the wrongs inflicted on Belgium, for what had occurred in Belgium would occur in Ireland if by any chance the Germans ever obtained a footing on the land'. He specifically appealed for farmers' sons to enlist.[38]

We can see, then, that atrocity stories figured prominently. How effective these appeals were in terms of stimulating recruitment is much more difficult to tell. Certainly the reception afforded to the Belgian refugees in Tipperary illustrated a humanitarian concern over their situation. It must be remembered that as 1915 wore on, the war became more brutal. The campaign at Gallipoli was struggling, casualties were mounting at the western front, especially at Ypres, and significant numbers of new volunteers were being killed along with pre-war regulars. Just as late August and early September of 1914 had seen a marked increase in 'atrocity' coverage, so did this period see 'a product of the intensification of the war and an intensification in the scale of actual atrocities'.[39]

These reports were carried in the papers, but it was not just the reports from Belgium, but German actions in 1915, closer to Ireland and Britain that also shocked people. Such reports were, in turn, used in recruiting speeches. The climax came during the spring of 1915 which saw the use of chlorine gas at Ypres by the Germans, the sinking of the *Lusitania*, air raids by zeppelins on British towns and the publication of the Bryce Report into German atrocities in Belgium, which 'established the image of Germany as having thrown aside civilized norms entirely'. The most widespread outbreaks of anti-German rioting occurred in British cities at this time.[40]

The latter half of 1915, particularly when the Department of Recruiting in Ireland took over from the CCORI, resulted in atrocity recruiting appeals being replaced with strident criticisms of farmers' sons and the threat of conscription. There were a number of reasons for this: the news was becoming increasingly stale; the Allies were beginning to lose the moral high-ground; and the image of Germany was becoming more fixed.[41]

CONSCRIPTION FEARS

Calls for the introduction of conscription were increasing. Some recruiters felt that rural districts could spare more men, and tried to intimidate or scare men into enlisting through threats of conscription. At a meeting in Nenagh following the sinking of the *Lusitania*, Lord Dunalley told the crowd that the only solution he could see was national service: 'It would be quite easy to bring in, and from what I have heard a great many people say would be very acceptable. It would give an excuse, which I am sorry to say is needed, to many who are wavering to enlist at once.'[42] He also believed that national service would put an end to what he considered was a very expensive system of recruiting, and useful men would be 'set at liberty'.

Dease said that Tipperary could send another 1,000 men. But he held different views from Dunalley on recruiting, and stated that 'one voluntary soldier is worth ten conscripts': 'Do not let it be said — for that would be shame — that an Irishman had to be flogged up to fight, let us go voluntarily forward and fight.'[43] Dunalley, however, continued his crusade for conscription at the meetings he attended. About a month later in Nenagh, he claimed the lack of progress at the front was due to the lack of men. The Chairman of the Urban District Council, J.L. Johnston, said:

I am not here tonight to preach compulsion, but we are here tonight to try and prevent compulsion. One volunteer is better than twenty pressed men. Thurles has given between 300 and 400 men, principally of the labouring classes, but we have hundreds more athletic men who ought prepare themselves to meet the enemy who may be upon us at any time… Think of the consequences of a German invasion. All our dreams of Home Rule, Land Purchase, Town Purchase, and all other reforms would be at an end.[44]

Johnston said that he was too old to go, but he advocated joining nonetheless, and linked those who enlisted with the fighters of the Irish Brigade.[45]

Sergeant Booth told a recruiting meeting in Dundrum that men would have to be fetched:

He saw around him as fine, strapping, broad-shouldered young men as ever he had laid eyes on, and it was up to these men to come and defend their country and the honour of their womenfolk and the lives of their children. If the men did not come voluntarily within the next three weeks they would have to be fetched.[46]

In Carrick, Captain Hughes of the Connaught Rangers told a meeting presided over by M. Power, the chairman of the Urban Council, that:

There were two classes in the country who had not done their duty… the farmers' sons and the shopkeepers and the shop assistants. If the Germans came to Ireland the prosperity and comfort the Irish farmers now enjoy would be very short lived… He did not like conscription himself, but if the men will not come forward conscription would have to be resorted to [to] beat the Germans, as there could be no other ending of the war, but a complete smashing of the Germans.[47]

J.J. O'Shee MP, however, defended the agricultural community, but then implied that conscription could be brought in if they did not respond to the calls:

> It should be remembered that the farmers' sons and the farm labourers are engaged in producing food for the army and for the people and this is a work of almost as great and vital importance as fighting or making munitions. Food is very necessary and important, important as munitions. The place for the farmer's son at present is in the furrow, and if he would not go into the furrow, and work hard there helping to produce food then his place should be in the trenches, and he should be sent to the trenches if he will not go into the furrow.[48]

The newspaper reports of such speeches came at a time when the debate about whether the National Registration Act should be applied to Ireland was at its height. Police reports in Tipperary continually deplored what they believed was a poor response by farmers, and said that they displayed 'considerable anxiety' on the question of conscription.[49] A month later, the RIC said there had been no reports of farmers' sons emigrating though fear of conscription,[50] but there is 'no doubt they are not now attending markets and fair days as heretofore. Their older relations go into the towns to transact business leaving the young men at home… The farmers are having a very prosperous season and the townspeople are commenting on their lack of patriotism.'[51] The local press actively supported recruiting but were against conscription, and made this clear throughout the war. In August, the *Nationalist* claimed:

> Knowing that the position of Home Rule is impregnable, it is the first duty of the people to take their part in ending the terrible war… The carping critics, who try for mean party purposes to belittle Ireland's services in the war, deserve the censure of all right thinking men. They do incalculable harm to recruiting work. It is an easy matter to get recruits in Ireland when our

young men are approached in the proper spirit; they can be led but never driven, especially by men who shamelessly subordinate patriotic principle to party purposes. Ireland's noble record in the war is the admiration of the civilized world and will illuminate the pages of history when her senseless detractors are buried in oblivion.[52]

A month later, however, it rejected any talk of compulsion:

As far as Ireland is concerned, she will not have conscription. Her record in the war is in full keeping with her great military traditions… She has given out of her sadly depleted population her best and bravest to fight in every phase of the great conflict and she will not submit to conscription or any other panicky scheme of the scaremongers. These very people have not spared themselves in the malicious work of belittling Ireland's part in the war. They try to minimize her recruiting work, shut out from proper recognition the heroic deeds of her gallant sons and give a false idea generally of Ireland's share in the conflict. They threw obstacles in the way of utilizing the Volunteers at home, they sneered at the formation of the Irish Brigades and when these brigades were eventually formed they endeavoured to starve them by sending the brigade men into other divisions. The same mean spirit operated against giving due recognition to the noble Irish fighters in the strenuous Gallipoli operations and in the sinister attempt to break up the Irish Brigade in that country. The scaremongers belong mostly to the old ascendancy party and they are as relentless in their antipathy to the Irish now as they ever were.[53]

The press also published letters from soldiers calling for conscription:

Dear Mother, I would like to hear of conscription coming out. It would make some of those farmers wake up… one of these days you will see all having to enlist. I should like to meet some of them out here. I would give them a hot reception. I expect those people expect that the world will be the same when the war is over but there will be a great change.[54]

Thomas White Royal Garrison Artillery (RGA), from Cappawhite, wrote of his experiences of the war. White had seen action in South Africa and rejoined in 1914. His brother, a RIRegt soldier, had sent him a copy of the *Nationalist* that carried a recruiting meeting report from his home town. His brother was invalided home after a gas attack in Ypres. White said:

I was grieved to see that the only response made to the appeals of the different speakers was by a few old men past military age. Undoubtedly, our little parish has done remarkably well, but in this war we are fighting for liberty and humanity, for Ireland just as much as for England, and a better response should have resulted… The people of Ireland should never cease to thank God that they are spared the dreadful, indescribable horrors of this war and they should be proud of their fellow countrymen who are laying down their lives so freely in such a noble cause.[55]

The national press began to report that recruiters were disillusioned with the progression of the campaign. A Reserve Defence Forces (RDF) lieutenant said it was 'pathetic' to have to 'beg men to do their obvious duty'.[56] One reporter claimed that 'sturdy young men… disappeared like rabbits into their burrows' once a meeting got under way.[57] The perceived failure of men to attend rural meetings was singled out by the *Irish Times* and one report claimed that men played pitch and toss when the recruiters were speaking.[58] Col Cooke also amplified this: 'Response good throughout the area but some classes fail to realize that "business (and pleasure) as usual" means ruin, and still hold back, in spite of inducements offered by formation of cadet companies.'[59]

At a recruiting meeting in Dundrum, the exchanges between a military officer and the crowd illustrated the vaudeville Punch-and-Judy style nature of some of the meetings. The band of the 7th Royal Irish Fusiliers came from their base at Tipperary to Dundrum under the command of Captain G. Robinson. Robinson told the recruiting meeting:

> Some of those in the crowd apparently did not realise the gravity of the situation and the great issues that were at stake for Ireland as well as for Great Britain in this war. It was all very well for some of these young men to come there with their hands in their pockets and lean up against the walls of the houses listening to what was said to them, but he could tell them there was something more to be done at the present time.[60]

Someone in the crowd retorted: 'We are doing our work for our country.' Robinson replied: 'You are not doing your work for your country standing there with your hands in your pockets and your pipe in your mouth... There are some hundreds of fine strong able men of military age in this crowd and out of their number at least fifty ought to come forward and volunteer right away.'[61] He then addressed some of the 'muttered remarks' from the crowd when they were speaking: 'There are one or two men in this crowd and they are not young men and we don't want them to spoil the show. If they have nothing else to do let them keep their mouths shut. This is not the time for laughing. It is far too serious a business we are up against for joking.'[62]

MacLaughlin claimed that the CCORI speakers relished hecklers: 'The voice of the hostile critic, it never passed the vocal stage, was music to our speakers. It gave the necessary stimulus and heralded recruits.'[63] But the inference from all this was clear: all the lieutenants and captains could talk themselves hoarse — it would make no difference.[64]

FAILURES AND CRITICISMS

At Nenagh Urban Council, a circular from the CCORI asking the council to establish a recruiting committee was refused. The chairman, Michael Guilfoyle, said:

> I think, gentlemen, as far as recruiting goes the district of Nenagh has broken all records, not alone in Ireland, England or Scotland, but in the whole British Empire. I do not think we require any committee for any further recruiting for the people of this district have done more than their duty as far as I can learn. And I have taken some pains to get information... I think Nenagh has the best record in the empire and [it] is only a small district with a small population.

Guilfoyle said that they had a good recruiting staff in the area with Captain Lefroy, Colour Sergeant Fitzgerald and Sergeant Frances, whom he said 'were qualified to take the names of any young men wishing to go to the front' and, therefore, he did not see the 'necessity for the formation of any committee'.[65] The members of the council agreed. One council member said: '...you have streets with no available men of military age. I think nearly all the men of military age have left the town.' Another said: 'There are towns in England from which very few are listed... Captain Lefroy, Colour Sergeant Fitzgerald and Sergeant Frances are quite capable to do the business.' The clerk of the council claimed: 'Something like 700 or 800 men have left the district out of a population of less than 5,000... there are streets in Nenagh with only two men.'[66] Therefore, no recruiting committee was formed.

The *Nenagh Guardian* reported on this council meeting a week later. It said: 'The people of Nenagh and district have well and gallantly responded to the call of King and country. Upwards of 800 men from the town alone have donned khaki and yet more are going every day and swelling the ranks of the men who will meet the hunnish hordes... Last week several old hands left for home service.' The report also mentioned the tribute paid to the recruiting officers who were 'worth a dozen recruiting committees'. It also said the clerk of Borrisokane Union, M.J. McKenna, 'has done, and is doing, his bit'.[67]

What local councils could do was collect information on the service record of local men. The family of each man was then presented with a 'Certificate of Honour'. This was something that far outlasted the CCORI but they were not presented in Tipperary until 1917. These were intended to unite 'mansions and cottages alike' by encouraging family pride and serving as an 'infectious appeal' to potential recruits.[68] At Nenagh Urban Council, the LGB wrote asking how many employees of the council had been released for military service. None were, but in a discussion one councillor wondered why 'have they not sent off the Ulster Division? … They must have got lost somewhere. They are sending off young men after three months' training and are keeping the Ulster Division at home'.[69] Guilfoyle, said that he had only received six certificates to give to the dependents of those who enlisted, which were supposed to have been given out after the last recruiting meeting, while many people had asked him for one. The chairman said: 'I think if we wrote for more certificates it would be a good idea, for Nenagh has done remarkably well'. The clerk said that if a representation was made for certificates 'he should ask for about sixteen hundred' and that he had 'travelled through parts of County Tipperary, County Galway and King's County and the majority of the people he had seen working in the fields were women; that, he said, showed that the farmers' sons had gone'. MacLaughlin, who had asked about the Ulster Division, said that he had been informed that the 'Royal Irish Regiment in Dublin is called the Nenagh Regiment'.[70] In theory, the practice of issuing the certificates was a private one to honour the service during the war, but this was eroded by the military when they used their presentation as a chance to ask for more recruits.[71]

At Carrick, MacLaughlin wrote to the Urban District Council, thanking it for the reception afforded to Mike O'Leary and asking that a recruiting committee be formed. One councillor said that if every town in England did as well as Carrick, there would be a 'couple of million more men in the army today. I would not be in favour of holding any recruiting meetings in

Carrick'. The chairman, Michael Power, said that there were 'no more men to spare from here'.[72] The response by Cashel UDC to such a CCORI request is instructive. The chairman, Michael Slattery, said that he had come across this before and that there was no point because enough had gone. Cashel had done its duty. Slattery said:

> There are lots of nonentities speaking about this matter and they don't know what they are talking about. I think that Ireland and particularly our own county of Tipperary has given as good a response as any other part. We are proud that Irishmen have done so nobly in this fight against tyranny. To my mind, the question of the crops is a most important matter... I don't see that there is anyone to be spared in the rural district.[73]

The council made an order: 'Owing to the number that have joined the army since the war broke out from the Cashel rural district there are so few available recruits left that it is unnecessary to form a recruiting committee. It is a matter of anxious consideration with the people who want the hands for saving crops and carrying on any local industry'.[74]

At South Tipperary County Council's annual meeting, the chairman surveyed the recruiting campaign. He said that nationalists had nothing to grumble at regarding the response by agricultural, commercial and working-class communities to the recruiting call, and the country 'had answered their leader's call in that respect'. He also rounded on those who he felt criticized the agricultural community for not doing enough – essentially, the landlords:

> It was his opinion and the opinion of many in Tipperary that the would-be recruiters would do better if they went about their recruiting in a proper manner than by indulging in sneers and grins at the agricultural community. If the men who shouted at the farmers' sons, and the farmers' sons who went into business in the towns, did their duty in the past instead of pulling down

the roof-trees of the farmers homes and driving the population
out of the country they would have more men to call upon now.[75]

Slattery also said that he had been asked to form a recruiting committee but,
mirroring the response given by the Cashel UDC, he said that there was no
point as in the country areas 'they could not find ten unmarried men between
the ages of 18 and 40 years and out of that number scarcely six would pass the
doctor for military service'. He said that in the face of this, what 'was the use of
sneering at farmers' sons? What was the necessity for a recruiting committee
when the men were coming forward voluntarily? The farmers had to remain in
the country to save the crops, and in that, they were doing their duty, because
food was as much a munition of war as were shells.'[76] Slattery dismissed what
he perceived as the hypocrisy of the recruiting effort, laying the blame for
Tipperary's depleted population at the feet of those now urging men to enlist
in the army, i.e. the landlords.

Thurles Urban Council met to discuss establishing a recruiting committee.
The council unanimously passed a motion condemning the German sinking
of the *Lusitania*: 'That we as a public body regard as infamous this last atrocity
of the German navy acting under instructions from their Kaiser in sinking
the *Lusitania* thereby sending into eternity over 1,200 souls without a minute's
warning — thus murdering helpless men, women and little children none of
whom had any party in the strike now raging.' The chairman of the council
bluntly said that they were now at war with Prussia[77] and it was their duty to
encourage people to enlist:

> This act of the Germans ought convince us that they are capable
> [of] doing anything. We have read the stories in the newspapers…
> I think it is our duty as Irishmen if we have a spark of humanity
> in us to condemn by every means in our power the action of the
> German navy which has shocked the civilized world. I cannot
> imagine for one instant how any Irishman is pro-German. As I
> have said, it becomes our duty to help recruiting in every way.

Some of us are physically unable to go out and fight, but I think we ought all do at home everything to encourage those who are able and willing to meet the Germans where they have a right to meet them — on the soil of France. This letter is an effort to get recruits by voluntary methods, and to my mind it is far better to get them that way then having recourse to other means.

The chairman supported the CCORI letter and acquiesced to the prospect of conscription if the voluntary scheme failed. One councillor went further, and said that he had two sons at the front, but the 'middle class' were 'laughing and sneering at the poor people going out' and the only way to get them to enlist was 'to force them out'. The chairman responded that 200 from the 'working classes' had enlisted, while another councillor said that if every town did as well as Thurles, there would be no problems. The police agreed with this assessment: 'Recruiting has been good from classes apart from farmers' sons and shop-boys. No additional stimulus will bring any large number to the army. The farmers' sons say they are wanted where they are or their mothers won't let them go, and the shop-boys have no taste for fighting.'[78]

The chairman wrote back to the CCORI stating that 200 had volunteered and there were no more left.[79] That was the crucial decision. The council was more than happy to support the recruiting campaign in words and to pass resolutions, but when it came to specific requests of help from the authorities, this was refused.

Henry MacLaughlin's role in the recruiting campaign was also criticized. John Cullinan branded MacLaughlin as a 'Carsonite henchman, who never let slip an opportunity of insulting the farmers and the farmers' sons of the south.'[80] Cullinan said that MacLaughlin had done more to damage recruiting than anyone else:

A recruiting meeting was called for Carrickbeg a few evenings ago and not a single local representative was consulted beforehand. The general suspicion in the minds of many was that a certain section of the recruiting agents were anxious that nationalists should not join so that it could be used against them later on. A protest should be made against men who, instead of inducing young men to join the army, were driving them away from it. If they wanted recruits in the south they should send officers and agents who were in sympathy with the people and not those who were their deadly enemies in the past and pledged to be their deadly enemies in the future. Nationalist Ireland has done remarkably well and would continue to do so, but they protested against those accusations and insults from men like Mr McLoughlin [sic].[81]

Slattery said that he would resign his position sooner than go on a platform with MacLaughlin, who was a direct injury to the cause of recruiting in Tipperary:

He got on a platform in Clonmel, and nationalists associated with him, and said that farmers had no excuse now — that they had the military to save the crops. What an absurdity to talk about saving crops with Englishmen who never saw a potato dug and Canadian horses that would not draw an empty cart along the road. He said before and he would repeat it, that for the twenty miles of the main road from Clonmel to Thurles there could not be found ten farmer's sons eligible for the army, and of those, six would not pass the doctor. They were exterminated in the past by those that now sneered at them.[82]

Therein lay one of the huge problems of the CCORI. The lack of screening saw 'locally unpopular' men on recruiting platforms, thus providing an excuse to nationalists who were 'loath to depart from all the tradition of their lifetime'.[83] It is unusual that Tipperary established no county committee, given its garrison nature. While one local committee was established in theory at Templemore, it never did any real work. A total of nineteen counties had established county recruiting committees, including two in the RIRegt district, Wexford and Waterford. It seems astonishing that Tipperary did not, given the amount of recruits raised, but the feeling among local bodies was that the county had done enough. Much damage had been done by recruiters, which led to a reluctance on behalf of local bodies to cooperate.[84] Even by the end of the CCORI's tenure, MacLaughlin himself had regrets about some of the tone of his speeches. He told *Irish Life* in October 1915:

> I do not think it would serve any useful purpose to discuss now the reasons why these classes [farmers/shop assistants] have failed in their duty. But I do want to say this and to say it with emphasis that I do not think there is anything to be gained and that there is much to be lost by branding whole classes as recreants or cowards because other classes have shown greater courage and patriotism. Perhaps I have been guilty myself in the heat of platform appeals of appearing to transgress this opinion. If so I regret it. If I have ever doubted, experience has taught me that the only really effective appeal is to a man's better self, to his truest and highest instincts and his innate love of freedom.[85]

INFLUENCE OF THE CATHOLIC CHURCH ON RECRUITING

The Church never made a formal statement on recruiting. The majority of the clergy in Tipperary, however, favoured the Allies. Many priests in the county supported the recruiting effort and spoke on platforms. We have seen how Dr John Harty, Archbishop of Cashel and Emly, supported recruiting after the Home Rule Bill was signed. Archbishop Harty was one of only nine bishops who continued to support the war into 1916.[86] The Archbishop was not alone among the religious fraternity in supporting recruiting: the parish priest in Tipperary town, Canon Arthur Ryan;[87] Archdeacon Flavin, the parish priest at St Peter and Paul's in Clonmel; and Father Edmund Kelly[88], an army chaplain, were all strongly in favour of the British war effort.

One priest in particular made a key contribution to the recruiting effort in Tipperary, and that man was Canon Ryan. Army recruitment could only have been boosted in some way by Ryan's passionate appeals. A major influence on Ryan were the connections between his family and the British Army, and it was the service of his nephews in particular during the European war, together with his support for Redmond, that led to Ryan becoming a major figure for recruiting in Tipperary. Three sons of his oldest brother served, one of whom died during the Somme battle. Three sons of another brother served, with one dying during the closing weeks. Furthermore, a son of his youngest brother was killed at Loos in 1915, and in July 1916, a professional soldier married to his niece was killed at the front. This concerned the family of his brother, Charles, a doctor who lived near Canon Ryan in Tipperary town. A stained glass window in the church in Tipperary commemorates this British officer.[89] Canon Ryan even managed a visit to the front in 1916, meeting with the commander of the 16th Irish Division, Tipperaryman Major General William Hickie,[90] Father Edmond Kelly and many Irish soldiers serving there. He even had a trench named after him: 'Canon's Trench'.[91]

Canon Ryan appeared frequently at recruiting meetings, but became the target of those who resented his efforts. One occurrence in particular made the national papers. At a meeting in Tipperary, Arthur Ryan was mailed 'anonymous letters threatening personal violence' if he took the chair.[92] A few days before the meeting, the people of the town were able to read posters denouncing the war effort and Ryan's activities. Ryan dismissed these 'personally offensive' threats and the meeting went ahead with Ryan appearing on the platform with Canon C.B. de Boinville, rector of Tipperary. The *Irish Times* claimed that the town was 'indignant' when such threats were revealed,[93] and the *Freeman's Journal* claimed that Tipperary town had defended its priest.[94] At the meeting, Ryan called the author a coward who deserved nothing but contempt:

> Were I to refuse to take this chair today I should be false to my
> people and false to my own past and false to my own dead... From
> this platform I will call him a coward, a mean and contemptible

coward who, afraid to show his face, writes anonymous threats and in the darkness of the night posts up his scurrilous placards.[95]

Ryan was undeterred by the threats and called for recruits to fill the 'vacant places' in three Irish divisions, saying that it would be shameful if the ranks were filled by Scottish, English or Welsh recruits. He would enlist if he could, and he had ancestors who fought with Sarsfield and the Irish Brigade. Enlisting, Ryan claimed, 'would save them from everlasting self-reproach and their country from the extinction of her fame upon the battlefield'.[96] 'There is only one way of bringing conscription and that is by the men of the country failing to do their duty as voluntary recruits.'[97] Essentially, for Ryan, this was about maintaining the Irish divisions and avoiding conscription.

This type of attempted intimidation was rare, and the anti-recruiting forces were usually reluctant to attack priests knowing that it could be counter-productive.[98] But the total embracement of the recruiting campaign in the way that Canon Ryan did was also rare, and some opposition from clerics existed in Tipperary. Father Michael Maher wrote regularly in his diary of the impact of the war and of support for the Allies, but he refused to speak on a recruiting platform:

> There was a recruiting meeting held in Ireland in the early part of July at which I was asked to preside… I refused to attend on the grounds that I had resigned from the volunteers and because I was the junior priest at Thurles. Then they requested me to attend if I thought well to speak at the meeting but I neither attended nor spoke.[99]

When Lt-Col Charles Dalton RAMC from Golden in Tipperary was killed, Father Matt Ryan of Knockavilla asked for prayers but then launched a stinging attack on MPs who asked for recruits, who 'wanted their sons to become maggots, meat in France and Belgium'. He was even more bitter regarding a recruiting meeting in his parish a few weeks later, and was reported as saying that: 'I don't want to stop ye if ye want to go to France and eat turnips. Ye can stop a bullet as well as any other and let John Bull stop at home.' These outbursts were reported to the police, who complained to Harty, who promised to order Father Ryan not to offend again.[100] The advanced nationalist press (separatists or republicans) also critizised Canon Ryan. Arthur Griffith's paper, *Nationality*, in a piece called 'The Two Ryans', gave the example of Father Matt Ryan,[101] who had been imprisoned during the Land War, a period, it claimed, when Canon Ryan had remained silent: 'He is not silent today. His fine rolling voice is working for England.'[102]

Generally, the clergy was seen as being in sympathy with the aims of the Allies. While the Church was officially neutral on the question of recruiting, it was often left up to individual members to make up their own minds, and there is no doubt that there was a vibrant pro-recruiting stance taken in Tipperary by the RC clergy, driven by Archbishop Harty and Canon Ryan. How much this affected recruiting figures is tempting to debate.

GALLIPOLI AND SERGEANT JAMES SOMERS VC

Irish losses at Gallipoli became a controversial issue as the descriptions of battle and the losses found their way into the national and local papers. Initial reports written in a touristy, almost sporty style gave way to more sombre and graphic accounts of the invasion.[103] The national papers gave much prominence to Gallipoli. Once news of the losses became well known in mid-August, newspapers were filled every day with photographs of dead, wounded and missing officers, usually with a pen portrait that included information about their family, their peacetime career and — in guarded detail — the manner of their demise.[104] The earlier assaults on Gallipoli did receive some praise from local papers, and they carried reports of Irish valour in Turkey. For example, in July the *Nationalist* reported on the despatches of Ian Hamilton, who wrote describing the Gallipoli landings and praising the 'magnificent heroism' of the Dublins, Munsters and Inniskillings in the landings.[105]

By the late summer of 1915, however, bitterness about the casualty rates made it a strongly contested political matter. The *Irish Independent* was troubled by reports that commanders felt the new divisions fighting at Suvla were not up to scratch. Redmond felt unease at the carnage in Turkey and was aghast at the way in which the actions of Irish soldiers were being ignored by the British establishment. 'Where were the Suvla medals and decorations?'[106] Redmond may have ignored the degree to which the military establishment was embarrassed by the debacle and 'inclined to perceive the lack of praise for Irish soldiers at Suvla as a deliberate snub, while it was possibly a symptom of the deep unease about the whole Dardanelles campaign'.[107]

Much of the information in Tipperary also came from letters or interviews with soldiers — much of it uncensored. Indeed, published letters were usually the only source of information. Action to enforce censorship at home was taken under the Defence of the Realm Act (DORA) and private letters, which by 1915 had to be submitted to the Press Bureau for vetting before publication, then declined as a source of news by the end of the year.[108] It was not until May 1915 that five representatives of the British press selected by the Newspaper Proprietors Association, and under strict military supervision, were allowed to send home censored dispatches from the front. Pte Lewis RIRegt (Pioneers) of Albert Street, Clonmel, wounded by shrapnel in the knee, wrote from a hospital in Cairo: 'The wound in the right knee is bad. I had a narrow shave of being killed. I well remember the fight, nothing but shell, shot and bombs flying about us. It was like hell upon earth.'[109]

A letter from a RIRegt officer said that the situation was badly handled by the authorities: 'The Irish are always at the front. Whatever is on they say "Send the Irish; they are the boys to get the Turks on the run". No one knows what we went through, only we who were there. We suffered much and were badly handled. But it's all coming out now. We were four to five days without a drink.'[110]

For the authorities, James Somers provided the perfect antidote to such press. Here was a man who had won the VC in Gallipoli and would engage in recruiting. Borrisokane District Council passed a resolution congratulating their 'hero' Sergeant James Somers on winning the VC.[111]

Dunalley chaired a meeting when he arrived back at the station, and Captain Lefroy said that he hoped more people from the town and district would try and attain the same distinction, but 'at any rate, they could go out and help those already gone'.[112] Landowner B.B. Trench said that they were all proud of Somers: 'This was the first Victoria Cross which had come to Tipperary in this war and he hoped it would not be the last. Only for the action of the gallant boys in khaki and navy blue they would be without a home. Their action had preserved the honour of their women.' Trench went out to call for recruits and he offered economic incentives: '50 acres of freehold land [to anyone who wins the VC] or to any employee of his who serves through the war, or their dependants, five acres of freehold land and a house'.[113] The *Irish Times* got in on the act, announcing that a special 'monster meeting' would be held later in October in honour of Somers and reporting that Nenagh had sent 900 to the colours out of a population of 5,000.[114]

The special ceremony in October was widely reported in the national press and several photographs were carried in the 18 October edition of *Irish Life*. A 'wide and enthusiastic audience' turned out for Somers.[115] Major General Friend, commander of the forces in Ireland, told the crowd that they did not realize that there was a war going on. Ireland was at peace 'yet some few hundred miles away shot and shells were flying and men were falling by the hundred'.[116] Friend said that many more Tipperary men could win the VC: 'The act which gained the VC for Sergeant Somers was not done on the spur of the moment. It was part of an action which lasted for many hours. There were many amongst the audience who were as brave and who might also, if they joined the Colours, receive such a distinction.'[117]

Trench said that he could not understand anybody who claimed to be pro-German.

> He did not know what these people meant, because if they wanted an instance of German rule they had only to look at Prussian Poland where the Polish people could not have an acre of land in their own name. In Poland, everything was under the rule of the military caste. He did not think the people of Ireland would appreciate that if they had to endure it. The brutality of the Germans was past credulity, but it was part of their doctrine of blood and iron.[118]

Trench also paid tribute to South Africa, and said that they had defeated the Germans in their own country and were now sending troops to fight with Britain. Could Ireland, he asked, stand by while the colonies sent men?[119] Reverend. R. Bourke, the church curate at Cloughjordan, said:

> It must be pleasing to General Friend to know Cloughjordan had done its best in the war. At present many of the bravest and best of the village and district were in training. Many of them too were fighting in the east and many in the west... [I will] conclude by assuring General Friend that should the fortunes of war so have it Cloughjordan would do a noble part in the future.[120]

Father Bourke paid tribute to Somers and to the role that Tipperary played in the conflict: 'Her sons have sunk their steel into the craven hearts of those that would ravage our homes and outrage humanity and Tipperary, always a hater of the bully and the tyrant, knows she is up against the greatest tyrant that ever disgraced humanity... [Somers] has given those at home an example that ought to serve them and to show them what Tipperary men can do'.[121]

But Somers was, as it were, the one bright spot for the authorities. The *Irish Independent* complained that it was only from private letters and occasional interviews with wounded soldiers that the Irish public had learned anything of the gallant conduct of the Irish regiments like the Royal Dublin Fusiliers in Flanders or the 10th at Gallipoli. Redmond considered it a scandal that up to the moment of withdrawal from Gallipoli in late 1915, there had been no detailed despatch from the force commander as to what had occurred regarding Irish regiments during the campaign. He thought it unworthy of the government that men who had faced untold sufferings and showed unparalleled heroism should have been left without any official despatch recording their deeds.[122] The *Irish Independent* added that there was 'bitter disappointment' over the Gallipoli withdrawal, which was a sorry end to the victory promised six months earlier and a beggarly return for the sacrifice of so many Irish lives. In the 'disastrous expedition', hundreds of the 10th Irish Division's lives had been sacrificed, yet there had been no official acknowledgement of their heroism and whoever was responsible for this appalling blunder had 'recklessly sacrificed' Irish lives.[123] The belated publication of despatches, while establishing that Irish gallantry was 'magnificent', also proved to the *Independent* that an almost impossible task had been set to unseasoned troops.[124]

A *Nationalist* editorial was devoted entirely to lauding Irish troops in the field:

> In the Gallipoli landing their efforts were magnificent, and won praise from all sides, while in the very latest phase of the war, the Allies' retreat towards Salonika, the 10th Irish Division has covered itself with glory... The official report deservedly marks out for special praise the marvellous work of the Irish troops, while the British press is ringing with unstinted praise of their bravery and dogged courage. One London paper suggests that parliament should vote special thanks to them... Orange and green have carried the day on the battlefield and the effects of the achievement will be felt far outside the Serbian frontier. The bonds of patriotism have been drawn more closely together between all classes in Ireland as the result of the heroic, praise compelling deeds of our magnificent fighting men in the Balkans.[125]

The paper was still carrying the slightly naive hope of Redmond that exploits on the battlefield would unite the two sections of Ireland. In Thurles, however, the junior priest wrote something more instructive:

> It was announced officially today that a portion of the force that had landed on the Gallipoli peninsula has been unsuccessfully withdrawn. There is great disappointment at this retreat as it is an admission of liability to overcome the Turk and it is likely to have been exceedingly humiliating... to have to turn their backs to the spot where so many of their brave comrades had fallen and to leave their remains there in nameless graves in an enemy

country. There is at least one Thurles man buried there. Private James Sheehan, who was a driver at Ms Hogan's hotel. He was a reserve man whose time had expired, but he volunteered soon after the war broke out. He leaves a wife and four young children to mourn his loss.[126]

CONCLUSION

The CCORI was established to tap previously neglected areas for recruits — to change the game as it were. From the start, it was clear that the council was not in tune with the unique recruiting landscape that existed in Ireland and in Tipperary. There is no doubt that the council operated in a difficult environment through 1915, beginning with Redmond's refusal to take a place in the Coalition government, an acrimonious debate over conscription and the Gallipoli disaster — a gross example of military bungling. Speeches given by men such as MacLaughlin had done infinite harm and worked against cultivating an atmosphere that was sympathetic to recruiting. It was steadily becoming apparent throughout 1915 that the government was edging towards conscription. This was manifested in the threats of compulsion that we have seen during recruiting meetings and, in turn, led to increasingly bitter criticisms of farmers' sons and shopkeepers' assistants, which alienated them from the recruiting campaign.

In essence, the CCORI proved hugely divisive. Their way of operating had not changed since the early days of the recruiting campaign, and still relied on bands and star speakers to convey their message. Many meetings descended into farcical to-and-fro battles between earnest speakers and hecklers. No CCORI county committee was established in Tipperary, which is astonishing given the support recruiters had from local politicians, the local clergy and given its garrison nature. The CCORI campaign had wide support from 'official Tipperary', for example the meeting with Mike O'Leary heard an impassioned call from the mayor for recruits. The refusal to establish a county committee is particularly remarkable, given that two other counties in the RIRegt area did so.[127]

4 RECRUITING AND CONSCRIPTION FEARS

The Collins brothers, Tipperary town. Tipperary People Publications.

A CONFERENCE WAS held at the Viceregal Lodge, Dublin, on 28 October 1915. The editor of the *Nationalist* told the Lord Lieutenant, Ivor Wimborne, that encouraging recruiting in Tipperary was merely a case of 'spurring a willing horse'. Brandon J. Long said that he felt certain Wimborne knew of Tipperary's record in the conflict: 'They had already done much and the result had been good. There were, however, still more recruits to be obtained. The ground was a fruitful one even if the supplies of men were limited and no stone would be left unturned to encourage the young men to follow in the footsteps of the brave soldiers who had already gone forth.'[1]

Representatives of the *Nenagh Guardian*, *Nenagh News*, *Cashel Sentinel*, and *Tipperary People* attended, along with a host of other provincial and national editors.[2] Wimborne was appointed president of this new recruiting group, which was known as the Department of Recruiting in Ireland (DRI).[3] The administration of the CCORI was ended swiftly — only one recruiting committee existed in Tipperary under the aegis of the council. Wimborne favoured a series of postal appeals, something that had been used in Britain. For the first three weeks, a nationwide postal campaign would be supplemented by a vigorous press campaign. Military bands would also maintain a high profile. The *Nationalist*, then, supported the DRI campaign, and the possible bias in the attendant media coverage must be borne in mind when determining the extent of public support for it.

THE DRI AND THE THREAT OF CONSCRIPTION

The postal campaign began on 29 October. In Cahir, hundreds of recruiting circulars were received by men of military age. 'They came as a surprise, and at first, created quite a sensation, especially in the country districts, and constituted the sole topic of conversation. Many persons thought that conscription had arrived and in places quite a panic was occasioned.'[4] The report felt obliged to state that the new recruiting scheme was not connected with any effort to impose conscription.[5] The police also said that they believed the circulars showed 'the seriousness of the situation to all classes, but it is too soon at present to say what effect they will have'.[6] It was this threat of conscription that destroyed any chance of the DRI meeting its targets. The department had not learned the lessons of the CCORI. In the October issue of *Irish Life*, just before the CCORI had been disbanded, a number of guidelines for recruiters were outlined. One key rule was this: 'Do not threaten men who refuse to enlist — even if they refuse rudely — with conscription. It is not honourable to attempt to intimidate by a threat which you have no power to enforce.'[7]

Many recruiters in Tipperary did the exact opposite and criticized voluntary enlistment whenever possible. This was most injurious to the cause of the DRI, especially when speakers 'wished for or threatened that conscription would be imposed on a recalcitrant population which deserved it'.[8] At a meeting in Thurles, the chairman of the urban council appealed for men to come forward 'and not wait for compulsion'. Captain Loftus, DRI sub-director of Recruiting for the eastern counties, Tipperary, Waterford, Kilkenny and Wexford, said that the appeal was the last attempt at voluntary recruiting: 'They were all in favour of the voluntary system both for England and Ireland, but if it failed something else should be tried… If recruits did not come forward the government would have to come to a decision… if the voluntary system failed then would come conscription.'[9]

This was black and white from Loftus. The mantra from the DRI was join now or else be conscripted. A number of days later, however, he told a meeting in Cashel:

> He could tell them directly and officially that that was not so…
> If the department of recruiting were in favour of conscription
> would they be sending speakers throughout the country, going to
> the expense of advertising for recruits, sending bands about the
> country at considerable expense and holding meetings to induce
> men to come forward voluntarily? Of course they would not.
> That was absolute and conclusive proof that the new department
> was out to support the voluntary system at all costs. He referred
> to a speech by John Dillon that promised the IPP's support for
> the new department. The lord lieutenant wanted all men to go
> forward as free men, not conscripts.[10]

Private Bernard Dempsey of the Irish Guards urged men to enlist that day and not wait until conscription. For Dempsey and the other speakers, conscription was a *fait accompli*, and he echoed the military's distaste for voluntary recruiting meetings: 'There are thousands of Irishmen fighting out there — come and give us your help — join now and don't wait for conscription. I wouldn't like to be a conscript… don't wait to be sent away like a waggon of cattle… These recruiting meetings are awful.'[11]

A former sergeant major of the Connaught Rangers 'asked the men of Thurles to join voluntarily and not be forced. If you don't join voluntarily… as sure as fate conscription will come and very soon, too.'[12] Another major seconded this: 'He was not there to make a speech, and all he had to say was, if we don't get volunteers they will be made to come.'[13] Lord Dunalley repeated something he had been saying from the start: 'Nenagh had done very well indeed, but it could do more. If the voluntary system did not come up to the standard of expectation some sort of compulsion would undoubtedly be necessary, but this they wanted to avoid if possible… he appealed to the farmers' sons to come forward and do their duty.'[14]

The IPP began to feel anxious about these threats of compulsion, and John Cullinan was forced to address them at a December recruiting meeting in Ardfinnan. With the Rising only months away, these DRI initiatives were effectively the swansong of the campaign. Cullinan accepted the negative impact some speakers had, whom he labelled 'stupid and malicious-minded people', but told people that the idea of conscription was absurd:

> In the first place he had to disabuse their minds of an idea which would never had existed were it not for the fact that parties addressing recruiting meetings were not in sympathy with the people and did not understand them. People were led to believe that if they showed themselves at a recruiting meeting they would be immediately nobbled by the sergeant; they were told that if they did not volunteer they would be forced into the army by the scruff of the neck. Nothing more absurd could be stated, for the simple reason that no one had the power to force a man into the army. There could be no conscription except through an Act of Parliament and if it came to a question of conscription in the House of Commons the Irish boys would be there, as they had been before, to prevent wrong things being done… By attending a recruiting meeting they were taking part in a campaign against conscription.[15]

But Cullinan did not hesitate to encourage enlisting at the same meeting. He told the crowd that Ireland was at peace because of the war, and there had never been a time when the country was so prosperous. This was due to the men 'who voluntarily went out to man the trenches and man the ships that defended the country and Ireland would be a most ungrateful nation and unworthy of her past traditions if she did not go to the rescue of the men who had fallen in her defence and whose sacrifice had brought such benefits to the country'.[16] Neither did Cullinan criticize the DRI campaign in general, saying that 'things were very much improved. It was arranged with the approval of Mr Redmond and under it no coercion would be applied to anyone.'[17] Even Loftus rowed back on his previous statements and said that conscription was not on the agenda and all they wanted were recruits to back up the men at the front.[18]

How real was the threat of conscription? An interesting way to look at this is through Wilson's Tour, a series of interviews held by a unionist with some 'prominent' men in the county. The consensus was generally that no trouble would arise. A recruiting director told Wilson: 'If a register were formed showing exactly who would be exempt and the thing explained by the government there would be no revolution.'[19] Col R. Cooke at the RIRegt depot took a different angle, and said that those who had contributed more to the army would be happy to see compulsion:

> There is nothing that the labouring classes and all those that have already come in would be more pleased with than to see compulsion. Women can be got to do anything in taking the place of men. Proper figures are badly wanted and these should be supplied. There would be no revolt. Not in the least. A lot of talk and so and so. It is easy to draw an analogy from the case of those arrested under the Defence of the Realm… where nothing occurred afterwards. No trouble arose when Lord Wimborne's letter calling for recruits was received and some people had expected great resistance.[20]

The town clerk said he did expect 'violent resistance. A section would preach it but the country is not in the humour for it.'[21] The editor of the *Clonmel Chronicle* said: 'There would only be some squabbling.'[22] A.W. Rochfort, a landowner based around Cahir, and who controversially appeared on a recruiting platform in Tipperary, gave this assessment:

> There would be trouble in places. A good deal would depend on how the order was carried out. Small classes should be taken up at a time. It depends upon what official did it. If the country people believed that real business was meant opposition would collapse. The people here are really the easiest governed in the world but there must be a sanction behind the law. They are easily terrorized.[23]

Some did not take the postal appeal seriously. In Thurles, one shop assistant had the form filled up by someone as a joke. When the military told him to report he had some difficulty in telling them he had not enlisted.[24] Police confirmed this: 'A number of cases of forging peoples' names to recruiting papers have occurred... There is no way of identifying each enlistment form and it was in all probability considered as an opportunity for what appeared to be a jest.'[25]

In the north of the county, the police felt the same way with the County Inspector stating: 'very little response was shown to His Excellency's [Wimborne] circular and in some cases... were filled in with bogus undertakings'.[26] Writing in his diary, Father Michael Maher mentioned the stir created by Wimborne's postal campaign in Tipperary:

> A few days ago an invitation was sent to most of the men of military age... from the lord lieutenant saying that Lord Kitchener wants 50,000 Irishmen to enlist for military service in Irish regiments. The man was asked if he were willing to join voluntarily and what regiment he wished to be attached to. There was no obligation imposed on the receiver to respond, but a good many will look on it as a mild command and I expect it will have the effect of bringing a large number of recruits to the colours.

> All the postmen and post office officials have received them and
> they regard it as a hint that if they don't join they must clear out.
> As the same time the Irish Party assures us that there will be no
> conscription.[27]

Of 12,000 replies received nationally by 12 November, 30 per cent said they
would enlist.[28] As we have seen, some of these were not reliable. In some
areas, the police felt that the appeal had the opposite effect and actually drove
people into Sinn Féin or the separatist Irish Volunteers: 'The IV are growing
in strength and the dread of conscription, a tool in their hands, would induce
many to join their ranks before too long.'[29] In the south of the county:

> The receipt of letters from the Dept of Recruiting has caused some
> little stir. It is too soon to say what the effect will ultimately be
> but it certainly had the effect in Clonmel of causing an increase
> in the ranks of the SFers. They were no doubt previously inclined
> that way. I am informed that these letters have been sent to boys
> of immature age in Clonmel which seems undesirable.[30]

At the same time, the police noted an improvement in recruiting, but this
was confined to the usual pool of urban-based labourers. In November, for
example, the County Inspector of Tipperary's North Riding district wrote that
'recruiting meetings have been held at different places in the riding and a fair
number of recruits have been obtained. Nearly all these recruits were from
the labouring classes.'[31] In the south, the inspector observed 'a steady flow of
recruits for the army. There are not, however, any shop boys or farmers' sons
enlisting.'[32] Col Cooke said: 'In Clonmel and the towns it is good, the same
as everywhere else. No countrymen are joining.'[33] The editor of the *Clonmel
Chronicle* stated: 'Clonmel and Carrick have done very well. Any number
could be spared from the grazing districts.'[34]

Farmers and their sons, then, were coming under sustained criticism from
recruiters for their refusal to enlist, or even consider enlisting in the military.[35]

CRITICISMS OF FARMERS' SONS

From the very beginning of the campaign, the authorities agreed that farmers' sons and shop assistants refused to enlist. Monthly police reports continually alluded to their unwillingness to join the army.[36] Police reported that the farmers 'who have received more state benefits than any other class, and shop assistants, are still unwilling to do their share in the trenches'.[37] A landowner, Rochfort, told Wilson: 'The farmers as a class are delighted at the high prices and hope the war will not be over until all their barley is sold.'[38] Efforts had been made by the CCORI to stimulate enlistment among both groupings and the DRI intensified those efforts.[39] Recruiters, however, told farmers that they were shirking their responsibilities in not fighting for their land. Farmers were also told that if Germany won the war, it would take their land by force. Irish farms were already mapped out in Berlin and it was unfair to let the labouring class bear the brunt of fighting. Captain Lefroy told a meeting in the Glen of Aherlow:

> I am ashamed of asking any more labouring men to join — we can't spare them; but we can spare plenty of the farmers' sons... Are you going to let future history say that you, the farmers' sons, refused to fight and let others fight for you... How are you going to face 200,000 Irishmen when they come back after the war, who will say to you 'We fought for you — what did you do for us?' Remember that when an Irish parliament sits in College Green the labouring men will have a very considerable vote in this country, and I tell you solemnly today that if I am spared at the end of this war I will back up every single one of the men who enlisted in getting some of the land that you won't go out and fight for.[40]

Lieutenant Patterson asked the same meeting if they could look on as their brothers had been fighting in the trenches for the past year to save Ireland, 'where farmers were at present getting such huge prices for their produce and cattle'. Patterson said:

The plain truth of it was that these enormous prices the farmers were now getting was blood money and it was up to the farmers and their sons to do something to help the men who were fighting for them in the trenches. The people who were going about Ireland saying the war was no concern of the Irish people were lying to their consciences and to their God.[41]

In Nenagh, Lord Dunalley launched a blistering attack on the farmers:

You are up against the war now and if we do not succeed we will be wiped off the face of the earth and it depends on you, the men of suitable age, to come and help… though the people of Nenagh have done very well the farmers… have not done very well. They are quite content to sit on their farm and live upon the fat of the land — not exactly the fat of the land, but on the blood of their neighbours and the blood of their friends and the blood of our sons and your sons who have died out there. That is what the farmers are living on — blood simply.[42]

T.P. Gill, Secretary of the Department of Agriculture, said that it was the first time he had stood on a recruiting platform but he nonetheless appealed to farmers to enlist and help save the farms they had purchased.[43] He said 'there was no getting away from the fact that farmers' sons must fight as well as every other class of the community'.

I feel sure of this — and I don't care what is said to the contrary — if after the voluntary principle has had full fair play there should remain any persons who ought to have volunteered, but who hung back with their thoughts on other men's jobs or other men's farms, or on their own skins, there will come from the trenches, where our men are fighting and dying, a yell for conscripting such persons, or for some means of getting them into the ranks, and securing that the whole burden shall not be laid upon the shoulder of the willing and that cry will be joined in by the fathers and families of our defenders of every class and party — nationalists and all.[44]

Lord Dunalley claimed that it was the refusal of farmers to join that would bring conscription:

[T]hey need not fear conscription when it did come, but it would be much better to keep it away. He did not think, however, that it would be so very hard. It depended very largely upon the farmers who had not responded yet to keep it away. The time was limited and it was solely a question of time. They had only got twenty days more to try the present system of recruiting... if the voluntary system did not succeed there would be compulsion of some sort.'[45]

Some recruiters took a different approach in trying to enlist farmers and used the position of Poland as an example of what might happen in Ireland if Germany won the war. Nicholas Maher JP told a recruiting meeting in Clonoulty that it was almost a case of better the devil you know:

Their government had been passing legislation to make them owners of their own land. That same government had passed many beneficent measures, notably the Old Age Pensions Act and it was only last year that the king sent his signature to the Home Rule Bill, thus giving to Ireland her legislative independence. During the same period let them look at what the German government was doing to their Polish subjects. Were they trying to give them justice — did they attempt to root them in their own soil? No, they made laws to crush them and to prevent them from owning a sod of Poland. As practical men of common sense, he was sure the farmers of Ireland had no anxiety to allow the Germans into their country to undo all the good work that had been done for them by the British government'.[46]

At another recruiting meeting in the Glen of Aherlow, prominent landowner Robert Sanders said that Germany was 'out for the destruction of small nations... if the Germans won they would destroy Ireland and pull down the great structure of land purchase... they would at once set about dispossessing the Irish people of their land as they dispossessed the people of Poland' and Ireland 'would be reduced to slaves'.[47] Cahir's curate, Reverend W.P. Burke, claimed that the war was one of conquest. This speech by Bourke made the national headlines:

> We are now, to my mind, confronted with the most serious crisis that has occurred for three hundred years — since Cromwell made preparations at Bristol for the invasion of Ireland. Don't think it is England's fight only. As sure as England goes down we will go down too... What has happened in Poland, that great Catholic country? Germany has set itself to crush it out of existence. They have uprooted some 25,000 Polish farmers and replaced them by Germans. To complete the destruction of Poland, the Germans passed a law prohibiting one Pole purchasing land, so that in the process of time the whole soil of Poland must pass into the German hands. Now, during all this period the English government has been labouring to reinstate and root the Irish people in their own soil. The Congested Districts Board and the Estates Commissioners have been busily engaged at work; great ranches have been divided up and no fewer than 4,000 evicted tenants have been restored. Tell me, as reasonable men, if the Germans are going to treat Ireland differently from Poland?'[48]

Farmers were not immune to the sustained criticism directed their way. The Thurles District Farmers Association sought to address the controversy. Hugh Ryan, a member of the association, was conciliatory and said that he supported the Allies. But he also said that the land could not be worked if more men enlisted:

> By inducing their sons and labourers to the army they would, he thought, be upsetting their efforts at home… he was totally in favour of the Allies being victorious — he was not opposed to recruiting in any way and he hoped every man would act according as his conscience… but as farmers they could not encourage their men to go to the front, because if they did the farmers would be unable to do what was necessary for the state… if they took more men away the land could not be worked at all.[49]

James Finn, who was also chairman of the Thurles Board of Guardians, told the meeting:

> In his district he did not know any young men of the farming classes who could be spared for the army… They were told day after day to till more land and not alone were they unable to spare men for the army but they had not enough of hands for tillage at present. At the same time he was not against recruitment and anyone who wished to join the army he would not oppose them.[50]

Mr Max, JP from Maxfort, said: 'No doubt some of the farmers' sons had gone into the towns into drapers' shops and other places of business and they could be spared but from a purely tillage point of view, none of the workers could be spared.'[51] The chairman, Thomas Duggan JP, also Chair of North Tipperary County Council, said the recruiting speakers had lost sight of the fact that 'young people in the towns, originally from the country, were joining the colours'. So a clear consensus existed among farmers. The most frequent response given was that no more men could be spared. Father Michael Maher seemed to agree with this:

> The military authorities are making desperate efforts to get the
> farmers' sons of this country to join the colours but they have not
> succeeded to any extent as yet. In fact, there are none to spare.
> There is not a sufficiency to cultivate the land chiefly, on account
> of the number of labourers who have already volunteered and are
> serving in the army.[52]

Farmers, of course, had difficulty holding on to labourers, and many left for
the munition works in England. Ryan pointed to this and said that farmers
had no guarantee they would be paid for their produce and criticized what he
termed munition 'slackers' in England who were given a 'great bribe':

> When the munition workers in England were asked to put
> forward their greatest energies they were at the same time given
> a great bribe — they got 50 per cent more wages than such class
> of work ever fetched before. Now the government were saying
> to the farmers 'produce more food', but what guarantee had
> the farmer that they would get paid for their labour now that a
> minimum price would be fixed on barley and wheat. They had
> to increase the pay of the munition workers in England who, he
> maintained, were greater slackers than the farmers in Ireland,
> but nothing was done to induce the farmers to increase their
> energies in the production of food.[53]

Generally, farmers appeared to agree with the Allied war aims. But when it
came to supporting the enlistment of their own sector the recruiters were
firmly told no. Wimborne tried to overcome this rural reluctance by having
the DRI send circulars to local bodies to try and get farmers' sons to enlist.
He proposed that each county council should raise sixty recruits to form
'pals' companies. To achieve this, each council member was asked to canvass

in their local areas and try to secure two recruits.[54] This had an element of deferred enlistment approximating to the group system in the Derby scheme. The nominated men would not have to go near any recruiting office, and if the idea did not come to fruition they would not be called.[55]

At North Tipperary County Council, Captain Loftus wrote regarding the scheme, which 'would show in a practical manner that the farmers of Ireland are anxious to prove their loyalty and their good will towards the Allies' cause'.

> The idea of a farmers' regiment is that all the young men who join it should be of a certain class and be nominated by a member of the county council. Every man who gives in his name would join as a private. If the regiment was formed there would be a class into which any member might go to qualify as a non-commissioned officer and then for a commission... There is no occasion for young men to go into the recruiting office.[56]

A Mr Sparrow, the DRI representative, made the typical appeals at the county council meeting, mentioning the atrocity reports in Belgium and stating that if Britain was not in a position to dictate terms after the war ended, it, and therefore Ireland, would be bled white through rates and taxes.[57] 'If [Antwerp] remained in [German] hands they would use it as a naval base as well as a port for the German trade with the result that Great Britain and Ireland would be flooded with cheap German goods after the war, which would militate against their own trade.'[58] He declared that Germany would not be content with that and would start a second war to annihilate Great Britain. He added that the farmers' battalion would be modelled on the 7th Battalion of the Royal Dublin Fusiliers — the 'Pals Battalion' — and he would be very pleased if the council would form a county recruiting committee that would help with the recruiting and pension scheme. Captain Lefroy told the meeting that he 'didn't wish to insinuate that the farmers had not done their duty. His private opinion was that they did not see the danger.'[59]

Chairman of the County Council, Thomas Duggan, however, claimed that men on recruiting committees were looked at by locals as 'spies and informers… The people thought that the duty of these committees would be to point out when the time would come all the eligible men. That was rather an awkward position to put any public man in even though it was not true'.[60] Duggan also maintained that no more men were to be spared, and those engaged in agricultural work were of great importance:

> Speaking for his own district he would certainly state that if they were to carry out the programme as they had been asked by several prominent men in the country to produce more food they would have no men to spare… He was of the opinion that the men who were engaged at present in producing food for man and beast were doing as useful work as the men engaged in producing munitions. His district was purely a tillage one and his opinion was that no man could be spared from his locality.[61]

The other councillors agreed with Duggan. Mr O'Meara said that he wanted an extra workman but could not get one. 'He had had to get a tradesman to follow a horse. He lived in a tillage district where labour was scarce and where the complaint of every farmer was that labour could not be got.' Another councillor named Mr Dwyer said: 'Roscrea had done remarkably well as Captain Lefroy could bear out. He did not think any good could be done by the formation of a committee. In the town and district of Roscrea labour was scarce and it was impossible to get a workman.' Sparrow then suggested a battalion for men of commercial interests. Mr Dwyer responded: 'As regards shop assistants, in Roscrea they have done very well.' No action was taken. No committee was formed; there was no quorum.[62]

Clogheen Board of Guardians also discussed the scheme. The chairman said that it was a good idea and that they 'would be glad to see the farmers represented so that they could not throw any disparagement on them or call them cowards, but we know they are wanted at home to till the land'.[63] The chairman urged the county council to see if it could be carried out:

> A good many farmers' sons have joined already and it was a pity that this was not started earlier… I think the landlords should give a guarantee not to evict the fathers and mothers of these young men during their absence at the war… The poor people ought to be terribly thanked for fighting. As a poor man said to me: 'I don't own the shirt on my back and still I must fight.'[64]

Another board member said that farmers had been enlisting: 'Look at Ballyporeen for instance, where the land has been purchased for years; a good deal of recruits have gone from there.' Another guardian closed off the meeting with this:

> There is no good dwelling too much on the past. There has been a change for the better; we are going through it now and I think we ought to do everything we can to encourage recruiting. In the towns the population has been increasing and in the country it has been diminishing. That makes it more difficult to get recruits in the country.

Loftus's letter was approved.[65]

The focus on farmers' sons and shop assistants reflected the authorities' belief that they were not doing enough. Farmers were threatened with conscription, which, in turn, only enflamed opinion. Farmers felt that enough recruits had gone, and if the government wanted more tillage then more men simply could not be spared. There were also prejudices felt by the agricultural class towards the army, and this was acknowledged by the attempts to establish farmers' 'pals' companies.[66] Even so, much damage had been done by crude and unsympathetic recruiting methods and speeches.

FORMING COMMITTEES

The DRI renewed the CCORI's system of sending representatives across the country to assist in establishing local committees. The reaction of local bodies was mixed; some expressing hostility, others indifferent to the campaign. The DRI, however, was more successful in this. The Tipperary South Riding County Council met to consider establishing a county recruiting committee. Captain Loftus told the councillors that the committee would firstly seek recruits and secondly, make 'inquiries with regard to the numbers who have already left the different districts so that the county would know what the county has done'. The committee would also note how many had gone from different trades, whether any trade had been injured from such, and also to see if any more could be spared. Loftus made it clear to the councillors that the war was not going to end soon and that the threat of invasion remained: 'The Balkan adventure made it probable that the conflict would be very much prolonged. Did Ireland stand in danger of invasion? The answer to that was what had happened in Belgium and Serbia. There was an unknown danger for Ireland.'[67]

The CCORI established just one committee in Tipperary at Templemore, and no county committee, but the DRI, despite opposition from some councillors (including the chairman), was more successful at the council and in general. The response from the county council is instructive. One councillor, Patrick Keating from Mullinahone, said that Ireland should wait until more went from England before sending further recruits.[68] Some councillors backed the idea that a recruiting committee could somehow prevent conscription. Edward Anglim of Killenaule said that no one could oppose the formation of the committee unless he was pro-German or 'one of the Northcliffe press fellows — a conscriptionist'.[69] Another said that he was in favour of the committee because it would be a bulwark against compulsion. However, Slattery claimed that by establishing the committee, 'you admit Irishmen are shirkers'.[70] Despite Slattery's diatribe against forming a committee, the council agreed to its formation with only two dissenters.

A recruiting committee was also formed at Thurles Urban District Council. Henry Poulter said that the military were now most anxious to get farmers' sons. 'The farmers' son,' he said, 'is the most reliable, he makes the best commissioned officer, he knows his business and one can depend on him.'[71] He said that he had met Thomas Duggan, Chairman of the North Tipperary County Council, and James Finn, Chairman of the Thurles Board of Guardians, who had both promised to co-operate. He also considered that having some ladies to canvass in the 'outlying districts' would help, as this had proved the case in Dublin.[72] This method had not changed significantly since the start of the war, and the DRI was simply receiving vague verbal promises of help without any tangible commitment to the recruiting campaign. The visits seemed to be successful on the surface, but these groups did little actual work. Mr Finn,[73] said that: 'He saw that he had been appointed on the local recruiting committee but he had not given any authority to use his name.'[74] The DRI also made no special attempt to include representatives from rural groups — where the department was trying to elicit recruits — that had shunned enlistment, identifying the recruiting movement with a merchant, commercial class.[75]

The reaction at Thurles Rural Council also illustrated those feelings, and the discussion at the council is revealing. John Hackett MP chaired a meeting at which G.H. Sparrow of the Clonmel recruiting area told the meeting:

> There were many reasons why the army attracted the labouring classes. The love of adventure was one, and another was that they earned very low wages at home and the separation allowances paid to their wives or relatives made the army an attractive occupation to them. It was quite the opposite with the farming classes, who gained nothing of course… the military authorities were very anxious to secure farmers' sons for the army, who made the very finest non-commissioned officers, being splendidly healthy fellows well fitted for the work on account of the healthy open-air life they led. This was well evidenced by the class of soldier found amongst the Canadian and Australian troops.[76]

Sparrow admitted that there was no financial gain for farmers' sons, but he appealed to them to prevent Germans from invading Ireland. Sparrow was looking for about 100 farmers' sons. One member asked: 'We're asked to till more land and to send men to the army — how can we do the two things?' Hackett said that he thought that a recruiting committee should be formed, which could ascertain how many men could be spared. There was no consensus on this from the meeting. One councillor, J. Stakelum, said: 'The appointment of such a committee would be equivalent to a declaration that Irishmen were shirking their duty.'[77] Sparrow said that Ireland, when compared with Britain, had only sent one-third of its share of men to the army. Another rural council member said: 'What answer did the Lord Lieutenant give to Mr Slattery, the chairman of the South Riding Council? He said "if you point them out we will take them". The resolution to appoint a recruiting committee was defeated nineteen to ten.[78] The police noted the disinterest in recruiting after the Thurles Rural District Council rejected forming a committee: 'The Thurles district council by a large majority rejected a proposal to form a recruiting committee. Two civilian members of Lord Wimborne's committee made Thurles their HQ for some weeks, but in view of the hopelessness of getting the country people to take any interest in recruiting, these members have now been withdrawn.'[79]

The fear over conscription was widespread across the county. Tipperary Rural District Council's clerk submitted notices on the necessity for increasing tillage. One member, M. Wall, asked how tillage was to be increased if the men enlisted. Another, William Power, said that he had heard that farmers had received circulars asking them to get their labourers to join the army: 'That is the thin edge of the wedge of conscription.'[80] Slievardagh Rural Council passed a resolution unanimously opposing conscription.[81] The feeling on the ground, however, never changed in favour of recruiting and was unlikely to in the face of conscription threats. When conscription was agreed by the Cabinet, Father Maher wrote in his diary:

> It is generally thought that there would be terrific opposition
> to any drastic measure of that kind in Ireland, that it would be

opposed even with arms by a section of the populace. We have done our part, we have given many more men than Ireland can afford with our depleted population, still the authorities are not satisfied because more farmers' sons have not volunteered. The farmers on the other hand claim that they have not enough men to cultivate the land and raise food for the people, which is an absolute necessity in the present circumstances.[82]

Maher said that it was believed that post office workers would be dismissed after Christmas and there was a rumour that the railway companies would do the same thing: 'There is no doubt that men are required and they will have to be got at all costs, but we hope still that Ireland will be saved from conscription.'[83]

CONCLUSION

The DRI failed to keep up the momentum of its earlier work with postal circulars. The speeches that threatened conscription turned people against recruiting. Another crucial factor was the strong war-weariness that had developed in Irish society. The war was now getting serious, the Dardanelles campaign had failed, Russia had suffered a number of defeats on the Eastern Front and Bulgaria was fighting with the Central Powers. In Templemore:

There was no more listening to the band. Something of the gloom of Flanders settled over the network of trenches dug for training in the parade field. Weeks, months and then a year and two passed without sign of the finish... The first fine surge of enthusiasm for the Allied cause had spent itself... At first we used to read the illustrated war periodicals, but grew tired of English bravery and German brutality. The war went flat. That first thrilling march to the railway station had led nowhere.[84]

The failure of the DRI's intensive campaign signalled the end of the valid expectation that Ireland could sustain the rate of enlistment during 1915.[85] The department's activity from October 1915 marked the end of any serious or sustained recruiting campaign until late in 1918, when another voluntary scheme under the aegis of the Irish Recruiting Council was established. Recruiting dramatically changed after the Easter Rising of 1916, and the army focused on schemes that were unlikely to raise the political temperature.[86] The failure to decide on a consistent pattern of recruiting stood as an indictment of the government's inability to fathom and tackle the crisis in Ireland.[87] The South Riding County Council's recruiting committee met in Easter Week 1916 and did not meet again. The Irish Guards visited Clonmel and Tipperary town in February 1917. Canon Ryan met them in Tipperary and said that the turnout would have been greater were it not for the fact that so many were at the front and hoped they might fill up the ranks with Irishmen.[88]

Another recruiting-related initiative was the belated presentation of certificates of honour to men who had enlisted from various areas in Tipperary. Presentations were made at locations including Clonmel, Carrick, Cahir, Clogheen, Cashel and Nenagh, and they passed for quasi recruiting meetings. Major de la Poer asked the women present at a presentation in Carrick 'to see that the men who were fond of them proved themselves so by coming forward and doing their duty to their country'.[89] Lt Col Richard Butler Charteris echoed this at a presentation in Cahir:

> It is up to you to make the young men of this country go out and do their duty. You have the graces and charms to make them do so. There are thousands and thousands of young men in this country — able bodied men — who ought to go out. When this war is all over we shall be looked down upon if we don't go out. I say also it should be the ambition and pride of every Irish girl to marry a man who has fought for his country.[90]

At Cashel, it was perhaps the dean who gave the most perceptive analysis of the entire recruiting campaign since the start of the war, its political implications and how the situation could be exacerbated. Dean Ryan complained that sufficient recognition had not been given to Irish soldiers and that Ireland and Cashel had done their duty in the war. Ryan said that they were not there to ask for recruits, and foresaw the crisis of 1918 when he stated that the imposition of conscription would be a disaster:

> There is not, or at least there should not be, any necessity for a campaign of recruiting or an agitation for conscription in Ireland. Some sections of the press are again full of this subject. The forcing of conscription on Ireland would be a disaster for Ireland, but a far greater disaster for England. It would lessen instead of increasing England's manpower; would alienate and embitter the minds of all England's Irish soldiers, whether from Ireland or the colonies; it would be a blighting curse.[91]

The voluntary recruiting campaign, to all intents and purposes, had ended.

ROYAL NAVY
J.CAREW   P.CLAVIN
J.ENGLISH
ROYAL NAVAL VOLUNTEER RESERVE
A.E.MALONEY
        LIFE GUARDS
C.E.MOULSON
9ᵀᴴ QUEEN'S ROYAL LANCERS
F.SULLIVAN
        ROYAL ARTILLERY
J.LONERGAN   J.WALL
P.MAUNSELL   M.WALSH
E.O'BRIEN
        ROYAL ENGINEERS
J.MA   J.G.WALSH
    SCOTS GUARDS
H.R. JONES
        GUARD
M.F   D.MA
J   J.MA

P.FITZGIBBON J.O'BRIEN
J.HOGAN   J.QUIRKE
M.KENNEALLY
        ROYAL FUSILIERS
W.ANDERSON
        NORFOLK REGIMENT
E.H.CUBITT
KING'S OWN SCOTTISH BORDERERS
T.NUGENT
DUKE OF WELLINGTON'S REGIMENT
M.WALSH
OXFORDSHIRE & BUCKINGHAMSHIRE
        LIGHT INFANTRY
J.L.BURKE
        MANCHESTER REGIMENT
J.D.COONEY
        ROYAL IRISH RIFL
J.HA

5 PATTERNS AND MOTIVATIONS

Names of the dead listed on the World War One memorial, Cahir, Co. Tipperary.

THE RIRegt RECRUITING area held 9.4 per cent of the Irish population in the 1911 census and provided about 7.8 per cent of Irish wartime recruits, which was the fourth highest total by district in Ireland.[1]

The RIRegt district's proportion of Irish recruitment was, however, closer to its share of the Irish urban population, from which so many wartime volunteers came, and official wartime estimates of manpower availability show that urban males tended to be more available for military service than their rural counterparts.[2] Thus, the RIRegt district share of the urban population was 7.1 per cent, corresponding to the wartime enlistment rate.[3]

Illustrating this were a number of presentations made by the military to families and relatives of soldiers from urban areas who enlisted in the armed forces in Tipperary. The local papers listed the names and addresses of the men who received them. On 31 May 1917, for example, 594 certificates were presented to families and relatives of the men of Clonmel town, and similar ceremonies were held in the urban areas of Carrick (460 certificates),

Cashel (275) and Nenagh (389).[4] About 3,500 men from Tipperary enlisted in the armed forces during the war, and the county experienced about 700 casualties.[5] The majority were Catholics, but that is not to downplay the significant contribution made by Protestants in the county. By the end of 1914, for example, the proportion of the Church of Ireland population in the Cashel diocese serving with the armed forces was 6 per cent. Casualties were also heavy. From the sixty-five who enlisted from St Mary's Church of Ireland parish in Clonmel, fifteen lost their lives.[6] Table 1 shows a six-monthly recruiting index. These figures represent recruiting totals to the end of June 1917, when the authorities stopped district figures and instead gave an overall total.

Table 1: Six-Monthly Recruiting By District to June 1917[7]

Depot —	Clonmel	Birr	Tralee	Galway
1st Period	2,645	1,524	4,525	1,700
2nd	2,914	1,543	3,439	1,156
3rd	1,684	1,463	2,457	1,035
4th	749	442	1,526	613
5th	581	219	1,713	370
6th	405	96	917	227
TOTAL	8,978	5,287	14,577	5,101

Almost two-thirds of those who enlisted in the RIRegt recruiting area did so in the first year of the war. Clonmel managed a significant increase in the second period. Birr increased too, but only by a minute portion when compared with Clonmel. That is significant. It shows that people enlisted when it was not simply a cake walk to Berlin, when Kitchener's prediction that the war would last three years was circulated, and when the brutality of war was widely accepted. This also shows a certain degree of calculation as separation allowances increased at the beginning of March. Figures fell away dramatically in the third period, coinciding with the DRI campaign and the increasing fear of conscription, exacerbated by recruiting speakers' frequent reference to its imminent imposition, the lure of munitions work, and war-weariness. But within these figures are county-by-county fluctuations. This is particularly the case in analysing the recruiting numbers in Duke's 'Manpower in Ireland' report dated 16 October 1916 (Table 2).

Table 2: Duke's 'Manpower in Ireland' Report — October 1916[8]

County	Men of Military Age at Oct 1915 Register	Men Considered Indispensable	Unfit for Service	Men Enlisted Since the Register	Available for Service	Percentage Who Joined the Forces During the Period
Tipperary	21,351	9,566	4,159	1,387	6,239	18%
Waterford	10,542	3,961	2,442	476	3,663	12%
Wexford	13,559	6,203	2,767	440	4,149	10%
Kilkenny	9,882	4,716	1,950	291	2,925	9%
Limerick	19,728	7,994	4,367	816	6,551	11%
Kerry	21,724	11,068	4,157	264	6,235	4%
Clare	14,095	7,272	2,557	430	3,836	10%
Offaly (King's Co.)	8,143	4,103	1,458	393	2,189	15%

Duke's report details the number of men the military authorities believed to be indispensable for agriculture in the country, the number who had joined since the date of the national register on 15 August 1915 and how many they believed were available for military service. The figures are instructive. 1,387 enlisted in Tipperary during the period, which was particularly high when compared with the other counties in the recruiting area. Waterford, for example, had a total of 476, Wexford, 440 and Kilkenny, 291; however, Tipperary was believed to have considerably more available men.

Tipperary also had a much larger overall population than the other counties in the regimental district, with about 152,000 inhabitants in 1911, compared with 83,000 in Waterford, 102,000 in Wexford and 74,000 in Kilkenny.[9]

Why did men enlist in the army? The motives of recruits will always remain uncertain. The brutality of the war was widely known and anyone who thought about serving knew that there was a very good chance that he or she would be killed, disabled, injured or psychologically damaged. This was even more the case in Tipperary than other counties with the presence of the depot for wounded soldiers. We can speculate on the reasons why a man joined the army: money, adventure, peer pressure, military tradition and travel, to name a few. But what the First World War brought, for the first time, was an idealistic dimension for Tipperary soldiers: democracy, Home Rule, and a fight for small nations against 'German brutality'.

One Tipperary historian has argued that at least three factors led to a man joining up in 1914: the universal appeal of guns, the impact of anti-German atrocity propaganda, and Redmond's argument that fighting Germans served Ireland's political interests.[10] All three probably played a part. But the reasons for enlistment were complex and we will never be able to know for certain the exact motivations due to a lack of direct evidence from other than a handful of articulate and literate men such as Tom Kettle, Stephen Gwynn and Willie Redmond. The thoughts and feelings of ordinary men in the ranks have to be largely deduced from the writings and sayings of others.[11]

And of course identifying a regular soldier's decision to enlist, or at least attempting to, is not a matter of scientific classification but historical analysis and speculation. The Irish recruit was generally an unskilled labourer. In 1911, unskilled labourers formed the second largest group of Irish workers.[12] Unskilled men had traditionally supplied the bulk of recruits for the army. Despite some early optimistic predictions that a middle-class surge into the forces would transform the social composition of the army, the vast majority of servicemen came from the unskilled sector, the urban poorer classes.

ECONOMIC MOTIVES

Much has been attributed to economics as a motivational factor. Indeed, it is probably the most easily identifiable factor. The average weekly wage for an urban unskilled worker was 14s. The basic pay for ordinary soldiers was 1s. But most soldiers got extra allowances, for shooting proficiency for example, and 1s 9d was more normal.[13] On top of the basic wage, the pay and separation allowances available to those who enlisted were attractive to a potential recruit who had experience only of intermittent and low-paid employment or no work at all.[14] Thomas P. Dooley, in his study of a Waterford soldier, illustrated how a general labourer with a wife and five children could increase his family's earnings by 154 per cent by enlisting in the army when separation allowances were taken into consideration.[15] In Tipperary, the living conditions of many people in the towns were tough. This was not helped by the sharp increases in food prices at the onset of war and worsened by poor wages. In Roscrea, it was claimed 'the only way for many young men to make a living was to join the British Army… They joined because they wanted jobs and this was the only way they were sure of getting money, as little as it was'.[16] Seamus Babington wrote of the recruits in Carrick: 'Most of them joined from sheer necessity, no industry, no employment'.[17] And a Carrick historian has claimed: 'Adventure and the desire for steady money dictated the move. They were mercenaries'.[18]

The money paid out through the separation allowance system increased in March 1915, enhancing its appeal. A recruiting poster in the Nenagh Guardian advised Tipperary men to join at once as 'your families will get good pay'.[19] Even senior military officers pointed to the separation allowances as the reason for enlistments. Colonel Cooke, the General Officer Commanding (GOC) at the RIRegt depot, said in 1916: 'The joining of the army is purely a case of money and separation allowance'.[20] A magistrate said that people living in the Bansha Road area of Tipperary town seemed to survive on separation allowances.[21] The payments were also criticized as blackmail by advanced nationalists who said that they were 'demoralizing' and resulted in families losing interest in Irish affairs.[22] This, in turn, led to significant social problems.[23]

Some employers promised to keep jobs for any worker who enlisted. Tipperary North Riding County Council, Borrisokane Board of Guardians, Clonmel Brewery, and the Nenagh Guardian newspaper, for example, promised employees their jobs back if they enlisted.[24] The Board of Guardians let enlistees keep half their salary.[25] It had also been claimed that some employers who had young gardeners and horsemen fired them in order to force them to enlist,[26] while on the other hand a military intelligence report claims that an offer by one landowner of five acres of land to any person who enlisted met with no response.[27] Clearly a conflict existed. Economic coercion, an indirect pressure to enlist, or simply bribery, is difficult to prove. As Pat Callan states, 'if the space devoted to it in the press was an indication, then it was a significant factor'. He suggests, however, that it would be impossible to assess the number of men who were encouraged to join because of employer incentives.[28]

There is little evidence to suggest that the motivation to enlist was exclusively construed in these terms. It is difficult to find a soldier admitting that he joined because he needed the cash, and the level of recruiting in Tipperary was of such a high extent that economics cannot explain comprehensively why so many still took that dangerous, uncomfortable yet voluntary decision to enlist. Whereas peacetime soldiery could better the living conditions of an unemployed, poverty-stricken man, the risks and horrors of the European war made the trade-off unfavourable.[29] However, as Table 1 illustrates, recruiting actually increased in the second period and declined in the third. From the summer of 1915 onwards, the establishment of a Ministry for Munitions, with the chance to work with high wages in England, provided more choices for any would-be recruit. The huge casualties at the Dardanelles and war-weariness in general added to this decline in recruiting activity. But from August 1914 to the following summer, unskilled labourers faced a grim future. There were considerable increases in prices and wages did not increase to meet them. For a labourer with children, the army was still an enticing option.[30]

ADVENTURE, MILITARY TRADITION AND MARTIAL SPIRIT

Would-be recruits during the war years were offered a chance to join Irish regiments. Those enlisting in Tipperary could join the Royal 'Irish' Regiment, one filled with history and tradition, echoing past campaigns and victories in far-flung outposts of the Empire. The RIRegt were known as the 'Old Namurers', derived from their storming of Namur in 1695. Recruits could feel continuity with previous Tipperary men and consider themselves part of a long lineage of military tradition — and of course, as we have seen, this was the subject of much recruiting rhetoric from military officials, local politicians and MPs. The tradition of military service was strong in Tipperary, and no doubt helped by the presence of so many garrisons, anchored by the RIRegt depot at Clonmel. This gave the army a high profile in these areas with troop marches, parades, and even military funerals representing a pomp and glamour that was attractive to the mundane drudgery of life in provincial towns. This was heightened during the early months of the war with the flurry of troop movements and mobilization of local reserves, at which crowds gathered and cheered, Irish Volunteers provided guards of honour and in some cases were inspected by British officers.

The British Army uniform had been considered by some as one of oppression. Seamus Babington, a future brigade engineer of the IRA, wrote:

> The First World War broke out when I left school. There were divided thoughts about the all-powerful propaganda of the British — poor Belgium and small nations attacked. Up to then, any man who joined the British Army could never appear in uniform; he either remained away or his people sent clothes to his station, the danger being that his uniform would be stripped from him and burned; even his parents, brothers and sisters would do it before neighbours, so much was the British uniform hated, giving a true insight into the spirit of the people.[31]

A report from the *Nenagh Guardian* on the reception afforded to the Irish Guards (albeit an Irish regiment), illustrated how the British Army uniform had apparently turned from one of oppression to freedom:

> [The reception] showed the remarkable change that has come over England's government of Ireland. What person in the vast crowd twenty years ago or even ten, thought that such a scene would ever be witnessed in a town thoroughly nationalist or that representatives of the British Army, coming on such a mission would be so well received and that such a Tipperary welcome would be extended to them. Not one we dare say. Times have,

however, changed since then…Then, the man who donned the scarlet coat and took the Saxon shilling was considered a renegade and a traitor to his country. Today the khaki coat of England is symbolic of patriotism and bravery and thus it was that the Irish Guards received a hearty cead mile failthe, and the cheers — not the groans — of true hearted Irishmen and gallant Tipperary men.[32]

Local papers also praised the 'great county regiment' and lauded 'gallant' soldiers from Tipperary who had won honours in battle.[33] 'Enthusiastic scenes' were witnessed in Borrisokane when twelve men enlisted and left by train: 'The local Volunteer band turned out and gave a discourse of national airs, while the local corps of the National Volunteers under the command of Capt M. J McKenna, the… clerk of the union, escorted the brave young men through the town. Everywhere, they received the wholehearted approval and the blessings of the populace.'[34] Recruits did not become soldiers of the Crown but 'the lads in khaki… we wish them all sorts of good luck'.[35] This initial blurring of the demarcation between Irish nationalist and British soldier would not have decreased the army's attractiveness.

Military funerals also held a morbid potency. For example, Sergeant John O'Brien of Barne died in late March leaving a widow and four children. He had served twenty years in the army. The funeral in Clonmel was full of powerful formality. Fifty RIRegt soldiers formed a guard while the coffin was removed from St Peter and Paul's church. It was covered with a Union Jack and placed on a twelve-pounder gun carriage sent from the artillery at Cahir. A firing party of twenty headed the cortege and behind them came the 3rd Battalion RIRegt band that had travelled from Waterford where they were on recruiting work. A detachment of the Army Service Corps also attended. The dead march was played, and the press reported a huge turnout from the townspeople 'comprising all classes'.[36] When the remains were lowered into the grave, the firing party discharged three volleys and the 'Last Post' was played.[37] One writer remembered these funerals he witnessed in Tipperary as a child:

> We never missed a military funeral... They were wonderful affairs to us. The flag-covered coffin on the gun-carriage, the band playing the dead march with muffled drums... The most important part of the funeral for us was the firing of the volleys over the grave. Then, after the Last Post was sounded, all the soldiers and the band assembled on the road, the band struck up a really lively air and all marched back to the barracks.[38]

Even in death, the military could lend gravitas to people who may have had little else. This worked both ways, however, and the reckless and sometimes cavalier attitude of the authorities led to resentment that they did not care about Irish troops, which was the case when no military guard of honour turned up at the funeral of Private Martin Nevin in north Tipperary.[39]

FRATERNAL MOTIVES

There was also a fraternal aspect to enlisting. Friends could join battalions with a strong local flavour and receive training at camps full of familiar faces. This was the case in Tipperary, with the 49th Brigade of the 16th Irish Division, commanded by Tipperary man William Hickie from 1916, based at Tipperary barracks.[40] However, this brought its own problems early in the war as the RIRegt suffered heavy casualties during the retreat from Mons. When certificates of honour were given to a number of soldiers in Tipperary during 1917, the commander, Beauchamp John Colclough Doran, underlined this with a series of speeches lauding the RIRegt for its tradition.

Family tradition was also an important factor, and those with brothers, fathers, or uncles with military experience may have been more inclined to enlist. The pages of local newspapers are littered with examples of multiple enlistments from one family. Veterans with Crimean or Boer War experience were often followed into the military by their sons or nephews. For example, two sons of a Clonmel army pensioner were serving in the RFA and the Royal Canadians. Norah Tobin, of Catherine Street, Clonmel, had four sons in the army: one died and one was gassed and suffered shell-shock.[41] George Maher of Nenagh had five sons in the army, one of whom had been killed, while eighteen families in Nenagh had three sons serving.[42]

For those belonging to militias, fraternities or sporting clubs, the presence of so many Volunteers in the ranks showed that there were those susceptible to collective pressure. For example, about 30 per cent of all the recruits who joined the army in Tipperary from 15 December 1914 to 15 December 1915 were believed to be INV.[43] Camaraderie was also important, and for many, the army offered the promise of adventure. Some joined regiments affiliated with their employers, for example three from Clonmel post office who joined the Post Office Rifles.

As we have seen, recruiters put pressure on women to shame men into joining. Men were expected to be masculine, and the way to this, the way to prove manliness, was joining the army. This motivation is hard to quantify, but recruiters made frequent reference to it. Whilst this type of pressure was frowned upon in guidelines for recruiters published in *Irish Life*, it was a factor.[44] The attraction of adventure was also a factor, and was connected to the new-found vibrancy for all things military and the lack of opportunities at home.[45] In Carrick, it was held that 'the very young — seventeen, eighteen and nineteen years — [enlisted] for adventure, like all youth, very few for the sake of helping England'.[46] Those who enlisted in Carrick have also been described as mercenaries:

> It is said that as many as a thousand men joined the British Army from the Carrick district alone. This did not denote any love for the British Empire. Adventure and the desire for steady money dictated the move. They were mercenaries.[47]

The same author was more generous in a later work on south Tipperary, however, describing those who fought as the 'adventurous, the young and the unemployed, as well as those who wished to fight for the freedom of small nations'.[48] Jack Moyney, a VC winner who saw out his days in Roscrea, told of his decision to enlist:

> I signed up because everyone else was going. I wanted to see a
> bit of life and I felt sorry for the Belgians to a certain extent...
> When I went to be a soldier, I was a young fellow and I wanted
> plenty of excitement. Well I got more than I bargained for. War is
> a cruel and wicked thing. When the end comes it leaves no side
> better off.[49]

That is revealing, and illustrates how one factor was rarely at work. The most convincing explanation of adventure as a motive for enlistment was that munitions work was both better paid and safer than soldiering.[50] Sinn Féin complained in 1915 that men were being recruited 'not by the recruiting sergeant's shilling only, but by a cunning appeal to our traditional valour', and also claimed that recruiting authorities were attempting to fill young men with a 'wondering admiration' for marching men and military bands.[51] Soldiers who were awarded medals for valour, such as James Somers, participated in recruiting drives, and Tipperary men were urged to emulate such deeds. It would have been surprising if some Irishmen had not responded to such an appeal.[52]

GLORY

Some newspaper reports portrayed death at the front as a noble thing. The *Nenagh Guardian* for example, reported that Phil Hynes, fighting with the 2nd Leinsters of Nenagh, the son of a Crimean War veteran, was killed in Flanders. His brother was in the same regiment and his mother was a widow. Hynes was thirty-three, and the newspaper said that 'he died a soldier's death on the field of glory, upholding like many another gallant Tipperary man, the flag and honour of his country'.[53]

As we have seen in Chapter Three, Sergeant James Somers was hailed as a hero and someone for any man to emulate when he won the Victoria Cross.[54] Private Patrick Murray of the Irish Guards was killed by a German sniper. He was a member of the Nenagh Shamrock Club and it passed a vote of sympathy: 'That we, the committee of the Nenagh Shamrock Club, beg to tender our sympathy to Mr Michael Murray and family in the great loss they have suffered by the death of their gallant son who nobly fell fighting the German huns on the battlefield of France.' Three of his brothers were also fighting in the war. The *Nenagh Guardian* called Murray 'a fine type of Tipperaryman'.[55] These descriptions may have spurred some men into the army.

IDEALISM

The continued flow of recruits throughout 1915 in Tipperary must be ascribed, then, to a combination of motives and loyalties. Idealism also constituted one of these. Recruiters made frequent reference to German brutality and aggression, and the appeal to patriotism and defence of the 'freedom' or 'rights' of one's country was the foundation of official recruiting rhetoric. The fate of Belgium was also much commented on and reported in the press with many lurid and exaggerated atrocity stories. Redmond's pledge of support to England and encouragement of enlistment from the volunteers also played a role as IPP members made recruiting appeals based on idealism, and we have seen, in Chapter Two, how Tipperary MPs made passionate cases for enlisting. In Carrick, most of the rank-and-file 'joined the British Army at the behest of John Redmond'.[56]

Figure 1 (see Appendix 1) shows the number of daily enlistments for the Clonmel depot during August 1914–May 1915. Two days after Redmond's Woodenbridge call, there is a spike of thirty-four, by far the highest since 11 August when seventy-two enlisted on one day — something that was never matched.[57]

Redmond's call, then, had some effect. The cause of the Allies was consistently referred to as a just one. When twelve men left Cloughjordan for the front in 1915, the local newspaper reported that cheers were given 'again and again for the cause of right and justice'.[58] Corporal C.J. Kennedy of the Army Service Corps was back in Clonmel, having seen action at Mons, and emphasized this:

> In the battle of Mons the Irish fought bravely, and showed to the world what Irishmen could do, especially in a war where right and justice and also freedom of nations are at stake... All through France you can hear the soldiers sing the famous song 'It's a Long Way to Tipperary', and even the French soldiers join with the civilians in singing it. We, Tipperary soldiers, like to hear it, for it called to mind our own dear old country.

Enlisting as a way of showing gratitude for the granting of Home Rule was possible. It is probable that idealistic motivations were usually taken with others, as Moyney explained. Other motivations are beyond the reach of analysis. For example, Cashel man Pte Patrick Dempsey of the 6th RIRegt, aged twenty-two, was motivated to join the ranks of the 16th Irish Division by the 'silent appeal'. He appeared in the columns of the *Clonmel Chronicle* in 1917 when he won the Military Medal.[59] Former soldiers also re-enlisted. These men most likely had no reserve commitments. Their reasons for joining could have included loyalty to the Crown or a chance to catch up with old comrades and taste the martial life once again. A protection scheme for ex-soldiers during the War of Independence illustrated this.[60] The army had generally given them a better life than anything else society could have offered and they were among the first to enlist in 1914, some sources going as far as to say that virtually all former soldiers tried to re-enlist before the war was a month old.[61] We have seen how much criticism was aimed at hostile speakers who threatened farmers' sons and shop assistants with conscription and accused them of being cowards. We have also seen how the authorities deplored what they perceived as the poor response from farmers and shop assistants. These appeals or threats fell on deaf ears, and it was generally held that they often stayed aloof, which had also been the case during peacetime.[62]

Irish agriculture experienced a wartime boom, and the profits gained by staying at home, combined with a policy of protecting agricultural occupations, resulted in an unwillingness to enlist. Another interesting point to note is that farmers, particularly amongst the wealthier echelons, regarded joining the army as a drop in status. The army was not a favoured occupation for farmers' sons with 'prospects', and the idiom 'gone for a soldier' was a disgrace if it applied to a farmer's son.[63]

A repugnance towards the army on social grounds was also evident among the urban middle classes. Despite that, there were a number of commissions from this group. In Clonmel for example, the son of the late mayor received a commission in the RIRegt, as did the son of the sub-Sheriff, Arnold Power; the borough surveyor's two sons received commissions in the Welsh Fusiliers; and Lieutenant R. Byrne of the RIRegt, promoted from colour sergeant, was formerly the instructor of the Clonmel National Volunteers.[64]

Cities and towns continued, as before the war, to supply the army with a significant amount of recruits.[65] Imposing classifications almost one hundred years later is extremely difficult. The relevance of various motives can vary. Economic motivations, and the desire for adventure are crucial, as the separation allowances were attractive and adventure was the motive most easily justified and could easily disguise others.[66] Idealism played a role, and military tradition and martial spirit were also important. Men may certainly have persuaded themselves, or may have been persuaded, that fighting was a noble profession and that Irishmen were good fighters.[67] It is likely that combinations of all of the various factors applied.

WHO WERE THE RECRUITERS?

As Pat Callan has argued, there was a general belief that somehow 'prominent individuals' in an area could persuade their neighbours to enlist. The conservative and sometimes inconsiderate selection of men who proceeded to deliver speeches to a nationalist audience was responsible for a considerable feeling of ill-will, disengagement and disenchantment with the war. Recruiting work attracted the 'scions of the establishment' but did not attract the rural farmers and peasants.[68] Who were the recruiters? They could invariably be doctors, town clerks, Protestant and Catholic clergy, town and county councillors, bank officials, bank managers, county and deputy lieutenants, government employees, resident magistrates, solicitors, mayors, county sheriffs, sub-sherrifs, guardians and hunt masters. This list underlines the formal and conservative nature of those advocating enlistment. Some speakers were not screened, and this gave rise to 'locally unpopular' men on recruiting platforms.[69] The appearance in Cahir of a disliked landlord was noted with distaste at Tipperary South Riding County Council. Ballyporeen Councillor, W. Fogarty, said:

> A great number of men had gone from the parish he represented and in the parish of Burncourt there were very few recruitable men at all. The people of that parish had noted unfavourably that Mr Rochfort of Cahir had appeared on a recruiting platform lately. The farmers of that district could not forget Mr Rochfort once boasted that he could depopulate the county with one bottle of ink. He was in favour of a recruiting committee if only for the purpose of keeping men like Mr Rochfort off recruiting platforms. Fully half the members of every family in the parish of Burncourt had been driven to America by Mr Rochfort and it was a mockery to have a man like him talking to the people about recruiting.[70]

This was something the CCORI struggled with. The appeals from these speakers did not go down well with those whom they were trying to recruit. In conjunction with this, the focus on conscription and on the hectoring attempts to enlist the sons of farmers alienated people. At Ardfinnan, Reverend Canon Sheehy chaired a recruiting meeting. Two points he addressed were the new recruiting scheme and conscription:

> Reading newspaper reports made at recruiting meetings throughout the country they sometimes found that in reality they were anti-recruiting speeches, calculated to make the audiences antagonistic rather than sympathetic. The gentlemen

who made such speeches did not understand the people or the circumstances of the country... From what he knew of the gentlemen about to address them he knew that such would not be the case that evening... He was very much against the idea of conscription, for which the only substitute was successful recruiting.[71]

Cullinan, meanwhile, agreed with Fogarty's assessment and expressed frustration with the poor choice of recruiting officials. He said that the establishment of a committee would be the best way to remove recruiting from such people and it would also prevent conscription.

Many on the popular side did not go on those platforms in the past on account of the objectionable parties who worked the system of recruiting. That system was an anti-recruiting system in reality. The appointment of a county committee under the new system took the recruiting out of the hands of those objectionable gentlemen. To his mind, the appointment of the committee would be a safeguard to the industries of the county, such as the woollen mills at Ardfinnan and the agricultural industry. There was a general cry throughout the country against conscription, but the surest way to defeat conscription was by having an organization like the proposed committee, which would be managed by the popularly elected representatives of the people.[72]

In the north of the county, Lord Dunalley, a prominent member of the landed gentry, played a central role by appearing on platforms throughout 1915. Dunalley, however, made no secret of his desire to see conscription. The gentry were seen as influential men, but were, or had been, landholders and landlords, and in turn, became associated with the recruiting drive. This sowed tension and had the potential to backfire. Stephen Gwynn also felt 'the choice of a man locally unpopular' hampered the drive to enlist men.[73]

Some military officials remained popular. There is evidence to suggest Captain Lefroy was regarded highly in the towns and villages of north Tipperary. When the CCORI wrote to Nenagh Urban District Council regarding a recruiting committee, it said that none was necessary as they had 'a good recruiting staff in the area with Captain Lefroy, Colour Sergeant Fitzgerald and Sergeant Frances'.[74] Lefroy was on another occasion referred to as the 'popular recruiting officer for north Tipperary'.[75] Lefroy was also subtle, thanking the 'public men' of north Tipperary for the help they had given him over the past eighteen months. 'From Newport to Roscrea he had not received an offensive word.'[76]

Local officials strongly made the case for recruiting along with senior IPP members such as MPs, with John Cullinan the main driver. IPP support melted away after the Rising but it was Cullinan who was recognized as one of the recruiting campaign's most vital supporters. A recruiting agent in 1916 said that John Cullinan was 'the only man who has given any real help'.[77] As we have seen in Chapter Two, the Roman Catholic church also played a role in the county, with Canon Ryan the central figure in Tipperary town. The lack of any representatives of the agricultural community reflected the attitude of the farmers, or indeed the apathy of the farmers, on the question of recruitment. Recruiting work ultimately attracted the establishment and was effectively ignored by the farmers and working class.

OPPOSITION TO RECRUITING

Opposition to recruitment was nothing new. William Myles, IRB member in 1913 and future vice commandant of the Clonmel Battalion, IRA, wrote of anti-recruiting activities pre-1914:

> The first job I remember was the posting of anti-recruiting literature in the town. These were small handbills which were supplied to us from Dublin and the wording of them was something to the effect that this was a warning to Irishmen who thought of joining the British armed forces or the police, that

such an act was one of treachery to their country, the intention being to discourage the recruiting of Irishmen into the British forces.[78]

During the First World War, there were those who did not view this as their conflict and engaged in anti-recruiting activity, although on a very small scale. On 30 September 1914, a series of anti-recruiting posters were removed from various locations in Tipperary town.[79] It was also reported that 'pro-German and anti-recruiting leaflets' were handed out on the Volunteers' drillfield.[80] By December, Tipperary South Riding County Council felt the reach of anti-Redmond propaganda. Slattery repudiated a circular posted to him from San Francisco and stated that they were 'strongly and unanimously in favour of the party and its policy'.[81] RIC reports detail the lack of pro-German feeling but the presence of 'advanced nationalists' who cry 'We are not at war with Germany. This is England's war', was noted.

This attitude was dismissed as a mere excuse for those who would do nothing to defend their country.[82] At Clonmel, William Wall was charged with tearing down and destroying three recruiting posters.[83] In Tipperary town, Roger Kennedy was arrested for removing recruiting posters. At the beginning of the war, he had been arrested on suspicion of being a spy.[84] Recruiters were frequently heckled, and, indeed, it seems that in Tipperary anti-recruiting activity was more often than not limited to heckling and tearing down posters. Seamus Babington writes: 'The national spirit seemed dead or dormant. Frequent British Army recruiting meetings were held, yet there was some heckling from behind big men. I gloried in this activity.'[85]

Some advanced nationalists felt regret at the nature of their activities. However, Eamon O'Duibhir, IRB member and Irish Volunteer organizer, felt they had succeeded in frustrating recruiting activities:

This great recruiting meeting was called for Tipperary town and we decided we would make things lively. We did our own hand printing as no one would print stuff for us and we put up a lot of anti-recruiting posters around the town and neighbourhood, some of it fairly strong, because, unfortunately, some of the men in control of that meeting on the other side were good Irishmen and it was a pity what happened, but we bitterly opposed that meeting and bitter and terrible things were said and posted up both the evening before and at the meeting... Other recruiting meetings held in Dundrum and Clonoulty were broken up by our fellows. In fact, they were broken up so quickly that most of us could not get around to the fun in time... We made British propaganda impossible.[86]

While this seems exaggerated in a county context, the area in which O'Duibhir operated, around Knockavilla (also the parish of Father Matt Ryan, who had come to the attention of the authorities for making speeches opposing recruitment), the IRB organizer's belief may contain some degree of truth.

It seems that local anti-recruiting efforts did not have a significant impact on recruiting returns. The police felt not enough Volunteers had enlisted and this was 'due in some measure to circulation of seditious and anti-enlisting literature and ideas'.[87] But when, in 1915, police seized anti-recruitment literature, they were unsure if it had any effect on the levels of enlistment.[88] Those most likely to circulate dissenting opinions, or to take them to heart, would not have been prime candidates for the recruiting call. Anti-enlistment movements were not very important in stemming the flow of recruits.[89] The intermittent character of the anti-recruiting exercise was effective only when it coalesced with other deep-seated disillusion about the war, such as conscription, particularly in late 1915 and early 1916.[90]

CONCLUSION

The military authorities consistently lauded in public the contribution made by Tipperary during the war. Indeed, a considerable number of Tipperary men fought in the war — about 3,500. While the authorities undoubtedly felt that many more could be spared, as illustrated in Table 2, it was still a huge contribution. Economics, military tradition, and adventure all existed before the war and played a role in the decision to enlist, particularly for unskilled labourers, while farmers' sons and the commercial class largely stayed aloof. The First World War brought idealism into the range of motives for the first time, as articulated by Figure 1 and the recruiting campaigns, where local politicians, clergy and officials claimed that fighting in France equated to fighting for Ireland.

It is most likely, however, that combinations of various motives applied to the same individual. The men who enlisted in the army were not dupes or carried away by an initial surge of anti-German or nationalistic feeling. As one man who had joined the army as a doctor put it, when applying for a job in Tipperary in 1918: 'I don't think somehow the Meaghers are in my favour since I went out to France, but I'd have gone just the same at that time if the Japs and Chinese were at it, besides my work was an act of mercy. But you never know in what light some of the guardians may look at it.'[91]

A recuperating soldier in Tipperary town, c.1916. Tipperary People Publication.

6 HOME FRONT

IN DECEMBER, NEWS filtered through to Cashel that a soldier from the town had won the prestigious French Legion of Honour. Driver James F. O'Brien had enlisted in 1909 at the age of nineteen and had been fighting with the Royal Field Artillery during the retreat from Mons. He won the decoration for saving a field gun from capture despite heavy German fire. In a letter to his mother at home in Tipperary, he wrote:

> It is like the Victoria Cross, but of course not quite so great. I am asking my major to get it sent home to you so that you may be able to see that I have done my duty... Irishmen are never afraid to die. I would gladly give my life if I knew I had been the cause of killing a few of my 'chums' the Germans. Now, how are all the old friends in Cashel? I trust you will not worry, because we must be all reconciled to whatever happens. God's will be done... I hear Ireland has got Home Rule. I am proud of it. Well, good

luck to our beloved country; may all her sons join in the happy times to come.[1]

O'Brien, however, died of wounds received at Ligny, the battle where he had won the award.[2] But if the war could claim a decorated Irish Catholic soldier, then it could also claim a member of the arch-gentry. Captain Reginald Prittie of the Rifle Brigade, son of Lord Dunalley, also won the Legion of Honour at the beginning of December. Prittie would be killed in action three weeks later.[3] His father received the telegram confirming his death on Christmas Eve. Along with other organizations in north Tipperary, the recently formed Nenagh Belgian Relief Committee sent its condolences to the Lord and Lady Dunalley. In Tipperary, then, the war was indiscriminate and cold. A soldier who had been honoured one day was killed the next. That was the most obvious impact the war had — the thousands who had enlisted, those who died or who were injured (whether physical or psychological), and the families that suffered as a consequence. There was not a town or parish in the county untouched by the conflict.

Tipperary, of course, had a military history and tradition. Garrisons at Cahir, Clonmel, Tipperary town and Fethard among others emphasized the Crown presence. This led to interaction: military weddings, parades and tendering of army contracts along with the pomp and ceremony of military life — displayed so vividly during the opening months of the war — served to blur and distort the demarcation between British soldier and Irish civilian. Band recitals, military games and dances were also held regularly and civilians involved in the welfare of soldiers were usually invited to social functions in the barracks.[4] Major Cliffe Vigors, commanding officer in Clonmel for much of the period between the Boer and First World Wars, greatly encouraged such functions as a bonding exercise between military and civilians, and as a fund-raiser for the Royal Irish Memorial Fund.[5] This was confirmed by a future IRA volunteer:

Clonmel was not then a very strong Irish-Ireland town because of the fact that it was and had been for generations one of the strongest garrison towns in the south of Ireland and a lot of marriages with British troops took place down the years. A further reason was that the Irish party was up to 1918 strongly entrenched and the local MP, the late Tom Condon, largely dominated local politics.[6]

Kitchener's new armies, raised in the autumn of 1914, vastly increased the number of soldiers in Tipperary — the 49th Brigade of the 16th Irish Division was stationed in Tipperary town. From the outset, injured and disabled soldiers were seen on the streets of towns and villages in Tipperary. Masses were said for local soldiers who died in the war. Father Michael Maher, writing in his diary at Thurles, noted how one 'could not take a walk out at any time without meeting a number of khaki-clad men, either at home on furlough or recovering from wounds received at the front'. He also noted that people relied on religion to get them through: 'It is edifying to notice how the faith of the people shows itself in this crisis. The parents and the wives of the soldiers are continually getting masses offered for them and saying prayers for the safe return and the soldiers themselves come to confession and ask for badges and Agnus Deis or other religious emblems before they go away.'[7]

In Thurles prayers were said for James Dwyer who was killed at the front:

This is the 9th or 10th Thurles man who has lost his life in the Great European war and so it cannot but be admitted that the small town of Thurles has sent its contribution of fighting men to the terrible struggle now raging between the nations. A few days ago a fine young fellow, the second son of Michael Keogh of Church Lane, arrived home on crutches having lost a leg in battle. The meeting between his parents and himself was a sad one.[8]

Two Nenagh men were also reported killed. First was Pte Patrick Murray, 2nd Battalion RIRegt, who was killed in France. The Shamrock Hurling Club sent their condolences to the family. From Chapel Street in Nenagh, three of his brothers were also serving. From the same street was reported another fatality, Pte Thomas Kelly. He had been a rural postman before the war.[9] A casualty list reported Pte P. Christie and Pte W. Mohilly as being wounded and gassed. Both were from Dublin Road, Nenagh. Father Maher admitted that the situation was difficult:

> It was sad to try to console the widows of some of the slain, they were heartbroken when they learned that their little children were fatherless. The loss of the unmarried men was not felt as much; it is astonishing how the poor people resigned themselves to fate when they heard that a son or brother had ended his career in France or Gallipoli.[10]

He also admitted that many did not want to return: 'None of the soldiers who returned from the front seemed anxious to go back, but one of the worst features of the war is that it seems likely that they will have to go back as long as they are able to fight.'[11]

These are just a sample of the casualty lists that appear in the newspapers. Reports of German atrocities were *de rigueur*, as was praise for Belgian troops, and criticism of French discipline and application.[12] Every day brought news of an injured, incapacitated or dead local soldier. There were also public lectures designed to give some impression of what was happening in Europe. At Cashel, Canon Hardy of Ardmayle gave a lecture illustrated with lantern slides to a crowded house on the 'Great European War'. At St Mary's Temperance Hall in Clonmel, people heard about 'Belgium Before the War'. This was to highlight the 'happiness and prosperity' enjoyed by the Belgians prior to the outbreak of hostilities.[13] This continued into 1915 and people were made aware of what was transpiring in Europe. A lecture was held in Nenagh on 'The Present

Conditions of Russia and the War'.[14] In Tipperary, therefore, people did not escape the trauma of the conflict, although its collective expression was muffled by the surge of emotion occasioned by the conflicts of 1916 to 1923.[15]

Another development that brought the war home to Tipperary was the establishment of a command depot for sick or wounded soldiers who were available for light duties in Tipperary town.[16] By October 1916, about 2,000 soldiers were recovering there from wounds, physical and mental, sustained in the war. The brutality of the conflict and the horrific injuries sustained in it were reported from the start. With the establishment of the depot, men, women and children in Tipperary could see firsthand the awful reality. As the *Chronicle* reported:

> Tipperary, whose name has been a trumpet call and an inspiration in the great war, has recently had brought home to it, in a vivid and striking way, some of the havoc to humanity which war inevitably brings, for it has been selected as the great depot in Ireland for our Irish wounded soldiers, and one needs but to see some of these maimed and broken men moving through the streets to comprehend in some measure the terrible experiences they have undergone. Especially is this [the] case on Sunday mornings when the men are passing to and from the various churches... Surely Ireland owes it to these men who have come back to us — and perhaps still more to the men who have not and who never will come back — to see that their sacrifices shall not be in vain?[17]

The composition of the joint committee of the depot indicated the cross-community support it received. The committee was a mix of local nationalist politicians, clergy and military officials, including Canon Ryan, who was president, Canon de Boinville (rector of Tipperary), Daniel Kelly (Chairman of the Urban Council) and P.J. Flynn (secretary to the Joint Tipperary Instruction Committee). The depot placed emphasis on 'mental' and 'moral' treatment as much as regular methods. It had manual instruction classes such as French polishing, auto repair, and typing. Concerts were held, along with cinema screenings and artistic performances. The Tipperary Technical Instruction Committee gave the free use of their schools and its manual instructor gave two hours' free instruction every morning to the soldiers.[18] In terms of treatment, there were gymnastic exercises, massage treatment and 'radiant heat baths'. The work Canon Ryan did for the depot was praised by Major General Lovick Friend, commander of the forces in Ireland, when he visited the depot to open a YMCA hall which cost £800.[19]

In October 1916, the *Chronicle* visited the command depot and ran a long piece on what was being done for the soldiers. It was punchy, with a number of photographs of the men engaged in shoemaking, mechanics and woodwork. It said that the depot was neither a hospital nor a home for convalescents, but was aimed at getting soldiers back to the front: 'We are at war, and the depot's primary purpose is to fit as many men as possible for return as soon as possible to the front or, failing their attainment of the necessary standard of fitness for active service in the field, then to get them ready for garrison duty at home or abroad.'[20] The paper noted 'that there must be a certain proportion of cases who, no matter how promising at first, might not recover during the period of treatment'. The injuries — mental and physical — that some of these men sustained prevented a return to their pre-war job, or duty they performed in the army, so the depot provided instructional classes to help them find a job in civilian life. The *Chronicle* emphasized the Irish nationality of many of these soldiers (though many were not from Ireland) and said that after the war they would no longer have to take up menial jobs:

> It gives these Irish soldiers — they belong exclusively to Irish infantry regiments and to every quarter of the country — a chance to become really useful citizens 'when the war drum beats no longer', if not in their own calling, then in some other, and it should go far, by imparting training and instruction in productive work, to open a way out of the 'blind alleys', in which

so many discharged soldiers heretofore have had, to the national disgrace, to find a means of supplementing a meagre pension. Trained as chauffeurs, as electric wire fitters, as musicians, as boot repairers, or to some extent in carpentry, there should be no compelling reason why a man broke, more or less, in the wars should necessarily enter the ranks of the light porters or casual labourers, which heretofore has been the ex-soldier's portion.[21]

Despite the enthusiasm for the project, the command depot was later shut down by the War Office because it felt that type of training worked against returning to the front. This decision was criticized by the local MP, John Cullinan, who said that his correspondence with the War Office 'was enough to try the temper' of any man.[22]

There is conflicting evidence of how these troops were welcomed by the locals. One of the soldiers was accosted by a prominent Donohill farmer and district councillor who fingered him in the chest and charged: 'You (expletive deleted) who are you fighting for? Why don't you fight for Ireland instead of fighting the Germans?' In 1917, Canon Ryan had to defend the people of the town against charges in a British newspaper that a 'wounded British Tommy' was abused.[23] An English newspaper, the *People*, claimed a soldier on crutches was 'hooted and howled at and bespattered with all kinds of filth' by the locals. Ryan wrote back rejecting the allegation, and saying that £1,000 had been collected in the town for the treatment of the soldiers.[24]

Horace Ham, serving with the Middlesex Regiment, was sent to Tipperary town on convalescence in 1917. He recalled how soldiers were warned not to go into the town alone and to travel in groups. Soldiers were also confined to barracks anytime there was a hurling match due to fears of unrest.[25] Another Middlesex Regiment soldier, Charles Ward, spent time at the same barracks in 1917, and said that while he had good relations with most, there were some 'nasty people about'. He said that soldiers were not allowed into grocery shops in the town, and were forced to wait outside while the shopkeeper got the order together and brought it outside.[26]

One soldier's story was different, however. Private M. Meades of the 2nd Middlesex Regiment was posted to the command depot for five weeks in 1917, and in a series of letters to his wife, wrote how he felt about the place and the town during his recuperation. In one, he writes: 'I went down into the church last evening. It isn't a bad sort of place for the size, seems to be all one street. Have been for a stroll this afternoon out in the country… It is very pretty too and it turned out very nice and sunny. Am going again this evening.'[27]

ABUSE OF SEPARATION ALLOWANCES

At Newport, a soldier's wife appeared on drunk and disorderly charges. The sergeant said that the woman's case was the worst he had seen for a long time and she was 'in receipt of too much separation allowance'. The judge fined her 5s and issued a strong caution, saying that she 'like many of her kind were spending their money on drink instead of putting it to better advantage.' In reply, she said that her son was 'shot in the war' and that was the reason she sought 'comfort in a few drinks'. Her husband was also at the front.[28] In Roscrea, two women were jailed for nine months' imprisonment for neglecting their children. The Justice of the Peace said that there was an 'understanding between the magistrates to give six months to all women who treat their children in an unchristian-like way'. Both were getting separation allowances of about 30s a week.[29] Such stories appear frequently in the court columns of local newspapers throughout the war. The provision of separation allowances was seen as an incentive to enlist, and in turn, the perceived abuse of these allowances was controversial at the time.

Some of the cases received extended coverage. At Clonmel Petty Sessions, NSPCC Inspector Beatty brought a case that he described as the worst that had come before him. A woman was charged with cruelty and neglect of her three children aged eleven, four and ten months. Her husband was fighting in France and she was in receipt of an allowance worth 23s. On various occasions, the inspector said, he found her 'drunk, the children in a dirty and neglected condition, no food in the house, no furniture except the broken frame of a bed and no bed clothes. She took a blanket out of the pawn shop one week when she got her money and it was in again the next day.' Beatty said that she spent the entire allowance on alcohol, was a bad influence on other women, and there was 'no hope for her'. Her children were not sent to school and were out begging, as was she. She got six months 'in her own interest and in the interest of her children'.[30] At Clonmel Borough Court, a woman was charged with neglect of her nine-year-old daughter. She lived in the workhouse and her husband had left her. Another child had died and another was in hospital. Beatty told the court:

> For some time past, military money had been rather flush in the town and defendant and two other or three other women adopted the systematic course of coming out of the workhouse in the mornings, staying about the town looking for a drink during the day and returning to the institution at night. The child was deprived of the dinner she would get in the workhouse and was also deprived of the opportunity of going to school. While the mother was drinking, she was standing at the corners in wet and cold. On one night, he found the woman and a number of others drinking in a house with the girl looking at the 'squalid orgy'.

The presiding officer at the court said that the woman 'and her class were a disgrace to the town'.[31] She was jailed for three months and the girl was committed to an industrial school.

Finally, a woman was jailed for a month for cruel treatment of her three children all aged under seven.

> Defendant was the wife of a soldier... the man himself had come back from where he had been stationed and when he saw the terrible state of the children asked the society to protect them. The defendant was drawing £1 per week for herself and the three children. She lived in a room in Peter Street, and since November,

it was found absolutely impossible to get any good of her. Under
the threat of being prosecuted, she promised to take the pledge,
but did not carry out her promise.[32]

The court heard that when the money was gone, she pawned everything the
children had including boots, stockings and bedclothes — leaving one bed of
about three feet wide, in which they slept. The woman had fallen into a 'self-
destructive cycle of drinking, pawning, and drinking' and the children were
'utterly neglected'. The prosecution told the court that wives of soldiers were as
a rule exemplary, but this case had to be highlighted. The mayor of Clonmel,
presiding, said that it was a squalid case and the defendant was an 'unnatural
mother to treat her children in the way she did'.[33] He ordered that when she
got out, the £1 would not be given to her until she got a certificate stating that
she was 'behaving herself'.[34]

The annual meeting of the Soldiers and Sailors Families Association in
Clonmel heard one committee member try to counter the perception that all
separation allowances were abused: 'There was a common misapprehension
about soldiers' wives which should be dispelled, namely that they put their
separation allowances to an improper use. Out of the hundreds of soldiers'
wives in Clonmel only half-a-dozen or so were not living respectably. The
others should not be judged by the few who appeared at irregular intervals
in the police court'.[35] The Roman Catholic curate in Nenagh, however,
condemned from the pulpit the spate of separation allowance abuses by
soldiers' wives in the town: 'It was disgraceful to observe the wives of soldiers
(who were risking their lives on the field of battle) going about day after day
from one public house to another spending on drink the money which should
be spent on the children and in the homes of the brave soldiers who were
fighting to defend their country'.[36] The priest asked for more respect from
the women who had been exhibiting 'unchristian conduct'.[37] The *Nenagh
Guardian* endorsed the priest's call, saying that it regretted the need for it but
that these women 'think that it is their duty and their right to let the money go
as easily as they get it and consequently they throng public houses and indulge

to excess in beer, without perhaps a thought or a prayer for him that is risking his life in Ireland's cause and for Erin's honour'. It also said it was 'wonderful that the government departments which are so careful and so well organized in many respects never considered this question'.[38]

Enlistment also provided respectability and immunity to people who would not otherwise have had a high status in society. The army took advantage of a grey area of tolerance when soldiers went to court, and magistrates sometimes treated miscreants leniently.[39] At Borrisokane Petty Sessions, a man accused of being drunk said he had two sons at the front and had not heard from one since Christmas; when he did hear, the man said, he drank whiskey. The judge let him off as he agreed to take the pledge. At the same sitting, another man was let off with a caution for drunkenness because he had gone drinking to celebrate his brother-in-law's return from the front.[40] However, this could work both ways. The *Nenagh Guardian* criticized a court ruling in December.

> We cannot acquiesce with the recommendation of Mr Justice Todd to the prisoner, Toohey, to apply to the military authorities with a view to enlistment and thus be released from what we consider a totally inadequate sentence for his participation in the death of the man Collins in Abbey Lane. Collins was done to death in the most brutal manner possible and when the jury found Toohey guilty his sentence should have run into years and not months.[41]

The paper said that in a previous case, a postman who was charged with embezzling three shillings and offered to join the army if he was let off, was told, according to the paper, 'the army did not want men of his class'. The paper claimed: 'Surely a young man, who in a weak moment embezzled a small sum, would be more acceptable to his comrades in Kitchener's army than a man who had another's life on his hands.'[42]

In March 1918, at Carrick, an ex-soldier was before the court on charges of drunkenness and disorderly conduct: 'He gave a good deal of trouble to the police,' a constable told the court. The defendant said he had been 'at the front since 1914 and was suffering from shell shock' and when he takes drink, 'he loses his head'. The constable said that ex-soldiers 'should be given to understand they cannot do as they like'. The resident magistrate said that such conduct by soldiers could not be allowed. However, he adjourned the case to see if he would take the pledge.[43] In Cahir, four boys were charged with letting off fireworks in the streets. One of the lads told the resident that magistrate his mother was dead and his father was fighting at the front. He was discharged without any penalty.[44] At Clonmel Borough Court, a soldier's wife was charged with drunkenness in public, and the police asked if she might be dealt with leniently on the basis that she had taken the pledge and her husband was going to take her to Dublin. The judges adjourned and said that if she was still in Clonmel in a month, it would be taken into consideration. Sometimes, nothing redemptive was found by the judge. For example, a British Army Service Corps soldier serving at Fethard was convicted of stealing chickens. His captain produced his army records in the court. Pte Bertie Heap said that he was a marked man in the army and that was the reason for the poor records. The judge asked would he be taken back into the army and the captain said no, as he would be useless at the front. He was duly jailed for six months.[45]

COMFORT DRIVES

The First World War brought with it a surge in charitable activity. Women, in particular, participated in voluntary war work in considerable numbers.[46] First-aid training, providing comforts for the troops, and fund-raising took place all over the county and continued throughout the war.

The *Nationalist* launched a fund-raising campaign to send cigarettes, tobacco and other comforts for Tipperary prisoners of war in Limburgh. The paper reported that more than 100 of the prisoners were from Tipperary and about £38 was already acknowledged. The *Nationalist* urged its readers to contribute to the fund for 'our gallant soldiers'.[47] Different towns also organized their own parcels, with Carrick sending out items to the prison camp for 'the Carrick boys'.[48] The issue of prisoners received considerable coverage in the press. The *Nationalist* devoted several editorials to it, claiming that the food the prisoners received was worse than that given to the dogs'. The Germans, hit badly by the blockade, had resorted to robbing Belgians for food, and but for the parcels sent out, the prisoners would die:

> It would be terrible to think of them suffering the rigours of another winter, insufficiently clad and fed without the help of those at home who can render them assistance. Hunger and torture have failed even to shake their loyalty and devotion to the cause in which they risked life and liberty. It is our duty then to see to their well-being and, as far as we can, to assuage the conditions of their dreary existence.[49]

It called for full support of a race meeting in Powerstown Park in aid of the fund for the war prisoners of 'our great county regiment, the 18th Royal Irish Regiment, which has played such a noble part in the war since the very beginning'.[50] The race meeting raised about £500.

Tipperary was praised in 1916 for its commitment to the issue of prisoners of war. The *Chronicle* published a letter from Father J. Crotty in Limburg, thanking Tipperary people in particular for their response:

> The amount of goods that come from Tipperary for the exiles from that part of our dear native land is an assurance that our appeal has struck a 'Golden Vein'. At any rate the boys look upon Tipperary as the 'El Dorado'… somehow it must be said the supplies that arrive for 'the boys of Tipperary' exceed in bulk and in frequency the abundant gifts that flow into us from other places. Besides the excellent bread that comes to us and the tobacco etc, weekly and monthly, we often receive supplies

of meat, sausages from Holland, which come from the funds collected in Tipperary... The editor of the Clonmel 'Nationalist' is well known here, for besides his literary contributions in his popular journal, he has frequently contributed money for the boys. From Nenagh and Roscrea parcels are often sent from kind ladies and friends for the boys of these towns. So you see the Tipperary boys are having a fine time of it.[51]

Limburg camp is now better known as the site of Roger Casement's unsuccessful attempts to form anti-British units from Irish prisoners. In July 1918, the *Clonmel Chronicle* published letters from former prisoners of the camp stating that the efforts made by people in Tipperary helped prevent them from joining such units. Three sergeants imprisoned there said the clothing and food sent by Mrs Kellet and Mrs Bagwell, and the efforts to address the 'spiritual needs' of the prisoners, went a long way towards alleviating their suffering and prevented the formation of an Irish brigade from Irish prisoners.[52]

The most recognizable voluntary organizations at the time were the British Red Cross Society, the St John Ambulance and voluntary aid detachments. In Tipperary, the surge in voluntary work attracted support from across the political and religious divide. Dr Ella Webb, inspecting thirty members of the Clonmel Nursing Division of the St John Ambulance Brigade, paid tribute to Clonmel and the mayor for their efforts: 'She was glad to know that the people of the town and district had given such valuable assistance to the division... They had the mayor of the town, Alderman Condon, the representatives of the army and of the people.'[53]

The annual meeting of the St John Ambulance Association and British Red Cross Society, Clonmel, heard in 1916 that in the preceding year, the work depot had sent 2,792 articles of clothing to 'the Dublin depot, Serbia, the Dardanelles and to the Tipperary command depot'.[54] The local Voluntary Aid Detachment (VAD) had sixty-four members, eighteen of whom were doing work in Dublin, Serbia, the Dardanelles and at the Tipperary command depot. The meeting also heard that the War Hospital Supply depot had sent

12,000 articles for hospitals, including swabs, bandages and pneumonia jackets. Michael Slattery, chairman of the county council, paid tribute to the work of the women:

> The cause in which they were engaged in was one in which every true Irishman could join heart and soul and while they had brave men in Tipperary to go forward and fight for the cause of justice and right, they also had lovely women in Tipperary who did not forget the soldiers and who work for their comfort in trench and hospital.[55]

Another initiative that developed was a free food buffet for soldiers travelling through the Limerick Junction rail station in Tipperary. This was suggested by RIC County Inspector William Langhorne, who had been on duty at the station and saw that the hundreds of soldiers travelling through it every day were forced to endure long waits without any food or drinks — except at high prices. The station's sergeant also said that 'he had met soldiers at the station who admitted they were actually hungry, that many of the men had no money and that sixpence for a cup of tea and a small piece of bread was more than most of them could afford'. When the facility was opened a number a weeks later, the *Chronicle* published a large column on it. The paper correctly noted the station's bleakness:

> At the best of times the junction is not an exhilarating place to have to spend an hour or two waiting for a train, but to men suffering from wounds or tired out after a long journey, its wind-swept platform is... a dreary... halting place... The work is hard, but it is willingly undertaken by the ladies of Clonmel, Cahir and Tipperary. In the first week they supplied refreshments to almost 1,500 men including three troop trains.[56]

By November 1918, the free buffet at Limerick Junction had served 339,233 since it opened in January 1916.[57] Workers of the Clonmel War Hospital Supply depot were lauded after a dramatic and musical recital in Clonmel.[58] Women were at the centre of all of these initiatives. In Clonmel, £130 was raised by 'zealous... lady collectors' in aid of Red Cross work.[59] In 1916, a series of gift sales held in Clonmel, Fethard, Carrick, Roscrea, Thurles, Cahir and Cashel raised the considerable sum of about £6,000. The funds were donated to various recipients including the RIRegt prisoner of war fund, the Red Cross, the Clonmel fund for the relief of the Belgians, St John Ambulance Brigade, the free buffet and the command depot at Tipperary.[60]

The local press attempted to play towns against each other. Before the gift sale held at Clonmel, the *Chronicle* said:

> Those poor fellows [prisoners] are our own... and if their fellow townsmen and women forget them, they cannot expect strangers to remember them. They have risked life and limb that we at home may live in security... For that reason we would like to see the list of gifts much bigger than it is... There has already been a great sale in Cashel and a greater one in Thurles. Is the county town, the headquarters of this county regiment to fall behind? [61]

In Carrick, it was reported that the town was determined to look after its soldiers through these comfort drives: 'Carrick has established a proud record in the matter of recruiting, having done better than perhaps any other district of its size in the United Kingdom and having provided the men it now shows a grand determination to stand by them and see that they need nothing.'[62] In Clonmel, particular reference was made to the wealth of the country, and one paper noted that it was glad their contribution had been high: 'The country people contributed as well as the much collected town.'[63] In Cashel, a gift sale for the Red Cross heard the auctioneer in charge pay tribute to the 'patriotic response the farmers of the country had made to the appeals on behalf of the Red Cross'.[64]

It is difficult to state exactly how much was contributed to funds like the Red Cross during the war. The war record of the Red Cross, however, shows the level of contributions to the British Red Cross Society, St John Ambulance Brigade and the VADs for 1917 and 1918. Tipperary increased its donations from £4,726 to £5,168 during these years. The county came second in terms of donations, and was beaten only by Dublin — a considerable achievement at a time when public disenchantment with the war was held to be considerable.[65]

The fund-raising and comfort drives were supported by a cross-section of society and continued throughout the war and beyond. In Tipperary, voluntary work was supported by Catholics and Protestants, nationalists and unionists. Sending comforts to troops, raising money for injured soldiers and first-aid training offered a tangible way for people in Tipperary to alleviate some of distress arising from the war. But the St John Ambulance Association admitted at the end of the war that 'a proportion of the population stood aloof and offered no help'.[66] Enthusiasm for volunteering does seem to have declined somewhat as the war progressed. The Irish War Hospital Supply Depot HQ said that there had been a falling-off in attendance at the depot in Clonmel.[67] In Templemore, one observer claimed that interest dwindled and died from 'one half-hearted jumble sale to another'.[68] The strain of so many collections also seems to have made an impact. The falling-off in subscriptions to the Cashel Nursing Association was attributed to the demands placed on people by the number of collections,[69] and the RIRegt fund was also experiencing problems in 1917.[70]

Many of those involved in those organizations came from the upper echelons of Irish society: gentry, the wives and daughters of senior officials, businessmen, politicians and clergy. While members of the gentry certainly played a central role in many of these efforts, they involved a cross-section of society, and appeals were made to all religious affiliations.[71] The work undertaken was 'no mere expression of Christian piety or Imperial zeal'.[72] People across the county also donated considerable amounts of money to the many different charities, funds and soldier help societies. It all was driven by a genuine desire to help.

STRAIN OF MILITARY LIFE

In May 1915, a RIRegt recruit committed suicide at Clonmel barracks. Charles Merritt, a recruit from Cloughjordan aged twenty-eight and unmarried, slit his throat with a knife. At the inquest, a soldier was interviewed who had enlisted and shared a room with Merritt on the night he died. James Hayden of the RIRegt said that he was unaware anything was wrong with him: 'I did not know anything was going to happen; we had all been so jolly coming down, and his young brother was with us, but not in the same room; twenty of us joined from Cloughjordan.'[73] The coroner replied that Cloughjordan must have done well: 'If there are many more like him in the Royal Irish they ought to give an account of themselves when they meet the Germans,' and asked him if he was sorry for enlisting. 'No, I am satisfied to do my share of the fighting.' The *Nationalist* expressed its sympathy to his parents over the suicide, stating that the tragedy had 'cast a gloom on the entire town and surrounding parishes of Cloughjordan.'[74]

Another tragic suicide at Cahir barracks highlighted the strain military life could place on soldiers who had rejoined. On Saturday 2 January 1915, Battery Quartermaster Sergeant Thomas Craig RFA slit his throat with a razor in the double room he shared with another soldier. At the inquest into his death, it was heard that Craig, aged about fifty-six with a wife and fourteen children in Liverpool, had left the army about ten years previously, had re-enlisted on the outbreak of the war and was put in charge of stores at Cahir barracks. The inquest heard that he had been having difficulties with his duties and his commanding officer felt it was beyond what one was capable of at the man's age, despite the fact that he could have asked for discharge at any time. His roommate told the inquest he had been feeling depressed and worried about his wife who had been unwell, but he also said he had gone to bed quite cheerful the evening before. Craig's suicide note read: 'God help me. I do not know what I am doing. Everything wrong. Love to wife and children.'[75]

Another soldier attempted suicide by taking poison. Police were called to his house, and the man said: 'I got nothing out of the army... I wish I was killed in India.'[76] At Carrick in July, an ex-soldier was before the court on charges of assaulting a station master, who 'had trouble with men like [the] defendant at the station on several occasions'. The defendant said that 'since he returned from France he does not know what he is doing when he has drink taken' and appealed to the judge not to jail him or he would lose his pension. The man had been in court previously charged with damaging a woman's shop. The judge sentenced him to two months in prison.[77] Such incidents highlighted a darker side of military life during the war years.

BELGIAN REFUGEES

By the middle of October 1914, tens of thousands of Belgian refugees had arrived in England and, in turn, the county mobilized to provide aid. The *Nationalist* regarded German operations in Belgium as evidence of their inhumanity. It claimed that Belgium's soldiers were modern-day Spartans fighting in Thermopylae and protecting Ireland from invasion. The paper also claimed that Ireland had sent 'thousands of her sons to fight for Belgium's liberty'.[78] In October 1914, the government issued a circular appealing for help in accommodating Belgian refugees, and the media, clergy and local distress societies moved to help them.[79]

We have seen in Chapter One the efforts made in raising money for the Belgian refugees, but also how there was concern that Belgians should not take local jobs. One of the largest public gatherings took place at Clonmel Town Hall on 19 October 1914. Here, it was moved that a rate be struck by Clonmel Corporation and the Local Government Board to finance the cost of accommodating Belgians in Tipperary, but this was later shot down at a meeting of the South Tipperary County Council.[80] Local residents (mainly gentry) offered accommodation, food and supplies for the prospective refugees; fifty were believed to be earmarked for Tipperary. Subscriptions were taken up at the meeting and a charity drive was started.[81]

At a Board of Guardians meeting on 24 October, however, the gentry were criticized for their inaction on the matter and their reluctance to provide direct assistance to the refugees. They directed the most vitriolic comments towards the Deputy Lieutenant, Richard Bagwell. Bagwell had been in the chair at the meeting in Clonmel and at one point had broken down in tears at the plight of the Belgians: 'He did not cry much when the Irish people were being driven from their homes and exterminated',[82] one board member said.

The efforts to help the Belgian refugees were extensive throughout the country. Some reports claimed that it 'united Irish society in a way that is not often seen in accounts of the period'.[83] Political and religious leaders from both sides were involved in the campaign and local firms offered support. Many local families also offered to help. It was believed that accommodating refugees was a short-term sacrifice.[84] Archbishop Harty held a collection in all churches of the diocese, and read a letter at all masses, reminding people that Belgium 'came to our aid when Ireland was a victim of the penal laws' and the 'Irish exile found a warm welcome and a hospitable home on Belgian soil'.[85] Harty's collection on 25 October raised £100, with the total expected to reach £150.[86]

Clothes, food, cooking utensils and financial donations poured into charitable organizations across the county, and concerts and fêtes were a common method of raising money.[87] A flag day was held in Clonmel on Thursday 5 November: 'During the day a number of ladies, all wearing red, yellow and black favours were engaged selling tiny Belgian flags... we understand as much as a pound was paid for the tiny emblem, whilst one fair lady netted 10s. for a badge bearing an inscription consigning the Kaiser to the infernal regions.'[88]

A colourful atrocity story was published in the *Clonmel Chronicle* on 4 November as a spur to this funding initiative. A Tipperary woman (Madame Charles Naus), who had married a Belgian, was back in the county after fleeing the continent. 'She saw a party of Germans parade the village singing and playing melodeons, while at their head marched a stalwart savage holding aloft on the point of a bayonet the dead body of a fourteen months old infant. The little innocent's blood trickled onto the monster's head and shoulders.'[89] One Tipperary man who rebuffed a seller was told that 'if not for the Belgians he and his big bullocks would not be in Clonmel that day'.[90] It was reported that over £118 was collected. The gentry were again the major contributors in this case: the Grubbs, Moores and McClellands noticeable in the subscription lists.[91]

At a concert in Clonmel on 30 November, groups of miniature Belgian flags lined the footlights of the stage, and at Clogheen, the clerk of the union, M.F. Ross-Lonergan, claimed that Belgian sacrifices had guaranteed Ireland's freedom.[92] In Clogheen, the concert had raised £20; the Thurles fair day collection had raised £50; and the Belgian Refugee fund was the extra beneficiary of a sale of work in Fethard initially organized for soldiers' and sailors' families.[93] The *Clonmel Chronicle* lauded the efforts of Tipperary people for their philanthropy: 'No portion of the country has been more wide awake to their needs, quicker or more generous to offer help, than our own county of Tipperary. All classes volunteered to house the refugees, subscription lists were opened and entertainments were organized, all of which realized considerable sums.'[94]

Belgians arrived in Roscrea in October.[95] Two families came to Nenagh in December: 'They were met by the ladies and gentlemen of the local distress committee, who had them, amidst cheers, conveyed to O'Meara's hotel in motor cars.'[96] After the meal, the Belgians told 'harrowing tales of the cruelties practiced by the Germans'.[97] Ten refugees arrived in Clonmel and Cashel during January. A local woman, previously married to a Belgian who was 'murdered' by the Germans was among the party that welcomed them to Clonmel. None of the refugees spoke English. In Cashel, Belgians arrived to similar scenes. They were greeted by the Dean of Cashel, Reverend Innocent Ryan, in French, and were housed in the courthouse. In both towns, the committees were composed mainly of gentry and clergy.[98] Collections were held in churches of several denominations in Cashel for the refugees and a mixed hockey game was held between Clonmel and Waterford.[99] Refugees also arrived in Nenagh, with Suttons donating coal for them.[100]

Belgium figured prominently in war propaganda. People had heard from politicians and recruiters that they had been lucky — they had been spared Belgium's fate. Recruiters at times went further and warned people that they faced the same fate if they failed to enlist. The sight of Belgian refugees in Tipperary certainly would have added to the perception of a community at war, but it is difficult to conclude that this was anything other than a humanitarian response. The work of maintaining refugees was mainly voluntary, with some aid from the Local Government Board. Women also played a role in organizing help for the Belgians, worked during the flag days and met them on arrival. The response to the appeals came from all sections of society.[101] Collections were held amongst all religious denominations. Sports, fêtes, concerts and flag days were an expression of genuine concern for the refugees. The Belgian refugees' fund was finally closed in November 1916. Its total receipts were £388; the remainder if its surplus, £44,was transferred to the gift sales committee.[102]

TEMPLEMORE PRISONERS OF WAR

In September 1914, 300 German prisoners of war were sent to Richmond Barracks in Templemore.[103] The two squares of the barracks, which had been occupied for the three years previous, were divided into four compounds surrounded by barbed-wire and each fitted with high observation towers.[104] The prisoners arrived at the end of August and continued until Christmas. Locals turned out to witness these arrivals, some apparently experiencing shock that the Germans were 'human'.[105] Numbers rose to about 2,000 by Christmas. The local press noted their 'fine physique', while also claiming that they looked 'crest-fallen, war-worn and travel stained'.[106] Coverage also emphasized the exoticism of the prisoners and the fact that they presented a business opportunity. Prisoners were still paid allowances, and a local entrepreneur had a mobile store that he wheeled into the barracks.[107]

The prisoners did work around Richmond Barracks and there are accounts of German prisoners undertaking local voluntary work such as laying a parquet floor in the sanctuary of the convent chapel for the nuns.[108] The prisoners walked to and from mass every Sunday morning and sang their national songs. In December, a prisoner died of wounds. His funeral was an interesting spectacle. A large group of local people gathered at the gates of the camp[109] and the funeral received full military honours. A firing party of the Leinster Regiment escorted the funeral and the coffin was draped in the German colours. The dead German was a Catholic and the funeral was met by the local parish priest who read prayers at the graveside. German soldiers sang hymns, three volleys were fired by the Leinster Regiment and the 'Last Post' was sounded. The German prisoners there threw three handfuls of clay into the grave.[110] Another prisoner died later, reportedly of food poisoning from bad sausage.[111] He was a Protestant who was buried in the Church of Ireland graveyard, and one of the Germans prisoners played the organ at the service.[112]

The prisoners also collected goods from the railway station using a cart and went to the post office to collect mail.[113] One story, probably apocryphal, told of an occasion when a party of four Germans and two guards left the prison. When they came to a public house, the Leinsters went inside and told the prisoners to wait. They were so long inside, the Germans had to go in and found them inebriated. 'They lifted their two unresisting guards and placed them comfortably in the truck car, added their rifles and ammunition and wheeled the lot back to the barracks.'[114] One of the prisoners carved a poem about their time in Templemore onto a collar bone of cow, which indicated criticism of the food they were getting at Templemore. This was in contrast to local reports that they were receiving the best quality Tipperary beef.[115] A German abbot visited Mount St Joseph's, Roscrea, and gave a retreat for three days. He also visited the prisoners at Templemore and heard their confessions.[116] The German prisoners also lit up the barracks with candles on the night of the Kaiser's birthday on 27 January.[117]

Templemore would soon, however, be saying goodbye to its unusual guests. By early 1915, the authorities were planning to move the prisoners. There is some uncertainty as to why this was so. The official explanations seem to dwell on the fact that sanitation was not up to scratch and that the barrack was needed as a training depot. There were also some indications that the military was concerned over the presence of so many German prisoners, given the political situation in the country. It was also claimed that the new commandant of the Irish Volunteers in the area, Pierce McCan, drew up plans for an insurrection that included the release of these prisoners, and this might have got back to the authorities.[118] By March 1915, all 2,000 prisoners had been transferred to Leigh, outside Manchester.[119] When the Germans left, a regiment of Royal Munster Fusiliers came to Richmond Barracks, and it became a training camp for the front, complete with replica trenches that were dug and re-dug to give soldiers some experience of what they could expect. This may have been in response to the fact that training for the 16th Division was patchy and the 49th Brigade, stationed at Tipperary barracks, did not receive trench training before going to Aldershot in Britain.[120]

CONCLUSION

Families across the county were touched by the unique brutality of the conflict. The war could not be ignored or avoided, particularly with the establishment of the command depot, which saw wounded and maimed troops from across the British Isles converge on Tipperary town. The trauma of this convergence no doubt served to shatter some of the pomp and glamour of the military. The conflict also brought severe social problems. Many soldiers' wives, for example, received generous separation allowances, but had difficulty adjusting to life with more money. Some failed to look after their children, squandered the money on alcohol, and ran into trouble with the courts. Others with military links who found themselves before the courts were treated more leniently than might have been the case in pre-war days. The strain of military life also manifested itself in other, more tragic ways. Some soldiers felt unable to deal with the stress of military life and committed suicide, while some found themselves before the courts having struggled to deal with life after the front.

But the war also brought out good in many people. Tipperary behaved in ways similar to the rest of the Ireland, and indeed Britain, in terms of volunteering. Women trained as nurses, made bandages and swabs, and collected money for the Red Cross. If men made the decision to enlist, then women supported them in other ways.[121] Tipperary led the way in some respects, raising considerable amounts of money for the Red Cross. The plight of Belgian refugees led to an outpouring of sympathy and tangible help from all sections of the community. Refugees were given temporary homes. This was the home front — 'everyday life' during the war.

7 ECONOMIC CHANGE

Remembrance Day wreath on the Cahir World War One memorial, Co. Tipperary, November 2012.

JOHN FRENCH, COMMANDER of the British Expeditionary Force, staged an attack on the Western Front at Neuve Chapelle on 10 March 1915. The British infantry broke the German line, but then hesitated and lost the initiative and both sides went back to shelling each other. French, to conceal his failure, complained that he was short of shells. The government, in turn, blamed munitions workers, who were alleged to draw high wages and to pass their days drinking in public houses. Excessive alcohol consumption was a particular concern of David Lloyd George, who was Chancellor of the Exchequer from 1914 to 1915, and subsequently Minister for Munitions. Lloyd George believed that 'munitions and materials are even more important than men' and that excessive drinking was negatively affecting quality and output.[1] With this in mind, Lloyd George announced the imposition of supertaxes on whiskey, beer and wine in 1915, but these were shelved after protests. However, compulsory bonding of all spirits under three years of age was introduced. Legislation curbing bar opening hours and a 'no treat order' prohibiting the buying of rounds was also introduced.[2] There were also further restrictions on output, which included the Output of Beer (Restriction) Act in 1916.

Over the course of the war years, brewing and distilling were damaged by heavy increases in excise duty: thirteen fold in the case of beer and fivefold in the case of whiskey.[3] By 1918, Irish brewing output was half of what it had been in 1916.[4] Murphy's brewery in Clonmel experienced a significant decline in fortunes during the war, resulting in its eventual demise. The belief that drinking was unpatriotic while there was a war on was central to this. The effect on Murphy's was dramatic. Exports to Britain ceased. Output dropped from 87,326 gallons in 1914 to 21,103 in 1918.[5] While there was a slight recovery after the war, it was brief, and the brewery closed during the 1920s. Competition from larger breweries, Guinness in particular, was a factor in its decline, but the challenging war period terminally damaged the brewery.

Munitions factories were established across Britain in an effort to spur production in 1915. War production was immensely profitable. Every firm and every town wanted a share of what was going on. The demand was not confined to munitions. The armed forces needed vast amounts of foodstuffs and quantities of practically every product. The chambers of commerce, industrial development associations, trades councils and local authorities clamoured for contracts in their respective areas, and in some towns, local munitions committees were formed to lobby for contracts. The campaign was taken up in the House of Commons by the IPP and efforts were made in Tipperary to secure munitions work. The *Nationalist* suggested that with a munitions factory reportedly being established in Nenagh, Clonmel should lobby for munitions contracts:[6]

> Clonmel has a strong claim on the War Office authorities. It is known to them as one of the best recruiting districts in Ireland, having sent over 2,000 men to the colours... Hundreds of labourers from the county have been recruited for munition works in England and Wales whereas if such industries were established in a centre like Clonmel the men could be employed with benefit to themselves and their own country at home.[7]

The paper pointed to the woollen mills at Ardfinnan, which had received a number of war contracts but whose workforce had 'sadly been thinned by the enlisting of men in the regular forces'. It was felt that the making of such essential clothing should save the establishment from such depletion. In any case, the *Nationalist* advocated the setting up of local committees and urged the corporation and county council to maintain their efforts in attempting to secure war contracts.[8] Early in 1916, the All-Ireland Munitions and Government Supplies Committee was formed, with the Mayor of Clonmel as one of the vice-presidents.[9] Clonmel, however, was not to be successful. By 1917, only five state-run national factories had been established — at Dublin, Waterford, Cork and Galway. This lack of development led to claims that the country was being overlooked, but 'there was no practical reason to situate munitions factories in Ireland and there were significant logistical and security reasons' against it.[10]

There were also calls for greater use of Clonmel's military facilities. An indication of how important local politicians considered the military was illustrated by Clonmel Corporation requesting the Mayor, T.J. Condon, to ask the military to send troops and 'impress upon the military authorities the fact that the most friendly relations existed between the Army Service Corps, who lately occupied the barracks and the people of Clonmel'. The chairman said that while the Army Service Corps had been in the town, '500 or 600 men had to be fed while 200 or 300 horses had to be looked after' and the loss of money circulating due to this plus the 'heavy taxation' was a 'big hardship'.[11] One councillor said that there had been a depression in the town since the military left, while another councillor supported this saying that he had personal dealings with the ASC: 'The military while in Clonmel did spend a lot of money and as one who had profited to a certain extent while they were here he should say that a more respectable body of men it would be difficult to find. He had had dealings with a large number of them and they left him a clean sheet.'[12] The resolution was passed unanimously.

FOOD SUPPLY, PRICES AND DISTRESS

Concerns about the food supply and the rise in prices were prevalent in Tipperary during these years. The spectre of another famine was raised frequently. In October 1916, the Clonmel Board of Guardians criticized the IPP for being more concerned about 'winning the war for England' than a perceived food crisis at home. Ultimately, a resolution was drafted calling for a convention to address possible food shortages:

> That we desire to call the attention of the people to the serious situation that confronts the country through the threatened shortage of food consequent on the failure of the potato crop and the danger of the overseas supplies failing through the shortage of ships and the excessive freights by the shipping companies. We think that a convention of Irish interests, both agricultural and commercial, should be called at once to deal with the matter.[13]

Clonmel Town Tenants League made similar claims regarding potatoes, accusing some merchants of buying large amounts and hoarding them until the price increased. The League passed a resolution stating: 'That we, the town tenants of Clonmel call on the public bodies of the country to take action in bringing pressure to bear on the government to prevent the exporting of potatoes from this country and to prevent capitalists from cornering the potato supply and exploiting on the consumers.'[14] The government decided to act in 1917, and fixed prices for potatoes at 115s per ton for the main crop, 120s for those delivered in February and March and 130s for the remainder.[15] This came in for criticism. At Clonmel District Asylum, Dr Harvey said there were no potatoes and no tender in response to the advertisement they posted. The board blamed the government, the chairman saying: 'If there are no potatoes available it is due to the bungling of the government themselves. How can it be expected that farmers will bring them into the market now when they are promised better prices for them in February and March? I don't blame the farmers, but the poor people in the towns are suffering.'[16] A resolution bringing the situation to the attention of Lord Devonport, the Food Controller at the Ministry of Food, was passed.

The war resulted in an annual average rise of 25 per cent in the cost of living until November 1920, and the weakness of trade unionism in Tipperary did not help the workers to maintain their real wage rates. War bonuses were awarded, however, as the war progressed. Clonmel Corporation rescinded a motion of October 1916 refusing a war bonus to carters, surfacemen and labourers. Stapleton, the mover, said 'the price of foodstuffs had gone up to a terrible extent. Three weeks ago the value of £1 was only 10s 10d; it was now perhaps 7s 6d. Meat had gone up 2d a lb; it was never seen by the poor except in the shop windows. Sugar it was impossible to buy; tea had gone up and a bottle of stout was not to be got. He proposed that a war bonus of 2s per week be given to the men'. This motion passed.[17] The caretakers of the Ardfinnan, Newcastle and Cahir dispensaries received a war bonus of £3 per year.[18] Veterinary surgeons were granted a war bonus of 20 per cent and rate collectors 1.5d in the pound extra.[19] In March 1917, a war bonus was granted to Clonmel Corporation's carters, surfacemen and labouring men at the rate of 2s 2d a week.[20]

A discussion at St Luke's Hospital in Clonmel regarding rates of pay during the war years is instructive. The committee discussed a war increase of 2s a week for married attendants from August 1916. One committee member, Mr Ryan, said that some in the asylum had far better wages 'than some men in the country who had to work harder'. The cost of running the asylum had gone up very much, and in the interests of the ratepayers he did not think the committee would be justified in voting any increase to those men. Alderman Peters, who proposed the increase, pointed to inflation and said: 'The value of the 15s they used to bring home to their families in the week is only 10s now'. Ryan replied that 'everyone is hit by the war'. The increase was ultimately rejected.[21]

At Tipperary Urban District Council, the general purposes committee recommended a war bonus of 1s 2d a day to the council's carters and 2s per week for other employees.[22] The carters had their wages increased, again on 12 August 1918 from £2 to 48s per week.[23] This was a generous increase but many did not receive that level of pay and the cost of food rose increasingly higher. At the Board of Guardians in Clonmel, sugar increased by most, from 1.5s to more than 3s per lb — an increase of 95 per cent. Bread had jumped 58 per cent, eggs 30 per cent and oatmeal from 12s 2d to 21s per sack — an increase of 74 per cent.[24]

In 1916, Captain John O'Brien, living in Lakefield, Fethard, wrote to the Board of Guardians at Clonmel underlining his concerns. O'Brien felt that food had advanced as much as 70 per cent, yet the 'lower grades' of wages had only advanced 20 per cent. This would lead to 'absolute destitution' for some.[25] O'Brien called for local bodies or a committee to approach the gentry and the 'well-to-do farmers who have benefitted by the war to supply milk, wheat, oats and potatoes at a fair price, say twenty-five or thirty per cent above the pre-war prices which will be sold by the local bodies'. O'Brien said that the milk question was a serious one in the country towns and Clonmel and Fethard have attempted to address this with the establishment of milk depots.[26]

Concerns over the price and supply of fuel were also prevalent. An agreement was reached in Clonmel that families whose income did not exceed 18s per week, including old age pensioners and poor roomkeepers, living in the parish of St Peter and Paul's, would receive coal at 6 pence per cwt less than current prices. Tickets were issued for this.[27] The issue became more acute as the war progressed with significant coverage devoted to it in the press. By 1915, the supply of coal was reduced because large numbers of British miners had joined the colours. This produced a scarcity, which when combined with the increased wages for those still working, had driven up the price.[28] Further price rises were expected and Clonmel Gas Committee offered tar as fuel at cheap rates, which the *Nationalist* felt was a good offer 'as mixed with slack coal, wood chips and other debris it makes an excellent fuel and cheap too, compared with coal... at £2 a ton'.[29] There was undoubtedly an element of profiteering involved and dividends in some industries increased. Coal profits in 1916 were triple those of the average for the last five pre-war years and shipping profits were up about 33 per cent. There were reports of 'fairy tale' profits while British as well as Irish working-class families found life extremely difficult.[30]

A member of the Town Tenants League in Clonmel said that the poor were being hit hard with no potatoes at the markets and the high price of coal.[31] At the end of July, the *Nationalist* reported that the coal supply question was threatening to become 'very acute' and a 'coal famine' was expected during the winter. The price had trebled to 70s per ton: 'the coal yards are empty, and odd cargoes that come through are quickly cleared mostly to meet long-standing orders. Coal at 70s a ton is very dear buying, and, while all industries are very hard hit, the poorer classes find it almost impossible to buy, the cost being quite prohibitive.'[32] The paper claimed there was talk about fuel-grabbing by the wealthy but it called for a system of rationing to prevent any fuel shortages during the winter.[33] At the end of August, a coal shortage was reported at Emly, with coal costing £4 a ton.[34] At Clonmel corporation, one councillor said that corporation funds should be used to secure fuel. This was rejected, but one member, Alderman D.F. O'Connor, urged members of charity organizations to act and pledged that the corporation would help by lending their motor tractor and allow use of the yard if any turf could be secured:

> [He] understood that the charitable society — the St Vincent de Paul — had failed to procure coal this year. This was a very sad state of affairs for the poor... and made their position for the coming winter worse than before because in previous years the society got supplies of coal, which they let the poor have at somewhat below cost. Already they could see the effect of the winter and the shortage of fuel in the country parts. It was no unusual thing even now before the full blast of the winter's breath had come, to see old and young, ill-clad and ragged, picking up sticks to make provision against the inclemency of winter.[35]

The resolution was passed unanimously, with the mayor, O'Halloran Peters, claiming the real problem was that the St Vincent de Paul Society just could not secure coal and it was not a matter of money.

The *Nationalist* welcomed the meeting held in Clonmel by the corporation to secure fuel for the workers and poor of the town:

> Coal is terribly scarce and dear, and our native stocks of turf and timber, though available in certain quantities, are not regularly marketed, and it requires some organization to get them to the homes of the poor. The corporation cannot legally spend money in the purchase of fuel for the people, but they can do the next best thing in focusing public attention on this urgent question.[36]

The paper admitted that the St Vincent de Paul Society had been working for years to this effect through their 'coal fund' and considered that if this work was supplemented by local societies, the problem would be alleviated. It also advocated a meeting to secure supplies of turf and timber in Ireland, which then could be shipped to the country.[37] Despite these efforts, Cashel became gripped by a coal famine:

> The people of Cashel have been suffering seriously for over a fortnight owing to the impossibility of procuring coal. Not a bit of coal has been sent into Cashel for the needs of the community for more than two weeks and it looks as if the people will have to go without it for another week if the authorities do not do their duty to the citizens by seeing that Cashel gets its fair quota.[38]

The paper declared that this length of time was improper and that the Coal Controller should ensure that supplies of coal were secured. Fuel, then, was a continuing concern.

Sinn Féin claimed in September 1917 that a famine was imminent. The first resolution of the Clonmel Sinn Féin Club warned people 'of the grave danger of famine during the coming winter owing to the threatened commandeering of food for English people' and advised people to hold the harvest. This resolution was adopted at Tipperary South Riding County Council.[39]

A meeting to examine the extent of distress and the possibility of a famine was held in Clonmel, which was chaired by T.J. Condon. Pierce McCan, who won a seat for Sinn Féin that December, said that unless all parties, Sinn Féin and nationalist, join together they would face famine, starvation and death.[40] Condon, however, dismissed the idea of a repeat of the famine: 'The circumstances were totally different. The population, the economic conditions, the food in the country at the present time, the means of distributions at the present time did not tend towards it.' Condon said that he was not there as a politician, but as an Irishman, and he was willing to join with anybody 'for the protection of the people'. He established a committee to look into the matter of relieving distress.[41] In Tipperary, a depot to supply milk for free to the poor children of the town was opened at Christmas 1917, and another at Limerick by Cleeves, which supplied as much as 400 gallons a day.[42]

Allotments were another initiative to increase food production during the time. The *Nationalist* criticized large landowners in mid-Tipperary for not releasing land for use as plots and welcomed the Local Government Board and Urban Council's efforts to compel them: 'It is a shameful state of affairs in the present trying conditions that the small amount of land required should be refused to the townsmen to grow food for their families.' It said that about 150 people were seeking plots in Templemore alone.[43] At Tipperary South Riding Technical Instruction committee, a circular from the Local Government Board regarding tillage of plots in urban districts was read and the Local Government Board was prepared to send an organizer. This provoked an angry response from the chairman, Michael Slattery: 'They would send us imported Scotchmen to tell the workmen and practical men in the urban districts what to do. It is simply ridiculous... and then they would be saying that the Irish farmers' sons ought to be out in France fighting.'[44]

The *Chronicle* reported on Clonmel Corporation's allotment scheme, which now had fifty people participating with plots of one eighth of an acre on land totalling seven and a half acres and it hoped to increase this to twenty acres by spring of that year.[45] As of January 1918, Clonmel Corporation had 144 allotments. This initiative had begun as early as 1915, but gathered speed in late 1916 and early 1917 when food production became more vital. The plot scheme was self-supporting and the expenses and funds financed by the plot-holders.[46] In February, the *Nationalist* reported that the Clonmel Allotment Committee had provided 220 plots for Clonmel workers and it would secure another 100 the following year:

> The plot is now the mainstay of the worker's home. It gives him plenty of wholesome food at cost price for himself and family and lessens considerably the strain on food resources... War conditions have at last given town workers a right to a share of the land, they have made good in their new industry, which is conferring many benefits on the community, and it is only proper that plotholders should band themselves together not alone for mutual interests but for making the allotment system a permanent feature of urban industry.[47]

AGRICULTURE

Dairy was central to trade in the county. By 1904, the Irish National Condensed Milk Company was producing one and a half million pounds of condensed milk annually and fifty tonnes of butter, with the London market its strongest customer.[48] The war years were productive as Britain was forced to rely on its own market and large supplies of condensed milk were exported there from 1914 to 1918. Stocks were hoarded in Britain, and when they were unloaded on the markets at the end of the war, it caused problems at the company resulting in serious industrial unrest.[49]

In general, the price of milk, cheese and eggs experienced significant price rises during this time. Drangan creamery, for example, saw the price paid for its milk increase from about 4*d* (per gallon) in 1914 to 14*d* by 1920.[50] Eggs were sold for prices up to and including 3*s* 10*d* per dozen during the war years and the profit at the creamery went from £3 to £180 from 1913 to 1915.[51] Every creamery in the south was also urged to make cheese, and by 1919 two hundred creameries were involved in cheese manufacture nationwide.[52]

Another area that boomed during the war years was the bacon trade. Exports to Britain resulted in major increases in the price of pork per hundred weight, which rose from 88*s* 9*d* in 1916 to 151*s* 9*d* in 1919 and peaking at 187*s* in 1920. This price dropped back annually until it reached 73*s* 3*d* in 1927.[53] Farmers also came under pressure to till more land from very early on in the war. The question of tillage was a controversial one. Political leaders and the media had consistently called for increases in the amount of tilled land. The Tipperary Farmers Association held a public meeting on food production in 1915, and the Secretary of the Department of Agriculture, T.P. Gill, told the association that more land must be tilled, and by doing so they would win the war:

> The war imposed a special duty on the farmers to extend their tillage… The sort of land to put under cultivation was the sound second-class pasture land of which there is so vast a proportion in Ireland. They should plant it with grain, grow roots and forage and depend less on imported foodstuff. They should save the breeding animals and breed a little more from them and in particular to rear more pigs and poultry this year… it was not much but if every farmer did that much, it would be a mighty thing in its way, towards winning the war.[54]

Cullinan said that the Irish Party would hopefully be in a position to help the Chancellor of the Exchequer in making the 'useless big graziers' till more land.[55] The *Nationalist*, while claiming that the grazing system had been wrongly allowed to expand, again urged farmers to till more land: 'The war has imposed several burdens on Ireland — payment of war taxes, recruiting for the fighting forces and increased tillage operations to provide home foodstuffs... They [the farmers] owe it to themselves and the nation to till all the land they can and, if possible, to double the amount of land under the plough.'[56]

At the Tipperary Board of Guardians, a motion was passed asking the government to break up 'large ranches on [sic] the hands of the landlords such as Lord Barrymore and [the] Scully ranches and other tracts of land convenient to this town so that the great scarcity which presently exists of food for the people may not occur again in the country'.[57] In Nenagh, a huge meeting was organized by the North Tipperary Agricultural Committee to further the food production campaign. Father Cunninghan, the parish priest at Templederry, said that it was 'ridiculous' that Ireland did not produce enough food for its own people and it was 'outrageous' that the county had to import 'millions upon millions of foodstuffs':

> The land was the breakfast table and dinner table of the nation and that should be supplied. It was the business of the farmer to put upon that table a sufficient amount of food for their needs and for the needs of the people. It was very likely that the high prices which were obtained for the products of the land would continue for many years and considering the crisis through which they were passing the farmer should at least produce enough of food stuffs to feed themselves and their stock.[58]

Following persistent calls for increased tillage, the government finally decided to compel farmers with the introduction of compulsory tillage for Ireland in 1917. The German policy of unrestricted submarine warfare resulted in the order, made under the Defence of the Realm Act (DORA), requiring all occupiers in Ireland of ten acres or more of arable land to cultivate 10 per cent more than they cultivated in 1916.[59] The chairman of the Tipperary Junior

Farmers criticized the tillage scheme and the sanctions threatened under DORA:

> Some farmers who always cultivated their land and did something extra last year were threatened under the Defence of the Realm Act, while others who did nothing were allowed to go scot free. He knew one military officer in his district who had not broken a sod and he had as good a right to do his share of tillage as his neighbours. His land was not taken over by the department.[60]

The county agricultural instructor, Con Donovan, told the Tipperary Farmers' Society that in the first year of the war tillage had increased but a 'lull in the submarine attacks' meant that 'the world's harvest was good; and food was cheap' so that people eased off: 'the people who did not cultivate land laughed at the cautious people who produced the food and sneered at those who advised them to grow more and more'. He said that the fact that the world's harvest was not up to the average, the partial failure of the potato crop in the British Isles and the destruction of shipping by the German submarines 'had left us at the present time with food at famine prices'. Donovan said that the government would loan money to be used in acquiring machinery at 4 per cent, to be repaid in 'easy instalments' and again criticized the large landowners for the perceived refusal to increase tillage:

> There are the demesne lands at Knocklofty, Barne, Marlfield, Woodrooffe, Newtown Anner, etc. On these lands had tillage been increased since the war commenced? No, and on some of them there is absolutely no tillage... These and other such are the places which the government should first insist on being put under cultivation to produce food for the soldiers who are fighting our battles in France and Salonika and then the farmers will follow and the sooner the owners of the ranches

and demesnes learn that this is Ireland's war as well as England's and that the production of corn and potatoes has as much, and possibly more, to do with winning the war than the getting of a few recruits for the army, because, as I one time pointed out to you, a small number of men well fed and well clothed will be far more effective than a starving multitude. It should not be necessary for the government to use compulsion if the land owners had a sense of their duties. But have they? If there is not sufficient food in the country who are to blame? Who will be the first to suffer? The landowners themselves.[61]

Cullinan, who suggested employing surplus labourers from the west to achieve the 10 per cent extra land to be tilled, criticized some farmers for their unhelpful stance:

People who criticized and raised impediments were those who did nothing to help food production and who had not given a man to the army. They had the land and they did nothing, paying no heed to the warnings and advice that those in a position to know had given them. Now compulsion had come [compulsory tillage] and they were blaming the government and everyone else, quite forgetting it was they themselves who were to blame. Instead of carping criticism, picking holes, and placing obstacles in the way every man should be prepared to do his part.[62]

Cullinan also complained about the various munitions agencies offering Tipperary men jobs in England, which he felt worked against the aim of the tillage order. He said that he had written to the department regarding this:

It was a monstrous thing to be calling on the people to till the land when anybody standing at the railway station in Tipperary could see day after day lots of men leaving for the munition works in England. These men were getting 9 and a half *d* an hour and a war bonus and were tempted to go across for this wage. Was there ever such a farce as to see one department of the government calling for increased food production which meant increased labour while the other department of the government was taking the men out of the country.[63]

The fact that people were leaving for munition works in England was mentioned in other places. At the Clonmel District Asylum, the lure of British munitions jobs was revealed. Five were leaving, with Dr Harvey stating: 'They are going to English asylums and munition works.'[64] At South Tipperary County Council, Cullinan said that he considered this 10 per cent increase to be unjust and again criticized the big landowners:

What they should protest against was that, though the government wanted increased food production, they still kept sending men all over the country looking for munition workers. He thought it was simply monstrous and an enormous number had already gone from Tipperary and the representative of the Labour Exchange in Tipperary had told him that he had an order for thirty more men next Tuesday.[65]

Another councillor said that seventy-five went from Templemore. No motion was made after the discussion. Munitions firms were tapping the pool of labour in Tipperary. In Cashel, for example, a representative of the United Alkali Company visited to enrol munitions volunteers: thirty left for Huddersfield.[66] Ultimately, the farmers agreed to pay any farm-hands who came to work 15*s* with board and lodging.[67] In Cahir, Ballyporeen and Ardfinnan, local committees were established to assist poor people to carry out tillage. About ten acres of land was offered by Colonel Charteris, who was based in Cahir, and there were eighty applicants.[68] Farmers consistently complained about the lack of labour. Cashel District Council had this in mind when considering a letter from the Department of National Service on organizing labour. The Chairman, Mr P. Moclair, said:

> Labour will be hard to be got because a great deal of the fine young men of the country have joined the army. You will see by the Chronicle whole columns taken up with a list of young fellows who joined the colours and for whom certificates were presented. We all know there will be a shortage of labour, but we are not in a position to name the exact requirements.

Contrary to this assessment, another councillor, Mr Fryday, said that there was a good supply of labour in his district and said that the efforts to secure outside labour had not been successful:

> At a meeting some time ago we had a conference and a gentleman came down from Dublin to arrange about supplying labourers. Several farmers gave their names to take labourers and I was amongst the number for one labourer. That was six months ago and I was to have the labourer on the 1st July, but I never heard a word about the matter since.[69]

South Tipperary County Council felt the compulsory tillage order would lead to a scarcity of labour, which would hinder the Council's road programme. The County Surveyor said that normally 700 were employed in the road works, but during the year to March 1917, 'it was impossible to procure sufficient labour to carry out the usual work' and that 'it was not a question of wages, as the labourers are satisfied with the increases given by the council'. The surveyor came to a number of interesting conclusions regarding the availability of labour in the county. He noted that general labourers had either joined the army or gone to the munitions works, but there were still 'considerable pools' of unemployed labour:

> The cause is that the labouring man has enlisted and gone to munition work freely, those remaining consisting only of old men and boys. There is still a good deal of unemployed labour in the county viz., the sons of small farmers who have not, as a rule, enlisted or gone to munition work, but, as the council knows, that class never works for hire, although they freely help each other in times of pressure.[70]

This analysis conflicts with farmers' claims of a lack of labour in the county during the recruiting campaigns of 1915. The estimated manpower discussed in Chapter Five, in conjunction with the stoppage of emigration, also leads to a difficulty in accepting those claims. The compulsory tillage order, then, did have some success. There was a considerable increase in the amount of land tilled during the First World War. In Tipperary, the amount of land under corn crops — wheat, oats and barley — rose from 21,000 hectares in 1914 to 37,000 in 1918, with root and green crops such as potatoes and turnips increasing from 21,000 hectares to 24,000 by 1918. Hay and pasture, meanwhile, declined from 306,000 to 284,000 during the same time period.[71]

Tipperary farmers also complained about price fixing. The Tipperary Junior Farmers complained in September that the price fixed by the Food Controller for beef (at 60s per cwt) was 'unjust and unreasonable', and passed a resolution to this effect. It also passed another resolution: 'That we strongly demand that the producer should get fair and proper representation in the fixing of prices of food and the price of all stall-fed beef should be in conformity with the high price of feeding stuff'.[72] The resolution called for Irish input on this, in contrast with the 'advice of Englishmen who are totally ignorant of the economic conditions of the country', and the withdrawal of the food production order until this is done. The chairman, W. Heffernan of Knockgraffon, said that it was unfair that Irish butter was fixed at 206s per cwt while there was no cap on Danish butter.[73] The chairman also said that the manner in which the authorities dealt with the hay crop was another example of 'muddling':

> A man sold his hay and had to hold it over. When it was called up it had lost materially in weight and it was accorded to the weight after being pressed that he was paid. He had sold hay to be delivered at Cahir barracks and although the railway freight was only 4s 6d per ton, the authorities made him pay 10s per ton to cover the cost of carriage to the port of embarkation.

The honorary secretary, P.J. Quinlan, said: 'I know one man who sold hay to the government and between carting and the railway charges it cost him £20 to deliver it… They got 25s an acre in England for merely ploughing their land and more tillage was done in Ireland than in England and Scotland put together, while there was no recompense for it.'

The chairman felt that the farmers should not sell anything and hold the food 'for there is no doubt about it that a time of famine is before us'.[74] Quinlan claimed that the idea 'seemed to be to crush the Irish farmer for the benefit of the English consumers'. The chairman also seemed to imply that profit was the main concern of farmers:

> They are looking after their own interests and not considering the people in Ireland. Many articles absolutely necessary in the household, including tea and sugar, not to talk of meat, cannot be got even at three times the old price. There is plenty of money in England and they ought to be made pay prices for their food that would leave the Irish producer a reasonable profit.[75]

The two resolutions were passed, and copies were sent to local MPs, the Department of Agriculture and the Food Controller. The idea then was not that there was much concern over the quality of produce, rather that Irish producers should be able to make a profit no matter what. Farmers, however, were criticized during the war. At Tipperary Urban District Council, one councillor attacked some farmers claiming that some did not bother growing potatoes but bought them at the market when the poor of the town needed them: 'I say the farmer, especially in times we are living at present, who comes into the town and buys up in the markets the potatoes that he could and should grow on his own land is not good for king or country.'[76]

CONCLUSION

The First World War developed into one of grim endurance between the combatant countries and economic resources were central in sustaining the conflict to the bitter end. The British war economy was geared towards munitions, supplies and food and, in turn, those involved in these areas would have a good experience.[77] The war brought economic gains to Tipperary, but in particular those involved in agriculture reaped considerable benefits.[78] The war boosted the agricultural economy and provided large profits in certain industries, but it was working-class families who bore the brunt of food shortages and increased prices as wages failed to keep pace with war-time inflation.[79] Prices paid for agricultural produce such as butter, milk and bacon increased considerably. But farmers also had to face calls to increase tillage from early in the war, with the government eventually compelling them through the Compulsory Tillage Act in 1917. Farmers claimed there was a lack of labour and local MPs criticized the government for luring workers away with promises of higher paid jobs in English munitions factories. Men and women did take these job offers, but there was also evidence that labour was available. Emigration virtually dried up during the war years. As most emigrants came from rural rather than urban centres, the pool of unemployed increased in the countryside.[80] Despite those claims and counter-claims, the land under tillage experienced a significant rise from 1916. For their part, farmers criticized the government for its attempts at price control and the amounts and the way in which it paid farmers for their produce.

Others did not do so well. The price of food rose considerably while the wages of the labourers or working class did not keep pace. That is why in 1915, Reverend R.J.S. Devenish, Dean of Cashel, said that although wages had increased, there existed a 'certain amount of chronic poverty'.[81] The war was bad for some sectors, such as brewing. Tipperary also experienced a fuel shortage with the price of coal beyond the means of many working people. Attempts to restrict profiteering by controlling prices generally resulted in the rapid disappearance of designated goods from the shops. Generally, price regulation in Britain had only a limited effect in curbing rent and price increases, and it was even less successful in Ireland.[82] Farmer, trader and manufacturer did well. These were prosperous years in rural Ireland: a well-known poet was moved to claim that during the First World War, 'money grew on the tops of bushes'.[83]

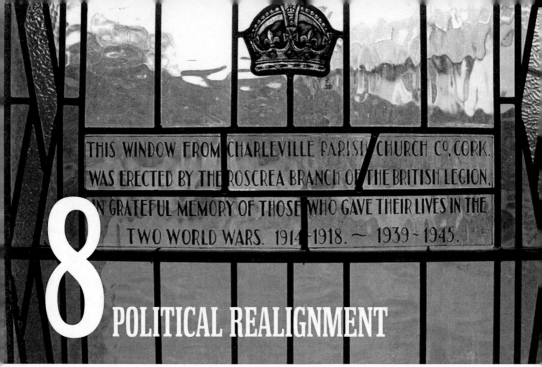

POLITICAL REALIGNMENT

Memorial window erected by the Roscrea branch of the British Legion,
St Cronan's Church, Roscrea, Co. Tipperary. Photograph courtesy
of Michael Lee/Irish War Memorials Project.

REDMOND'S SUPPORT FOR the war effort prevented systematic criticism of the government's activities.[1] By the spring of 1915, Home Rule was looking like an increasingly dim prospect, and when the war ushered in a coalition government in June, it illustrated Redmond's vulnerability. Carson joined the coalition as Attorney General and Redmond refused a position. While this was consistent with IPP policy, it was not inevitable at the time.[2] The decision was inconsistent with Redmond's own tactics since 1914. There was little logical justification for supporting the war effort but refusing office, even if the acceptance of office would have offered his critics some ammunition.[3] By remaining outside, Redmond got the worst of both worlds: responsibility for an increasingly unpopular war effort without any way to influence it.

In May, some of the discussions among local bodies illustrated the level of unease at a British coalition government that included Carson. On a vote to support this decision by Redmond at Clogheen Guardians, one board member said: 'We should wipe the English government off the map altogether after making Carson the attorney general... My opinion of Johnnie Redmond is not the same as it was two years ago. Why didn't he stand his ground and fight the same as he did with Lloyd George and the drink taxes? He weakened to the English government.' Another said: 'There is a great difference of opinion with regard to the attitude of the Irish party on this question.'[4]

Cashel Rural District Council commended Redmond on staying out of the Cabinet, but protested against the inclusion of 'orange rebel leaders'. The possible inclusion of J.H. Campbell was a 'wanton insult'.[5] It is difficult to measure how much of the unease over the coalition constituted anti-Redmondism, but a by-election held in Tipperary North around this time does prove instructive. John Esmonde, MP for Tipperary North, died on 17 April 1915.[6] He had been a key supporter of Redmond and the Volunteer movement, rowing in behind his call for recruits and the British war effort. As if to prove this, Esmonde had joined the RAMC as a captain at Tipperary barracks.[7] As the *Nationalist* put it: 'After the outbreak of the great European war, Dr Esmonde took a leading part in urging that Nationalist Ireland should do her share in curbing the ambition and frustrating the designs of Prussian militarism.'[8]

Esmonde's son, John Lymbrick, a lieutenant in the army, was returned as MP for Tipperary North at the end of June.[9] While an IPP candidate won, the fact that three candidates ran was criticized by the *Nationalist* as symptomatic of a growing malaise in the party. The newspaper claimed that the election revealed the state of affairs of the Irish Party in Tipperary and the 'laxity of national organization in the district not at all creditable to the people of the locality'.[10] It called for a convention in all future elections and felt that the 'turmoil, expense and trouble' of a contest could be spared if the convention was possible.[11] This was borne out as the United Irish League had practically ceased to exist in the constituency with only four functioning branches.[12] Esmonde had a decisive win against Pat Hoctor, a former IRB activist with separatist tendencies, and, taken with the residual vote for the third candidate, Richard Gill (who was a Redmondite with a son at the front), it was clear that north Tipperary supported Redmond and his policy.[13]

DECLINE OF THE IRISH NATIONAL VOLUNTEERS

While the IPP may have taken some solace from Esmonde's win, the limits of Irish commitment to the war driven by Redmond and IPP support was reflected by the decline in the Irish National Volunteers. This was encouraged by the split over Woodenbridge and its bitter polemics, the enlistment of committed activists and fear that military training might bring conscription. Throughout 1915, the question: 'What are they for?' regarding the INV was increasingly difficult to answer. In January, the Volunteer county board admitted that in some districts, Volunteer companies had practically disbanded. A huge problem was securing instructors as the best men had joined up.[14] Confusion over the Volunteers was evident: a statement from Eamonn Mansfield of the Cullen Company declared that the Volunteers had nothing to do with recruitment to the army, but if they joined, their training would be useful. It was clear that Mansfield was sympathetic.[15] On St Patrick's Day 1915, Canon Ryan also made it clear that he believed the Volunteers that had enlisted in the British forces were making a superior sacrifice.[16]

The Volunteers met sporadically in 1915, culminating in a large review in Dublin's Phoenix Park at Easter. During the preceding months, attempts at reorganization were made around the county. T.J. Condon attempted to keep the movement alive in Clonmel telling a meeting there that Volunteers were 'soldiers of the empire' and therefore should form part of any national army.[17] Smaller meetings took place at Knockavilla, Cappawhite, Thurles, Cashel and Fethard. These attempts to reorganize again raised the issue of what the INV was for. Some speakers were repeatedly forced to address the rumours of conscription after Redmond's controversial Woodenbridge speech. At an INV meeting in Thurles, Father Michael Maher said:

> Some time ago, it was thought, perhaps, that the Volunteers would be asked to go and take their place in the firing line in the present terrible war, but as far as one can judge nothing like that will happen. Even though a man is a Volunteer, it does not follow that he will be commandeered in the service of England.

If England wants men she will try and get them whether they are trained or not, but the Irish National Volunteers are for only one object.[18]

The MP for mid-Tipperary, John Hackett, said that Redmond had stated merely what other Irish 'rulers' had:

Some people took exceptions to pronouncements made by Mr Redmond in connection with the war, but Mr Redmond had said nothing, but what had been said by former Irish rulers. At the great Home Rule Confederation when Isaac Butt put forward his demand for Home Rule he said that when England recognized Ireland's rights Ireland would cheerfully become part and parcel of the great British Empire. That was afterwards repeated by Parnell and during the past seven or eight years since the Home Rule question was put forward the same statement was made in propounding the policy of the party in England, Scotland and Wales so that Mr Redmond had propounded no new policy and made no new departure.[19]

On St Patrick's Day, the INV participated in most of the parades, but their attention was also focused on the Phoenix Park review. Special trains were organized for Volunteer groups from Nenagh, Tipperary town, Carrick, Cashel and Cahir. In Fethard, the Volunteers got twenty rifles from Condon and 100 specially made caps were delivered bearing the Fethard coat of arms with the INV letters worked onto a shamrock background.[20] Clonmel INV also made moves to reorganize prior to the review. They had secured a former RIRegt soldier as a new instructor and agreed to hold a house-to-house collection to defray expenses from the Dublin trip.

The review was designed to showcase the might of the INV and argue that they could still be recognized by the War Office and deployed as garrison troops.[21] The press claimed about 27,000 attended. Tipperary turned out with the second-largest number of companies, fifty-seven. Canon Ryan held a special mass for them and the Fethard Corps carried a German rifle, captured in the retreat from Mons by Major Newland, RFA, son-in-law of Richard Burke, the master of the Tipperary foxhounds — thereby again linking the war in Europe with the INV.

> Tipperary county occupied pride of place and furnished a complete section equal to that of a province... the Irish leader seemed especially pleased with our men and spent some time viewing them on the field and in chatting with the officers and Monsignor Ryan at the head of the section. Redmond felt recruiting for the army would be enhanced if the Volunteers were used for home defence and reiterated that some were asking why don't all the Volunteers enroll [sic], which was an 'absurd and malicious' question as all the Ulster Volunteers had not gone.[22]

At the INV convention in the Mansion House the day after the review, Clonmel's mayor and Canon Ryan were present. Redmond said that Belgium was drenched in blood and Ireland would not stand in isolation. Condon proposed a vote of thanks and said that the day's proceedings would rank as 'historic in the annals of Ireland'. Ryan said:

> Sunday's demonstration from Tipperary was not only a demonstration of Tipperary's love for the old land and Tipperary's determination if needs be to fight for her liberties and her shores, but it was also a demonstration of her deep and determined trust in Mr John Redmond... When I looked up that splendid street yesterday over that sea of innumerable heads and saw that one figure standing there receiving the salute of his armed countrymen, I thanked God that man was what he is — one

worthy to receive the salute, to receive the love and appreciation and loyalty of old Ireland.[23]

One of those who went to the Phoenix Park review was Jeremiah Darmody, who worked as an agricultural labourer close to Bansha. He subsequently joined the Irish Guards and was killed at the Somme in 1916 trying to recover the body of his officer. His death received local press notice because the mother of the officer sent £100 to Darmody's father in gratitude for his son's bravery.[24] Timothy Tierney, another INV who attended the review at the Phoenix Park, wrote of his conversation with a relative regarding the review:

> When leaving the Phoenix Park after the review, I met a cousin of mine, named William O'Dea, who was then resident in Dublin. He asked me what I was doing there and, in rather forcible language, he told me that I was in the wrong volunteers. From him, I first heard of Eoin MacNeill and learned of the Irish Volunteers as distinct from the Irish National Volunteers, or the Redmondite volunteers, as O'Dea called them. Up to this, I had always looked on John Redmond as the leader of the Irish people — to me he was a little god — but this talk with my cousins opened my eyes; and after my return home I took no further interest in the company as it then existed.[25]

Edward McGrath, future vice commandant of the 2nd (Mid) Tipperary Brigade of the IRA, near Templemore, wrote that he was not impressed with the review:

> At the time I was a member of the Loughmore Company of the National Volunteers and I remained a member of that organization until Easter Sunday 1915, when I attended a review by the late John E Redmond of the National Volunteers in the Phoenix Park, Dublin. I was not very impressed by what I saw

and heard in the Phoenix Park on that Sunday and I concluded
that the National Volunteer organization was not likely to be
of any great service to Ireland. Sometime later, possibly in the
spring of 1916, I had thoughts of forming an Irish Volunteer unit
in Loughmore, but sympathizers were few.[26]

James Duggan, future captain A Company 2nd Battalion, 2nd Tipperary
Brigade, near Templemore, claimed: 'The company appears to have
disintegrated at the time, and a few pro-Redmondite individuals who attended
the National Volunteer review in the Phoenix Park on Easter Sunday 1915 did
so solely as individuals.'[27]

Easter 1915 marked the end point of any meaningful activity in the
INV movement. Thousands of its members had joined the army, and
added to this was the failure of many local units to pay fees; of seventy-five
registered companies in Tipperary, only five had paid up.[28] Despite this,
a county convention held in St Patrick's College, Thurles, in August 1915
aimed to reorganize the UIL and reinvigorate the movement in the county.
Redmond and Dillon attended. In Thurles, at a reception for the IPP leader, a
'magnificent body of Tipperary Volunteers' attended, though the press report
did not specify how many. At the convention was Canon Ryan and the three
local Tipperary MPs, Esmonde being at the front. Country representatives
presented an address to Redmond and Dillon, pledging support for the party
and Redmond's strategy, declaring that:

Home Rule would now be in operation but for the unprecedented
war on the Continent... Ireland, while striving hard for centuries
for the restoration of her own freedom, has given her best blood
for liberty and against tyranny in every land under the sun. She
is doing the same in France, Flanders and the Dardanelles and
her heroic sacrifices have won her the admiration of the world
and established her claim more firmly than ever to be 'a nation
once again.'

The address also dismissed any dissentients: 'But, thank god, they are a small and noisy section and while Ireland remains loyal and united their machinations will be futile. Destructive faction[alism] has no foothold in our midst. Tipperary is sound and loyal to the core.'[29] This address was signed by representatives of thirty-two elected bodies in Tipperary, including the Dean of Cashel, the chairmen of the south and north county councils, the chairmen of Urban and District councils and the mayor of Clonmel, T.J. Condon. John Redmond, in reply, stated:

> It [Home Rule] was part of the constitution of these countries...
> This awful war had tested the very soul of Ireland, and, thank
> God, so far Ireland had magnificently responded to the
> necessities of the crisis... She realized that they could not come
> into the full enjoyment of her national inheritance at a moment
> when the whole civilized world was engaged in a death struggle
> with despotism and barbarism... The victorious ending of the
> war is then the first necessity of Ireland. I say to you — let us
> help bring that about, not alone by our courage upon the field
> of battle, but by scrupulously maintaining the political truce
> and by promoting and inculcating wisdom, tolerance and unity
> amongst all classes of our people at home.[30]

John Dillon said that it was crucial to remain united behind the party to oppose any taxes against Ireland. He noted that after the war 30,000 Volunteers would be back, 'many of them with high records of gallantry' and he asserted that if a final struggle was forced upon them, 'the fact of having a large force of determined, organized Volunteers, stiffened by soldiers who have returned from the front will be a deciding element in the result'. Dillon believed that the Volunteers could not be non-political and should be closely allied to the Nationalist organization.[31]

At Cashel, a number of weeks later, another attempt was made to reorganize the INV. The Dean of Cashel said a strong volunteer army was needed to ensure Home Rule for Ireland:

> It would appear that prejudice has arisen in the minds of some against the Volunteer organization. It was suggested that the Volunteers would be picked up by the military authorities and compelled to join the army. We know how unfounded and foolish was that thought. In Ireland no man, even in the time of war, can be run against his will into the army of England. The volunteer is just as independent as the non-volunteer… the Irish party has pledged itself before the government, before the world, to offer all the opposition in its power to… conscription.[32]

He also said that the IPP would be in a much stronger position to oppose conscription with '100,000 Volunteer rifles'. The report of this meeting claimed that the Volunteer body in Cashel had only become apathetic because of the number of men who enlisted in the British Army: 'The action of these men was highly commendable, for their enthusiasm and courage have helped to maintain our shores inviolate from the blighting presence of the invader.'[33]

The impression that the INV was making progress was not accurate. As Maurice Davin, Captain of the Carrick Volunteers, wrote in early September, four months had passed since it was agreed that the two county boards would be set up. This had not taken place, and 'consequently this splendid movement is growing very flat purely for want of proper organization'.[34] Cashel still tried to keep the faith with the Volunteers. In late August, Cashel held a review that 1,000 Volunteers attended — this coincided with an INV rejuvenation attempt by a Captain Eckersley from Volunteer Headquarters. Amongst the Volunteer corps that participated in the parade were the Dublin and Limerick City Regiments, Cashel, Tipperary, Thurles, Fethard, Boherlahan, Rosegreen, Ardfinnan, Oola and Annacarty. The Dublin Pipers' Band, St John's Temperance Band Limerick, Tipperary's C.J. Kickham Brass and Reed Band, and Cashel Fife and Drum Band were among those who attended. At the reviewing stand were Captain Eckersley, Reverend T. Dunne, chairman of the Cashel Battalion Committee, and Cullinan, with the Inspecting Officer, Lieutenant-Colonel Fitzroy Hemphill. Hemphill said:

A year ago the country was full of Volunteers. We had 180,000 on the rolls of the National Volunteers. These numbers are considerably diminished now; the causes are not far to seek. One of the main causes of course has been due to the war and to the fact that many, many men from Tipperary and elsewhere throughout Ireland have enlisted and gone on active service. Tipperary, of all the counties in Ireland, has done its fair share in sending men on active service. But war has been only one of the causes. The war looks likely to be pretty soon brought to an end.

He added that because of this, it was more important to continue the INV movement. He compared the Volunteers to the territorials in England and said that they had to struggle for eighty years to get recognition. The INV should be prepared to do the same and it wanted 'professional men, the shopkeepers, the men of all classes'. He stated:

Well I am told in some parts of Ireland there are men who go swaggering about, looking on from the outside, and who laugh at the National Volunteer uniform; they laugh at the men who are Volunteers. I ask such men are they ashamed of their country, are they ashamed of their national colour? Or is it that they are afraid of conscription? Well, if they are afraid of conscription, their best way to get conscription is to sneer and do nothing. Conscription is not likely, thank god, to come, but if it does it will come on chaps like those who look on and don't do anything for their country. It is time that such men would make up their minds to help their country and help this national movement.[35]

Reverend Dunne was also forced to address conscription concerns. Voluntary conscription was slowly coming to an end in England and this had raised alarm that compulsion was to be introduced:

Over and over again I have stated that if ever conscription comes it will be applied according to age and not to profession. Colonel Hemphill has explained to you that there is no danger for the men in the ranks of the Volunteers, but the men not in the ranks of the Volunteers will be called up [Volunteer applause]. At the same time while this rumour of conscription is being worked for all it is worth by a group of newspapers in London it is admitted by some of the leading conscriptionists that they have not the slightest idea of putting it into force in this country. Why is this significant admission made? Why is this differentiation made as against Ireland? It is because of the active existence of the Volunteers.[36]

Cullinan also appealed for more to join the INV, and said that those who did so should not be ashamed:

I hope those outside the ranks will take his [Hemphill's] remarks to heart and remember that in the near future it might be necessary for them to show the stuff they were made of and to prove that they were ready to defend their country... One thing you ought to remember, any man who does not join the National Volunteers ought to be ashamed to call himself an Irishman.[37]

The Volunteer leadership were less than happy with the turnout, although the Tipperary Volunteers were praised. In October, Maurice Davin noted privately 'the lack of enthusiasm' in the county and that there were not eight companies at full strength. The Tipperary Battalion Committee of the INV met in Tipperary in October to reorganize the group. Cullinan again criticized those who 'sneered' at the INV: 'Such people were to be found all over the country and he had met them in the town of Tipperary itself — people whom one would expect to find decent respectable citizens.' Cullinan said Hackett had been more active than he, and was even prepared to visit north Tipperary, where Esmonde could not because of war commitments.

> The other day a man asked him [Cullinan]: "Is it possible you are going to attend a recruiting meeting in Tipperary on Saturday?" He said: "Yes." His friend said: "Are you going to ask our people to go out and fight and risk their lives?" He [Cullinan] said: "Have you joined the Volunteers?""Oh," he replied, "they have nobody to fight." This man's first complaint was about asking men to fight and his second about having nobody to fight. There was a certain section of the community who had not the courage to go out like the brave men who had gone to the front to try and make Ireland what she was at present — one of the happiest and most peaceful nations in the whole world — and had not the courage to come into the ranks of the Volunteers.[38] Cullinan also felt the Volunteers had been 'too energetic' at the start and this had been difficult to maintain but he also considered that a number of wounded soldiers, 'permanently disabled', who had returned from the front could be secured as instructors.

Hackett said he believed the meeting would represent a 'new epoch' in the Volunteer movement. He said, rather fancifully, that securing rifles would be no problem and used the example of Kitchener in raising the new armies to illustrate how the INV could secure weapons and equipment. Hackett also joined Cullinan in attacking the dissentients:

> When the Irish Party were fighting hard to take the burden of rack rents off the backs of farmers and were struggling to secure various measures of reform for Ireland these were just the people who gave the party very little help, but they were never absent

when the rent reductions were going on or when a big purchase came along or [in] partaking in any of the other benefits that were won by those who had fought and suffered in the cause.[39]

Cullinan finished off the meeting and said that the Volunteers must be armed and ready to defend Ireland's shores, and again rounded on the 'sneerers'. '[He] said it was a significant and remarkable fact that many of those who were sneering at the Volunteers and at the National Party were government officials — pensioners and pensioners' sons, and so forth — who spoke about receiving British gold but who themselves never refused to take British gold in their pensions and salaries.'[40]

The persistent problem with the INV had been a lack of guns and ammunition. A few weeks later, Tipperary was forced to request ammunition from Dublin so 'our lads' could at least practise for a forthcoming marksmanship competition.[41] The reality of Volunteer activity was starkly outlined by Eamonn Mansfield, head of the Cullen Volunteers. At this time, he had written to Dublin stating that the Emly group they were tied to had 'never enjoyed three months active existence', their military exercises had declined, and a 'slackness' existed — mainly due to around thirty members, including six instructors, joining the army. It was unclear what the INV were for, he claimed, and with the War Office hostile to the Volunteer movement, specifically its use for home defence, people were of a mind not to join an organization seen as supporting the war. Pointing out that the local committee had supported Redmond in 'the teeth of strong opposition', there was regret in Mansfield's conclusion that 'interest, earnestness and enthusiasm' had gone from the local organization. Dublin wrote back with plans for reorganization but these only existed on paper.[42]

1916 RISING

The INV had been in terminal decline since the Woodenbridge split of 1914. The RIC recorded 1,443 volunteers in the north of the county in May 1916, compared with 3,559 in October 1914 — and most of the 1,443 were on paper only.[43] The militant Irish Volunteers (IV) were, however, beginning to flourish. As we have seen in Chapters Two and Five, they rejected Redmond's endorsement of the British war effort and his Woodenbridge appeal. Some disrupted recruiting meetings and tore down enlistment posters. When the Fenian Jeremiah O'Donovan Rossa died in 1915 and was buried in Dublin, Irish Republican Brotherhood (IRB) men from Clonmel were deeply impressed by Pádraig Pearse's graveside oration.[44] The IV in the town stayed in contact with other key separatist figures in the county such as Seán Treacy and Pierce McCan, were visited by advanced nationalist figures such as Countess Markievicz and Ernest Blythe, and regularly met in the Workmen's Boat Club using the Gaelic League as a cover for their activity.[45]

Local Volunteers twice prepared for action during Easter Week. Plans were drawn up to attack RIC bases, but were never acted upon because of countermanding orders and poor communications. The police reports in the preceding months give no indication of any unrest in the county, and the report for April claims that the prompt action suppressing the rising in Dublin stymied any locally based insurgence.

> The promptitude of the suppression of the rebellion in Dublin and the want of success in other places prevented any general disturbance. The portion of the county affected by unrest and subject to the SF [Sinn Féin] influence entirely excludes the Cahir district and lies principally between Cashel and Clonmel... On 27 April (Thursday) word was received that the rebels were to march on the town. 50 troops (OTC) [Officer Training Corps] arrived in motor car from Fermoy between 8 and 10p.m. After a consultation in the RI Barracks, it was decided to hold the military barracks, police barracks and to throw a strong force

of police outside the Post Office. The rebels did not pursue their intentions however.[46]

The authorities arrested many Irish Volunteers in the county following the Rising including Frank Drohan, Eamon Ó Duibhir and Dominic Mackey. The INV did play a role during this time, and in Carrick they offered to fight the insurgents. The authorities politely declined but instead asked the Volunteers to give up their guns, twenty Enfields and twenty Martini-Henrys, and they duly obliged.[47] This kind of offer, however, was not confined to Carrick. The police reported that other INV groups were willing to assist the government: 'In Tipperary, the Irish National Volunteers readily expressed their intention to assist in every way possible. Cashel was quiet throughout. Here also the Irish National Volunteers, very indignant at the Sinn Féin proceedings, offered their services.'[48] The INV complaint that they had not been invited to join the Tipperary branch of the National Aid Association, which was established to provide assistance to dependents of those killed or imprisoned during the 1916 Rising, was, therefore, not surprising.[49]

The tensions over IPP policy in the previous years bubbled to the surface after the Rising. There was conflict at Carrick Guardians over Redmond's reaction to the rising. Dillon was credited with having 'upheld the credit of their countrymen' and 'having exposed to some extent the dishonest tactics now being adopted towards this country'. A number of board members felt that Redmond had taken his eye off the ball. One said: 'I was always a supporter of Mr Redmond, but I could not understand the leader of the Irish party going out into the trenches and leaving the Irish people behind him. We are told that he went out to the Irish soldiers because this is a war for the liberty of small nations. What about this small nation, Ireland?'[50]

Unease about the Rising and Redmond's stance on partition became evident at Clonmel Corporation. In November 1916, when a resolution forwarded from Kerry County Council protesting against partition and conscription was debated, a proposal to amend the resolution to include only conscription was carried, but only by a small majority.[51] Throughout 1917, Clonmel Corporation pursued a policy of concern for the welfare of political prisoners while at the same time remaining aware of the shifting political landscape. Some defected to Sinn Féin. O'Halloran Peters, a supporter of Condon, found himself at odds with some of the members who elected him mayor. Condon himself took no part in Corporation activities in 1917 and was legally expelled from membership of the Corporation in May because of his absence for six consecutive months.[52] The rise of Sinn Féin put pressure on the Corporation and this was underlined over the awarding of the Freedom of the Borough to Constance Markievicz. This proved to be a step too far, and most of the (still mainly Redmondite) Corporation refused to attend. Of the twenty-four aldermen and councillors, only eight attended; the motion was passed but proved to be a pyrrhic victory.[53] This incident also marked a trend whereby members of the Corporation absented themselves from meetings rather than facing up to controversy. Clonmel Corporation thus became unrepresentative in the years that followed.

Redmond, his authority greatly diminished, died in March 1918, before the collapse of an Irish Convention devised by Lloyd George in the alleged hope that the Irish could agree on a constitution. The convention was boycotted by Sinn Féin and was largely an academic exercise.[54] The *Nationalist* declared that Ireland had suffered a 'distinct loss', as his life was one of 'strenuous unceasing labour for Ireland's regeneration… Under his direction the Irish Party secured many ameliorative measures for Ireland culminating in the passage of the Home Rule bill'.[55] Motions of sympathy were passed across the county, from the Archbishop of Cashel, Condon, T.W. Russell, W.B. O'Donnell (parish priest at Clogheen), Canon Ryan (who told the *Nationalist* that Redmond loved campaigning in Tipperary, 'campaigning on velvet', and that Redmond had made his name in Tipperary defending the Plan of Campaign prisoners); while tributes poured in from across the political spectrum, including Lloyd George, Carson and Asquith.[56]

Behind the resolutions of sympathy, however, was a conflicting web of discourse on Redmond, his role during the war years and his legacy. At Clonmel Corporation, O'Halloran Peters noted the 'present-day differences'. He paid tribute to Redmond's oratory and his efforts to collect funds for the

IPP in Australia at the turn of the century, but did not discuss the conflict and discord of the previous years: 'I am not touching [on] present-day politics. This is a non-contentious matter — a matter that appeals to us all, and we all realize that a great and distinguished Irishman is no more.'[57] At Clonmel Board of Guardians, a vote of sympathy was passed but there were several objections. One board member, J.M. Lyons, objected to the vote aggressively: 'I regret very much that I have to object to a vote of sympathy with any Irishman, but I must do so on principle. I do so because after getting the fullest trust of the Irish people Mr Redmond betrayed that trust. He humiliated the cause of Ireland and lowered its flag.'[58] Another board member, Stapleton, said: 'I wish to associate myself with the vote of sympathy. I would not like to go as far as Mr Lyons. For late years Mr Redmond has not seen eye to eye with the vast majority of the Irish people, but no matter how we differed from him we sympathize with his relatives. He did make a political mistake.'[59]

CONCLUSION

By the time of his death in 1918, Redmond had long lost his grip. This had begun as early as 1915 as the enthusiasm of the previous autumn had receded, the war was turning into carnage, the prospect of Home Rule was growing ever more remote and the Ulster Unionists were widely felt to have out-manoeuvred nationalists at Westminster.[60] The split in the Volunteers also foreshadowed what was to come, the process of radicalization predating the Rising.[61] The party was not helped by government policy in its decision to extend conscription and multiple 'German Plot' arrests. These came not long before the watershed election of December 1918, which formally marked the collapse of the IPP and the overwhelming domination of Sinn Féin in the county. Two seats were not even contested by the IPP, and the others were decisively taken by the new political force. Redmond's support for the war played a considerable role in the waning of his and the party's fortunes. His decision to refuse a position in the Cabinet could be seen as fatal despite the fact that it was not party policy to do so. But these were not ordinary times, and it left Redmond isolated at Westminster and in Ireland.

IT'S A LONG, LONG WAY TO TIPPERARY

9 THE CONSCRIPTION CRISIS

Part of an advertisement for sheet music for the wartime song.

THE MORNING OF 21 March 1918 was a very foggy one on the Western Front.[1] The British gunners could not see what they were doing. At 4:40a.m, the German army began their offensive — a final attempt to end the war decisively in the west. The German bombardment, in seven phases, went on until 9:40a.m, with more than a million shells being fired. An especially irritating gas was used, which caused some of the defenders to tear off their gas masks to scratch the itch, whereupon one or other of the poison gases took effect.[2] The British rear areas were shattered and Hubert Gough, scion of a prominent Anglo-Irish family from Co. Tipperary and notorious as one of the Curragh mutineers, who was in command of the Fifth Army, lost control.[3]

The British Army suffered a stunning setback. On that day alone, British casualties were about 38,000.[4] Over a week, there was a rapid advance, the Germans pushing forty miles into enemy territory on a fifty-mile front and inflicting 300,000 casualties. The 16th Irish Division and 36th Ulster Division, both part of the Fifth Army, suffered heavy casualties, losing 6,435 and 6,109 respectively.[5] The British lost 1,300 guns. Dozens of battalions had ceased to exist, and as the 12th Royal Irish Rifles' war diary showed: 'Battalion surrounded. Twenty-two officers and 566 men missing.'[6] Behind German lines, Kaiser Wilhelm II's train pulled into a station where members of his staff were waiting for him on the platform. Unable to conceal his excitement, he rolled down the window and shouted: 'The battle is won, the English have been utterly defeated.'[7]

The offensive was an extraordinary success for Germany because mobility had been restored to the Western Front, something that had not been seen since 1914, when it had still been possible for cavalry to canter grandly over open fields.[8] The gravity of the crisis was correctly noted in Tipperary by the *Nenagh Guardian*, which claimed that the flower of European manhood was being annihilated:

> The imagination is utterly unable to grasp the intensity, the ferocity, and the reckless destruction of human life involved in the mighty struggle that is now proceeding in France. Nothing like it has hitherto occurred in this war; nothing to compare with it in any war known to history... [The Germans] appear to have been able to bring their guns, tanks, etc, into action with ease and rapidity... Another surprise of the great struggle is the bombardment of Paris by a gun of 75-mile range.[9] Experts are at a loss to account for the nature of this new device. There are theories of a new explosive of great power. We may have some faint idea of what this gun means when we mention that it would throw a shell nearly from Nenagh to Cork... All will watch the development of this struggle with care. It is a mighty effort of human skill, tenacity, courage, and resource. It grips the imagination by the stakes at issue, by the vast numbers engaged and by the huge quantities of guns, aircraft and every mechanical device in operation. Yet there is one saddening feature to it all. How many brave men have gone into this struggle never to return

alive. The flower of European manhood is being annihilated. Everything else may be replaced but human life never.[10]

The *Clonmel Chronicle* described the situation as 'very grave'.[11] The situation meant that the British government was forced to raise more men. The War Cabinet was informed that an extension of conscription in Britain could raise about 550,000 and in Ireland 150,000 men could be got, with the figure in Britain based on sending eighteen-year-olds overseas, conscripting boys of seventeen, although they would not be used for overseas service, and 'comb-outs' of exempted men. The government decided to extend conscription to Ireland. In doing so, they guaranteed the failure of any attempt to settle the Irish question on the basis of Home Rule, shattered the IPP's credibility and alienated much of Irish public opinion. A pan-nationalist front developed, which met at the Mansion House on 18 April 1918. The conference produced a Sinn Féin-inspired pledge, denying Britain's right to impose conscription on Ireland and pledging to resist its imposition 'by the most effective means at our disposal'.[12] The Catholic bishops issued a statement of support and ordered a 'public mass of intercession', while the IPP withdrew from Westminster, effectively handing Sinn Féin a huge propaganda victory as for years they had been proclaiming the uselessness of taking seats in the British parliament.

Outside Clonmel's town hall, home to the Corporation, a banner declaring 'Conscript means slave' hung across the building. The mayor, Patrick O'Halloran Peters, told a hastily arranged meeting at 3p.m on Wednesday 10 April that Britain had no 'moral right' to conscript the country and he blamed the development on those involved in the Curragh mutiny:

> He knew of no moral right in the English government to conscript Ireland... He should like to know who was to carry on... [the tillage]... scheme if the young men of the country were going to be conscripted. Were the ghosts of the men who were slain in Belgium going to leave their shroudless coffins and reap the harvest in Ireland? Conscription in Ireland would not raise a

single useful regiment for Flanders and it was only a base party move on the part of disgruntled politicians who had blocked the road to Home Rule since 1914 that it was now proposed. The Curragh mutineers were still behind the scenes.[13]

The meeting of the Corporation showed clear evidence of party division, with several members criticizing IPP policy, claiming the Party lacked any mandate to support the British war effort.[14] One member, Alderman Stapleton, struck a note of realism. He said that he represented the 'working' section of the town — those most likely to be conscripted — and from a meeting he was at the previous night, where about 400 men attended, he felt that conscription could not be implemented: 'From what he knew it would take five or six corps from the Western Front to take the young men out of Ireland, and he thought it would be better for Lloyd George not to carry out his project.'[15]

At Tipperary Board of Guardians, P. O'Dwyer said it was 'a monstrous thing to attempt such an act of tyranny on a small nation like Ireland, which had given too many of her sons to the war'. The resolution the guardians passed expressed similar sentiments, arguing that the food production campaign and the fact that Britain was supposedly fighting for small nations made the attempt 'an act of madness' that would be a 'disastrous failure' leading to 'chaos and turmoil and appalling bloodshed and loss of life'.[16] The conscription threat had mobilized considerable resistance.

In 1915, a huge recruiting meeting had taken place on Clonmel's Parnell Street with Michael O'Leary VC the star speaker. Local politicians, clergy and officials spoke and urged more recruits for the army. In April 1918, a similar meeting took place on the same spot. This gathering, however, was to prevent men being taken by force. O'Halloran Peters told the crowd that conscription was a blood tax, that Clonmel had already sent its quota to the army, and that England was trying to 'extinguish' the Irish race:

A dark mist seems to envelop our Irish valleys and a heavy cloud has already settled on our Irish hills. The British government has decided to apply conscription to Ireland. But here from this platform I tell Lloyd George and the coalition government that they have no moral right to inflict conscription on this country. Conscription is a blood tax and England has no right to impose that tax on this country, except with the free consent of the Irish people. Let England restore to us our ancient rights and free constitution and then if conscription should come let it come by the unanimous wish of the Irish people themselves... This is a huge political gamble and the coalition government are playing for high stakes. Does anybody here think that Clonmel has not given its proper quota in this war? Clonmel since 1914 gave eight hundred of its best and brawniest sons to the British Army — and Clonmel has paid the toll. Ireland has already contributed 170,000 of her sons, not to speak of all her exiled children who have rallied to the colours in America, Australia, and every quarter of the globe. Yet England considers that sacrifice not quite enough. She wants to extinguish the whole Irish race.[17]

Comparisons were made between the Irish situation and Israel, with the mayor claiming 'the same god that watched over Israel in the days of her sorrow and tribulation will also watch over this old country of ours in her day of affliction and trouble'. Monsignor Flavin, parish priest at St Peter and Paul's in Clonmel, who had also supported recruitment into the army, agreed with this: 'The Israelites, God's people, were persecuted and Pharaoh wanted them to make bricks without straw. Today Englishmen wanted to compel Irishmen to fight her battle while denying this country its rights; but as pharaoh and his army perished in the Red Sea, so the bad laws of those who sought to enslave Ireland would be buried in the deep.'[18]

The curate, Reverend Walshe, saw a different angle: 'They were not half-savages like the Hottentots or Maoris to be driven like slaves into the battlefield.'[19]

PEAK OF THE CRISIS

Towns and villages across Tipperary were gripped by anti-conscription fever. Seven hundred attended a meeting in Borrisokane's town square.[20] At Roscrea, thousands paraded through the town holding banners such as 'Death before Conscription'.[21] In Cashel, 4,000 men marched around the city,[22] and in Nenagh, an anti-conscription meeting overflowed by several hundred, at which there were reportedly 'Protestants and unionists present'. Michael Guilfoyle, Chairman of the Urban Council, presided and said they wanted a 'national scheme of action to oppose the brutal and callous measure'. He declared that they would stand united and 'sink all social and political differences in that great crisis — one of the greatest that ever presented itself in all the chequered history of their country'.[23]

On Sunday 21 April, thousands of people signed the anti-conscription pledge with bishops and priests heavily involved in the operation. The clergy had given instructions that a mass of intercession to avoid conscription would be celebrated that day, funds would be collected outside churches to be used against conscription, and the clergy would also organize the signing of the anti-conscription pledge.[24] The pledge stated: 'Denying the right of the British government to enforce compulsory service in this country, we pledge ourselves solemnly to one another to resist conscription by the most effective means at our disposal.'[25]

There was a palpably fevered atmosphere.[26] After mass at St Peter and Paul's church in Clonmel, a crowd assembled on Gladstone Street to subscribe to the pledge. Flavin addressed them from the Ormonde Hotel on O'Connell Street: 'There was no reason in the world why conscription should be imposed on this country. He remembered 48 and 67; he had been through various phases of Irish politics during the past forty years; but this was the greatest calamity which they had yet faced. They had God with them, and they were sure to win in the struggle.'[27]

At St Mary's church in Irishtown in Clonmel on the same day, Reverend James Walsh asked the people to repeat the words after him, who then signed the pledges. The *Chronicle* reported that thousands signed the pledge during the evening in Carrick.[28] Thousands also took the anti-conscription pledge in Cashel. Dean Ryan and three other priests addressed the meeting and another local defence committee was formed. This was followed by the rosary and benediction.[29] At Fethard, P.C. Ryan, parish priest, administered the pledge to 1,200 people and another local defence committee was also formed. At Newcastle, a village outside Clonmel, a defence committee was again formed, with 400 signing the pledge.[30] District Councillor Philip Brennan told an anti-conscription meeting at Cambonsfield:

> What did England ever give to Ireland that she should now claim the right to impose conscription on them? She had meted out nothing but persecution to them for centuries. When the Irish Volunteers were offered to her at the beginning of the war she would not accept them, because they wanted their own officers and would not be led by members of the ascendancy class. He had been instrumental in organizing the local volunteers and he would be glad now to reorganize them to fight for Ireland.[31]

The bishops were active on the day, and some went for the first time to the anti-conscription meetings. Among them was Archbishop Harty, who at mass criticized the hypocritical attitude of the main powers towards small nations, and at an anti-conscription meeting later that day made a warlike speech with 'definite revolutionary overtones':[32]

> I proclaim here that the Act of Conscription is unjust, hypocritical, and I shall now proceed to the Confraternity Hall to sign the protest against it. Every man with a drop of Irish blood in his veins should do so. We shall march to victory and shall plant the flag of Ireland in an impregnable position, proudly floating over this free nation.[33]

The move to implement conscription had also provoked strong separatist feelings. Canon Ryan, the great friend of Redmond and his pro-war policy, best defined the country's frame of mind: 'This pledge we take today in every parish in Ireland will ring like the tocsin of freedom through the coming centuries.'[34] Thousands attended a mass of intercession at Tipperary town celebrated by Ryan.[35] After the mass, the C.J. Kickham band played and he administered the pledge. All the clergy of the parish were there (four priests) and a number of Redemptorists who had recently given a mission. Ryan paid tribute to those who had gone out to fight in the Great War from Tipperary, but said the county would never send out anyone to fight as slaves:

> Tipperary was never afraid of a fight. We have proved it on a hundred battlefields. Many a sad Tipperary home is witness of that today; but they fought as freemen. We will never send out one Tipperaryman to fight as slaves. This pledge I now administer to you has been penned by your bishops. It has been endorsed by the leaders of all the national parties; it is the pledge, thanks be to God, of a reunited Ireland. Let no one by a reckless rush forward or by a cowardly lagging behind break the unity of our ranks in our orderly and unconquerable march to freedom.[36]

The report of the pledge read like a mass, a quasi-religious ceremony in itself: 'Monsignor Ryan then administered the pledge, and the spectacle was an impressive one as the great throng, with heads uncovered and uplifted hands repeated after him the solemn words.'[37]

Along with Ryan, Flavin and local MPs T.J. Condon and John Cullinan, who had been supporters of recruitment and the British war effort, embraced the new situation. Condon said he came back to meet his constituents and was now determined to fight the British:

> He was there to take the pledge against conscription and stand or fall he would be with the people. It was impossible for the

English government to force conscription on the country if the people stood together. There should be no panic; their duty was to keep calm, reserved and determined. He intended to make a tour through his constituency within the next few days and assist in forming defence clubs. They had fought the English government on previous occasions and they were determined to fight them now.[38]

A Redemptorist preacher, speaking at a mission in St Nicholas' church in Tipperary, said: 'Ireland was a land worth fighting for, because she had accepted and kept the faith and had not sold it for the world's material gain.' The priest said 'God was on their side.'[39] At the close of this mission, the pledge was administered and about 4,000 signed it in Tipperary.

The crisis escalated on Tuesday 23 April when a national strike against the measure was observed. All the businesses were closed in the county — only the banks and the post offices remained open. No trains ran either.[40] At a special meeting of the South Tipperary County Council, Slattery proposed: 'That we enter our emphatic protest against the attempt being made by the English government to conscript Ireland. We deny the right of that country to apply this blood tax to the Irish nation and we rejoice at the meeting of the Irish leaders in the conference and earnestly appeal to the people to be guided solely by their advice.'[41] Cullinan expressed fears that some were exploiting the crisis to advance their own means:

> He and his colleagues had agreed to come back to Ireland to help the people in resisting conscription, and, as they hoped, successfully resisting it. They also desired to guard their people against being led into a dangerous or serious position. He had personal reasons to know that things were not as pleasant as they would like to have them. He would like to agree with the chairman's words that they were all united now, but he was greatly afraid that that was not the fact.[42]

At Cahir, the local brass band played and Volunteers attended a meeting. The *Clonmel Chronicle* reported that 'during the meeting an aeroplane appeared and rockets were discharged, several of which exploded in the crowd, but the crowd stood firm and there was no excitement'.[43] This was an attempt by the authorities to break up anti-conscription meetings. Lloyd George advocated the use of aircraft to disperse them.[44] The police reported the Cahir meeting thus:

> A large meeting was addressed at Cahir on 21 inst by Count Plunkett. About 2,000 people attended. The large attendance was due to the belief that it was an anti-conscription meeting. Count Plunkett said that the leaders of SF and the IPP were divided in the conscription question and this produced a bad effect. An aeroplane flying over the meeting completed its failure.[45]

One of the difficulties with the response to the crisis was that there was no definite course of action. What would any given person do if the army actually began to enforce it? The success of the defence fund collection was noted by the police, but they claimed that some had been intimidated into contributing: 'Large contributions were made to the Defence Fund (Clonmel alone £2,133). A great number subscribed under compulsion and there is evidence of intimidation being used in one case. This fund being illegal and in defiance of laws, used as it will be for the support of families of rebels imprisoned and to bribe RIC, an object freely mentioned.'[46] But aside from financial aid, the pledge itself did not specify what action could truly be taken, only stating 'every means'. Many speeches called for calm, for people to follow their leaders and employ 'passive' resistance.[47] This problem was noted by Frank Drohan at Clonmel where he asked for clarification and hoped 'passive resistance would be properly defined... It was not a time for talking of passing resolutions — it was a time for determination and work'. Town Councillor John Morrissey claimed, however, that he had visited the country districts and the people were actually 'ready to give an account of themselves'. He didn't say if the people had received any training or weapons or, indeed, any information about what an individual could do.[48]

A more determined plan came from Seán Treacy, a leading advanced nationalist in south Tipperary, which gave some insight into the plans the Irish Volunteers had been considering, and which also foresaw some of the tactics that would be employed during the War of Independence: 'Barricade all roads, smash down bridges, fell trees on roads, burn station houses, destroy railway lines, cut wires, snipe at barracks. Hit enemy first and don't let him hit you. Fight under cover. Store lasting foodstuffs. Dig digouts, roof and prop underground chambers etc.'[49] This plan seemed a little fanciful but in some areas advanced nationalists had pikes made: 'Our company acting on orders received from the battalion headquarters in Nenagh, got a pike made for each man for use in the event of an effort being made to enforce compulsory military service in the British Army.'[50]

Another advanced nationalist explained how orders from the Irish Volunteer GHQ told the volunteers to acquire a gun or a pike. Guns usually being unattainable, they made pikes: 'After all the trouble and excitement which the making of these pikes entailed, they were never used. They may, however, have played their part in impressing upon the authorities through reports received from the RIC that an attempt to enforce conscription would meet with bloody and violent resistance.'[51]

The Nenagh Guardian acknowledged that options were limited, however, accepting that people who tried to stand against conscription had no weapons and were facing an 'enemy' with military capabilities beyond anything Ireland could compete against: 'We are out against an enemy armed with high explosives and aeroplanes and machine guns. Against them we may not have much chance… Finally let us say our prayers.'[52]

Despite the somewhat vague plans for resistance to conscription, the police reports for Tipperary's North Riding district claimed there would be much resistance. At a rally in Thurles, the RIC reported that John McLoughlin, an Irish Volunteer, drew a revolver and advised its use in case of arrests.[53] The

Inspector General of the RIC reported that north Tipperary was in such a 'turbulent' state that police had to be confined to their barracks on many consecutive nights to [protect] them from attack.[54] The County Inspector reported that any attempt to enforce conscription would be impossible and if attempted would lead to open rebellion:

> It is not too much to say that all this locality is prepared to break out into open rebellion at a moment's notice. The police can do nothing as they are practically always confined to their barracks, fearing an attack. The first step taken by the government to enforce conscription will be the signal for insurrection to break out in this riding beyond any question of a doubt.[55]

This was not the case in the South Riding, where the police reported that active resistance to conscription was considered unlikely and the scale of the crisis was put down to farmers' sons who didn't want to be made to do anything: 'Doubt is impressed as to there being a likelihood of active resistance to conscription… The reason that there is so much dread of it out at Tipperary is that there are a lot of young fellows… farmers' sons… who do nothing and want to do nothing and don't like being made to.'[56] Whether the police report was true or not remains uncertain, but there is no doubt that farmers joined the campaign.

The nature of the crisis resulted in the establishment of a united front against the threat of conscription. Farmers had largely remained aloof from the recruiting campaign, but embraced the anti-conscription one. At Drom, farmers guaranteed sums of £5 each for people who 'in the course of the struggle might be injured financially'. The *Nationalist* reported that at the Drom meeting, 'men who had taken different sides in politics for years came together on the platform as they believed that this was a struggle by Ireland against English tyranny and that it was every man's duty to stand by his own country against the common danger threatened'. At the Kilvilcorris

(Templemore) Co-operative Dairy Society, the farmers passed a resolution against conscription, condemning the actions of the government as 'suicidal and calculated to put a stop to every industry in the country'. It also said: '… we wish to inform the government that there are already too few people left on the soil of Ireland to till the land and to look after the general work of the nation'.[57]

Frequent references were made to Ireland's role in the war and the perceived hypocrisy of Britain in its claims to be fighting for small nations yet attempting to conscript the Irish against their will. Reverend T. Mechan told a meeting in Borrisokane that Ireland had given heroes to the war effort and Britain had no right to conscript the county:

> Today Ireland is plunged into a sad and desperate state by those hypocrites in the British cabinet. We are told that Ireland has not done anything in this war. Well I can tell you that north Tipperary alone has given between 1,500 and 2,000 of the young men since the outbreak of the war. Who fought like brave heroes at Gallipoli? Who stood the sword and the heavy gun fire at Mons? It was our Irish heroes.[58]

Reverend J. Cunningham, parish priest of Templederry, told a huge meeting in Nenagh that Britain had deceived Irish men and induced them into the army with promises they had no intention of keeping. Reverend Cunningham also claimed that Ireland would stop producing food for Britain if conscription were introduced.

> England — the British House of Commons by means of promises, which the world knew she never meant to keep, had induced upwards of 160,000 Irishmen to fight under her flag in the present great war. Now, if that were in any sense Ireland's war… but even if it were, considering her scanty population Ireland

could not be expected in justice to herself to contribute a larger contingent... men in Ireland were at present wanted to deal with the work of increased tillage. If the government attempted to enforce conscription which their bishops had declared to be inhuman and oppressive and disastrous... England would have to seek food... elsewhere than in the neglected and abandoned fields of Ireland.[59]

At Ballyneale, more than 100 signed the anti-conscription pledge and passed a resolution against the imposition of conscription by a 'foreign race', which also criticized what it saw as 'British hypocrisy and an affront to our national feelings to be asked to fight for small nationalities, while we are ourselves a nation of slaves'.[60] Reverend W.B. O'Donnell, parish priest at Clogheen, said that conscription would bring desolation to a country that had already given its fair share.[61]

The crisis led to a surge in support for Sinn Féin across the county. The number of Sinn Féin clubs and members increased significantly during this time.[62] For example, in the South Riding of the county, the number of Sinn Féin clubs and members increased from 39 and 2,594 respectively in January 1918 to 45 and 3,653 by December of that year — an increase in members of almost 30 per cent.[63] In Carrick, the intersection of support for Sinn Féin and opposition to conscription was evident. A branch of the party was formed in the district and 'a large number' joined. It was also reported that the Sinn Féin party had received a 'considerable addition' to its numbers because of the crisis.[64] There was more of a Sinn Féin colour to the anti-conscription moves in Carrick. The town hall was filled with people in response to a Sinn Féin poster campaign in the town calling on people to join the club and co-operate with it in opposing conscription.[65]

An interesting glimpse into the advanced nationalist psyche was revealed by Seamus Babington, Brigade Engineer of the 3rd Tipperary Brigade during the War of Independence. Babington claimed that he wanted to see conscription enforced as it would have been a form of 'purification' and would have revitalized Irish feeling: 'It was a tragedy, even to the present day, that conscription was not enforced, because it would have been a form of purification. It might have brought out some Irish feeling. It might have made men out of mice and even if they submitted to conscription, it might have put spirit into spineless men.'[66] Babington criticized what he saw as 'pro-British… anti-republican' people who donated money to 'save their carcasses', only then to take their money back after the threat had receded. He said this created a 'sourness' in him: 'To stand there all day and see the wealthy anti-Irish Irishmen take their £20, £30 and £50 and sneer at the people who saved their skin, created in me a sourness which I found hard to shake off.'[67]

At the same time, the crisis resulted in a huge increase in people joining the Irish Volunteers. One advanced nationalist said that it was their peak time for recruits:

> The conscription crisis period in the summer of 1918 was our peak period so far as numbers were concerned. The strength of the company more than doubled itself and parades and training were intensified and carried out openly. Anti-conscription meetings to which the volunteers marched were held in Templemore and Castleiney and at these meetings the volunteers maintained order and, generally speaking, did all police duties.[68]

However, an IRB member and vice commandant of the IRA's Clonmel battalion noted that while there was huge increase at the time, many subsequently dropped out:

> Recruits of this kind came in by hundreds… After the threat of conscription was removed, about the autumn of 1918, the number of men fell rather drastically, but still we had a fairly good number of men who were all reliable and loyal. A good few of those who had come in under the conscription threat

remained on as enthusiastic volunteers from then onwards, though others had faded away.[69]

Another advanced nationalist revealed that the new members that surged into the volunteers initially proved troublesome for the original members:

> During the conscription crisis period, huge parades and field exercises were frequently held. Thousands then thronged into the movement for fear of conscription and they caused any amount of trouble. Many of the newcomers had no respect for their officers, but with the passing of the conscription threat things resolved themselves, for thereafter we saw few, if any, of those who came into the movement at that time.[70]

Tipperary had been gripped by the crisis and a united front had developed comprising of nationalists, advanced nationalists and the Roman Catholic Church. The crisis had brought shape and focus to attitudes regarding the war, and provoked strong separatist feelings. A national strike had been observed. Across the county, the idea that Britain was fighting for the rights of small nations was rejected. Political and religious leaders said that Britain had no right to conscript Ireland; Tipperary had sent enough to the army and it could send no more as they were needed to cultivate the land. Ultimately, however, the dilemma as to what could actually be done to resist conscription never had to be faced — as it was never implemented.

The Church of Ireland Archbishops sent out an 'urgent appeal' to the men of the Church of Ireland to join the colours, and also hoped that conscription would be 'cheerfully accepted'.[71] On the other hand, the Roman Catholic Church in Tipperary placed itself at the centre of resistance efforts. The clergy followed the lead of their bishops by denouncing compulsory service, organizing the taking of the anti-conscription pledge and the collection of the defence fund, and by acting as the main officers on the local defence committees.[72] Nowhere was this more clearly illustrated than in Tipperary town, where the key supporter of the war effort in the region, Canon Ryan, called for a united front against the threat. At Cahir, the curate, W.P. Burke, called for passive resistance and gave advice on how to evade conscription: 'No shootings, the men to flee to the country, have them move by night, avoiding public roads and mass gatherings, and have women be vigilant.' The priest said that the county afforded great protection against aeroplanes and it would take 5,000 British soldiers to secure any recruits and that could not be sustained.[73]

At a protest meeting in Nenagh, four priests stood on the platform.[74] Reverend Dr O'Dwyer of St Patrick's College Thurles said to the reportedly 600 men present that he was with them 'heart and soul' and went further than most of the priests: 'He assured them that he would lay down his life to save each one of them and prayed God to bless them in their struggle against the cruel vindictiveness of their enemies.' He also warned against any rash action which might defeat themselves.[75] At Newcastle, at a meeting in the churchyard, the parish priest, Reverend T. Moran, assured the people that 'he himself would be with them even at the sacrifice of his life'.[76] The idea that priests would be shot defending their flocks was noted by the authorities. The Attorney General of Ireland told the Cabinet sub-committee on 2 April 1918 that the conscripts, when obtained, 'would have a consuming hatred of the cause they were conscripted to serve'. He also predicted that 'several priests would be shot defending their flocks'.[77]

A thousand people attended a meeting in Carrick. Reverend L. Ormonde, the curate, presided and said it was 'morally wrong for England to attempt to conscript Irish nationalists. Irishmen should be prepared to resist conscription even to death'.[78] After mass at Ballyneale, Reverend J. Quann, church curate, presided over a meeting at which 'all present pledged themselves to resist conscription and to die in their houses, fields or farmyards before they will consent to be conscripted'. At an evening mass in Carrick, the Very Reverend Canon Sheehy said that 'if they were determined to offer strenuous passive resistance there would be no conscription and the dark cloud would soon pass away'.[79] At the monthly meeting of the Sacred Heart Confraternity, Reverend

William Ryan launched a stinging attack on the threat, and perceptively said that the end of the war would more than likely collapse several empires, but Ireland needed to see it through:

> A dire calamity is threatened in this country... is the Irish race to be extinguished? ... I want you to keep cool and calm. I want you to keep up the hearts of the poor women at home. Their hearts are throbbing and their hearts are beating because they are feeling for their boys, their husbands, their fathers and their sons... One great result of this infamous threat from across the water is that it will assist the prospect of uniting all our people together as one man... Whether they are conscripted or not you will have your priests to sustain you... The world is an awful state just now. Nobody can tell when the end of this frightful war will be, but it will come sometime, and perhaps we may be nearer the end than we can see now... Empires may be changed, new nations may arise, but, please God, there will be one old country — one of the oldest amongst them — that will be found in that day faithful to faith and fatherland. When all the nations are starting on their new career beginning their fresh life, Ireland will be there and Ireland will take her place — and a high place — amongst the nations of the earth, happy and free.[80]

In Cashel, a banner stating: 'Vow of Tipperary — Death before Conscription,' hung across the podium of a meeting chaired by the Dean, Innocent Ryan:

> They felt, as did the people of Ireland the world over, that the attempt at conscripting the people of Ireland against their will was an untold and wicked act. It was an unholy thing and they were there to raise their voice against it and pledge themselves to offer it unending opposition... For every one conscript that

England would make she would need two men in khaki in our midst.[81]

Ryan advised people not to do anything rash. The role of the Roman Catholic Church was correctly noted by the RIC as crucial, but they said that the clergy had helped in preventing any serious outbreak of violence: 'The influence of the RC clergy has as a rule been exercised to calm the tempest and dissuade from forcible resistance and… violence.'[82] There may be an element of truth to this as the vast majority of clergy urged caution, restraint and for people not lose their heads.

Military intelligence reports also noted how the response to the crisis had become religious in nature. The military intelligence report for the southern district, of which Tipperary was a part, claimed that the anti-conscription meetings had taken on a religious aspect and this was a move to prevent the marches and protests being banned by the authorities: 'In most cases these meetings are now given a religious colour, and devotions held in churches, the object being to prevent the dispersal or proclamations of these processions or perhaps get them prohibited. It would then be possible to raise a howl that the religion of the people is being attacked.'[83]

The arrangements for the pledge, defence fund and local committees were dominated by the clergy. The priest announced the arrangements for the pledge at mass and then administered it. The way this was reported, as we have seen, took on the trappings of a religious ceremony. The pledge was usually administered after mass, and in some places, rosary and benediction followed it. The local priest led the people in taking the pledge verbally and was usually the first to sign it in a specially prepared book. The priest was traditionally the main fund-raiser in the community and 'almost invariably acted as trustee of the fund.'[84] Some pledged that they would give up their lives for the cause, but mainly the clergy in Tipperary advocated passive resistance.[85]

GERMAN PLOT AND THE IRISH RECRUITING COUNCIL

The police reports for May claimed that the crisis had abated: 'The general feeling is that they will not be enforced. There is also an appreciation of the fact by farmers that putting conscription into force does not necessarily mean herding up people like a lot of sheep. There have been exceptions to the peace of the county in the shape of raids for arms'.[86] But by 9 May, Lloyd George no longer wanted to implement conscription. Walter Long, however, advocated arresting all the Sinn Féin members. Long claimed that republicans had been plotting with the Germans to stage a rebellion in Ireland.[87] The arrest of Joseph Dowling, a member of Roger Casement's German Irish brigade, off the coast of Clare provided the final 'proof' of the German Plot, which some in the administration so eagerly sought.[88] Long also said that Lord French, the Lord Lieutenant, should issue a proclamation defending the arrests and stating that conscription would be ended so long as rates of voluntary recruitment improved.[89]

On 17 May, more than eighty Sinn Féin members were arrested, but this backfired as an attempt to separate the RC Church from Sinn Féin as they backed the prisoners. Archbishop Harty 'did not mince his words'. Harty welcomed Eoin MacNeill to Thurles stating that he was one of the few leaders who represented united Ireland in her fight against 'tyranny and inhumanity'. With regard to Eamon de Valera and Arthur Griffith, who were in English jails, he said 'those men had been deported because of a supposed German plot, which… Wimborne said he was unaware of until the British government discovered it'.[90] The *Nationalist* believed that Ireland was bled 'whiter and whiter' and then came the 'military screw' of the widespread arrests:

> Under cover of an alleged pro-German plot in Ireland wholesale arrests have been made and the country is thrown into a fever or unrest and excitement… It is a painful, a sorry picture to contemplate — this miserable torturing, blundering policy of alien mis-government and has not a single feature to redeem

it, and is wholly and hopelessly at variance with the accepted principles governing the world war.[91]

The paper said: 'The denial of fair trial and the withholding of evidence are the most sinister aspects of the case.'[92] The idea that the Great War was Ireland's war was completely discredited by this stage. The crisis had severed any link between the IPP and the government. The paper said that Ireland had won a moral victory and had defeated the conscriptionists 'for the present' as the English papers were reporting that conscription had been dropped.[93] Most of the British Cabinet believed there was a conspiracy in Ireland and they publicly defended the arrests, despite the absence of any real evidence.[94] The German Plot arrests were an attempt to remove from Ireland those seen to be at the root of Irish recalcitrance.

The easing of the situation on the Western Front, the arrival of fresh American troops to the battlefield, the new voluntary recruiting appeal that aimed to raise 50,000 recruits by 1 October, and the German Plot arrests 'let the government off the hook'.[95] British policy now swung back to a voluntary recruiting campaign. The recruiting proclamation was published on 3 June and it emphasized that the appeal was addressed mainly to those in the towns.[96] The Irish Recruiting Council (IRC) was organized in a different way to previous recruiting initiatives. The country was divided into ten parts and it came under the aegis of the British Ministry of National Service. Tipperary was part of the Waterford recruiting area and had recruiting office sub-stations at places including Cahir, Cashel, Carrick, Templemore, Tipperary, and Clonmel.[97] The Council sought the support of local officials and bodies, but this was not always forthcoming given the fraught political situation. At Templemore Urban District Council, the response to the IRC's circular was unsurprisingly hostile. One board member said that if England wanted Irishmen to do anything for them:

> ... they should treat them in a friendly spirit, but instead of that they were treating them in the worst possible manner... England

pretends to be at war for the purpose of freeing small nations, but she should begin at home. She preaches about Serbia and Belgium, but to the Irish she refused to give any concession, even Home Rule in any shape or form. What can she expect after the way she had kidnapped our people and deported them to English jails without any form of trial, while on our priests she is trying to cast every indignity.[98]

The Council passed a resolution: 'That we cannot see our way to give the English government any assistance in procuring recruits for them in this town and district until such time as England gives us a genuine proof of what she claims to be fighting for — self-determination of small nations — by allowing us the right to manage our own affairs in our own way.'[99]

At Carrick Urban District Council, the Town Clerk said that Carrick had probably sent more men than any other urban district to the war: 'There is probably no urban district in Ireland from which so many have gone… There will be a shortage of labour if more go.' The circular was dismissed by another councillor, who said 'to take no notice of it'.[100] At the end of September, Lieutenant Keating of the IRC sought the support of South Tipperary County Council in the new recruiting drive. One councillor walked out, claiming that England had not carried out its promises.[101] Keating claimed that the recruits were asked to fill up the gaps — 'not necessarily for immediate fighting purposes'.[102] Most of the councillors, however, while they were in favour of the Allies, waved away the recruiting appeal.[103]

The IRC received practically no support from local political or religious figures. The Conscription Crisis, German Plot and trend of events in the county had created a bitter feeling among the people. This was illustrated by the reception afforded to the circulars and also at the small number of meetings the council managed to organize in Tipperary. Less than a month before the First World War Armistice, an IRC meeting in Thurles demonstrated the apathy and utter dislocation between the people and the recruiting campaign.[104] This, of course, had already been accepted by the military authorities. Military intelligence reports noted the lack of support for recruiting: 'It is now supposed by the more ignorant of the people that it is against their religion to join the army, even voluntarily. With others this reason is merely given as an excuse.'[105]

About an hour before the meeting, the band of the 17th Lancers from Tipperary barracks played through 'practically deserted streets' and 'the proceedings seemed to attract very little attention and the attendance was small' with 'not more than half-a-dozen eligible men present'.[106] Lieutenant Owen Gill (son of R.P. Gill, the County Surveyor) did not see any reason to attempt conciliation, however, and launched a stinging attack on the men of Thurles: 'Thurlesmen, you all have seen if you could read during the last week the object of my meeting here tonight and I am very much surprised that a section of you either have not the pluck or the inclination to come here and listen to my view.'[107] Gill tried to establish a connection with the audience and said 'he and his people knew the Co. Tipperary before some of his audience were born'.[108] He also pointed to the fact that many had not come to the meeting because of anti-recruiting activity. The German sinking of the Leinster, a mail boat that was torpedoed by a German U-boat in the Irish Sea in October, also provided another opportunity to criticize German atrocities, telling the meeting that if Ireland did not help the Allies, they could not expect political salvation:

There was a thing called the Conscription Menace, but he had seen a worse menace — the sinking of the Leinster on Thursday morning showed the presence of a more dangerous menace and there was not a man in Ireland whose blood should not surge up in him at the diabolical outrage. The people who had sunk the Leinster wanted peace from them, but any man whom he knew who would not be filled with determination to punish the crime would be a coward. He wished he had the rest of Thurles there to tell them of the 500 men, women and girls, and little children, done to their death—it was one of the long list of German atrocities. The purpose of the meeting was to ask

> the people of Thurles to set aside their grievances, which were
> the same as those of the rest of Ireland and come and help...
> if Ireland expected political salvation they must help the Allied
> nations in the war; otherwise when the Peace Conference came
> on, the Allied nations would not listen to Ireland.[109]

Police reports from both ridings in the county reported that advanced
nationalists had claimed English submarines had sunk the *Leinster* in a bid
to boost recruiting.[110] In the South Riding: 'A notice was found posted up in
Cahir district on 15 October ascribing the sinking of the *Leinster* to English
submarines for the purpose of assisting the recruiting scheme. The origin
could not be traced, but the allegation was prevalent for a time though no
efforts could trace its source.'[111] While in the South Riding: 'The disaster to the
Leinster was largely discussed, the disloyal element pretending to believe that
the sinking was the work of a British submarine in order to further recruiting
in Ireland.'[112]

Lieutenant Henry Harrison, a recruiter in the Waterford area, told the
meeting that if enough recruits were forthcoming then conscription would
not be introduced, but 'he did not wish to be taken as conveying any sort of
a threat'.[113] He echoed Gill's thesis on the Peace Conference, admitted it had
ceased to be Ireland's war since the days of early 1914, but then asked:

> Could Ireland see their poor fishing boats and cross-Channel
> steamers sunk and their women and children murdered without
> wishing to strike back? Those were intolerable and unprovoked
> outrages on the people of Ireland. He referred to the thousands
> of Irishmen and men of Irish blood in the ranks of the British,
> colonial and American armies — how, then, could it be so...
> [that] this was not Ireland's war? Ireland would earn the ill-will of
> the Allied nations and of their countrymen on the Allied armies
> if they did not respond and fill up the ranks of the depleted Irish
> regiment.[114]

Harrison said that it was fair to argue that England had been inconsistent with the principles it was fighting for in terms of its Irish policy, but 'appealed to the men of Thurles not to let those men [Irish soldiers] think they were despised, rejected and abandoned by their kinsfolk at home'.[115]

Sergeant Denis Lenihan, who the paper reported as being in the army for twenty years, also agreed that the War Office had not been consistent: '... they all know Ireland got unequal treatment, but two wrongs did not make a right and arguing on that would not settle the war'. He finished off by criticizing those who did not enlist, still failing to learn the lessons of the 1915 recruiting campaign:

> There were men who were not actually engaged in any work — loitering around corners and they would not join up — they should be ashamed. He hoped the result of the meeting would be that they would have a large number of recruits. He was proud after such a long absence from Thurles to see how courteously the speakers were received and were not interrupted as in other places.[116]

The police reported the Thurles meeting thus: 'A recruiting meeting was held in Thurles on the 11 ult but the townspeople boycotted the meeting and the attendance was chiefly composed of soldiers and police'.[117]

The success of any recruiting campaign is measured by how many enlist. The Council did attract some recruits. Police reports noted, however, that there was no significant increase: 'Some recruits have joined the army but there does not seem a general disposition to enlist. The feeling against conscription remains strong but a majority are convinced that it is inevitable'.[118]

The IRC campaign attracted a steady stream of recruits generally, raising about 10,000 out of the quota of 50,000 set by the government. The monthly returns of recruits during the IRC period surpassed the monthly average of the DRI, from October 1915 to May 1916, a considerable return given the fraught political situation and the crisis over conscription. The area in which Tipperary was included, the Waterford area, raised about 600 recruits during this period and the quota for the county was 5,200. Thirty recruits joined in the north during September, but this was considered unsatisfactory.[119] Eighty-eight recruits joined in Tipperary during this time.[120] More than half of the recruits nationally, however, joined the Royal Air Force (RAF), where they were no doubt attracted by the technical and training opportunities. The RAF also gave individual lectures to stimulate enlistment in their ranks. A Lieutenant Alston of the RAF gave a 'lantern lecture' at Nenagh's town hall on its work: 'The attendance of young men was small.'[121]

Unlike other meetings organized by the IRC, which were largely shunned, people did attend the RAF meetings. This was confirmed by the police, who reported that the Nenagh meeting was 'well attended—the audience were appreciative and nothing unpleasant took place'.[122] The benefits of specialized branches of the military such as the RAF were emphasized in an 'interview' given to the *Clonmel Chronicle* by Lt Keating:

> The training afforded in the specialized branches is a valuable one, both physically and mentally. In the air force, for instance, the training a man receives must be a very valuable one, in view of the enormous importance of aerial service in after-the-war days. Similarly the opportunities of specialized training offered in the Royal Engineers and Motor Transport should appeal strongly to those who look forward to their own advancement in the days of peace and the navy has also peculiar attractions.[123]

He added that these branches of service were currently open to Irish enlistees, which was not the case in Britain, but this option would no longer be available in Ireland 'once the period of voluntary recruiting has passed'.

Other novel recruiting efforts employed in Tipperary included bill dropping from an aeroplane and exhibiting war trophies.[124] One other instructive meeting was held in Clonmel in the Magner's theatre, scene of an earlier recruiting appeal in 1915. Anti-recruiting posters appeared in the town before the meeting and the tone and format proved considerably different in 1918.[125] The *Chronicle* reported:

> When Lieutenant S J Keating appeared on the platform in Magner's theatre on Wednesday evening, accompanied by Arnold de la Poer, a member of the local gentry, Lieutenants Harrison and O'Riordan and Mr E A Hackett, county surveyor for Tipperary, he was accorded a stormy reception from the back of the hall, where about 150 young men had gathered in the answer to the summons of a recruiting poster which for about a week previously had been extensively displayed in and around Clonmel.[126]

The speakers were constantly interrupted, and it is useful to take just one example. When Lieutenant Riordan stepped up to speak, the report went:

> When he declared that the Irishman was true and comes of a fighting race, a voice shouted: 'You shot a lot of them in Easter Week'... I love Irishmen first and everybody else after. It was for Ireland I myself donned the khaki. I gave up home and comfort and put on this uniform — the uniform of liberty — ('Of Prussianism' — a voice from the back of the hall) and my children and children's children will be proud I did not stand back... the speaker appealed to the interruptors' sympathy with ravaged Belgium, but all to no purpose. 'What about Dublin?' came the hoarse reply again. If the Hun came to Clonmel tomorrow, said the lieutenant, you would see the same things perpetrated again and again. The hoarse was incorrigible — 'The Hun is here,' it shouted. The police then moved in on the 'interruptors' to cries

of 'What about the Hun now?' The Soldier's Song was then sung three times.[127]

What followed then was a bizarre question and answer section, with the agreement of the recruiting platform, between Dominic Mackey, Sinn Féin Secretary, and one of the recruiters. This immediately gave those intent on breaking up the meeting the initiative. Mackey criticized what he perceived as the hypocrisy of Britain's war aims in relation to Ireland and said it had no right to deport people following the German Plot.[128] The Lieutenant was clearly in a difficult position and tried to deflect questions on the basis of his rank and the civilian nature of the Council. As we have seen, conscription had always been a controversial tropic from the days of the CCORI. Once the government decided to go with compulsion, it would remain a battleground issue for the remainder of the war. Accordingly. it dominated this exchange along with the German Plot. The Lieutenant could not hope to emerge victorious from this debate. Mackey left the hall after the exchange and was followed by most of the audience — thus ending the First World War recruiting campaign in Tipperary.

CONCLUSION

For the British, events on the Western Front and a consequent desire to 'force through a workable conscription policy'[129] superseded all others. However, this came at a price. The policy to extend conscription was a highly cynical act and effectively meant the loss of Ireland to advance policy on the mainland. The news of imminent compulsion led to a public outcry and a mass mobilization of support by the Irish Parliamentary Party, Sinn Féin and the Roman Catholic Church. The pan-nationalist front that developed denounced the British, claiming that the country had no moral right to conscript Irish people; it was a blood tax, Tipperary had sent enough, and any remaining were needed to work the land. The government was denounced as hypocritical for claiming to be fighting for the rights of small nations. Tens of thousands of Tipperary men and women took the anti-conscription pledge, which was administered usually by a member of the RC clergy. The clergy was central to all aspects of the anti-conscription movement, with the movement itself having strong religious overtones. Indeed, some priests pledged to die along with the people.

A mass strike was held, which illustrated how serious people were in their opposition. Beyond such measures of passive opposition, however, it remained unclear how conscription would ultimately be resisted. When the situation on the Western Front eased, and the government saw how unified and strong the opposition was, it returned to a policy of voluntary recruiting. While this led to a significant increase in recruitment compared with previous months, many opted for the RAF and other technical corps (such as the Tank Corps) in order to gain training. The recruiting meetings in Tipperary were largely shunned and heckled.

The Conscription Crisis confirmed for the majority of Tipperary people that they could expect nothing from a British government and it alienated all shades of political opinion. Religious leaders who had once supported John Redmond's policy and the British war effort in Tipperary (such as Harty, Flavin and Ryan) all rejected the attempt to introduce compulsion and ignored the new recruiting drive that followed. This move played into the hands of advanced nationalism with IPP policy perceived to have failed.[130] The involvement of the church also gave Sinn Féin respectability and merged Catholicism and nationalism. Some reports suggested that Protestants were involved in the campaign against compulsion[131], but as the RC Church became involved centrally, 'inter-denominational relations… had gravely deteriorated and every Roman Catholic Church had become a political centre for resistance'.[132] Irish Party support for the war had much to do with this turn of events as Cullinan and Condon had given crucial support and called for recruits to the army, which, in turn, would allegedly guarantee the rights of small nations, i.e. Ireland. This policy, the policy of Redmond, was considered to have resulted in the exact opposite. Association with the war effort was a huge liability and Sinn Féin now had the initiative.

CONCLUSION

WHEN THE ARMISTICE was signed on 11 November 1918, celebrations occurred at the military barracks in Nenagh, the north Tipperary club, big houses such as Castle Otway and various centres associated with the Crown. The Allies had emerged victorious and the *Nenagh Guardian* noted dryly that the celebrations there ignored 'the work of America and the sacrifices of the twelve hundred men who enlisted from Nenagh… [but] no angry word was heard from the people nearby'.[1] Criticisms were also made of men who celebrated the end of the war but who did not fight:

> Most prominent in the celebrations were a number of young men of military age who, when fighting was to be done and flag of the Empire held aloft, preferred the security of their homes to the bloody battlefields of France, Belgium, Gallipoli and Mesopotamia. The dangerous work they left to their nationalist fellow countrymen both at home and in the United States. To use

a well-known phrase: 'They were invisible in times of war, but invincible in times of peace.'[2]

The *Nationalist* continued its repeated denunciations of British policy, attacking the British Prime Minister, Lloyd George, for his support of Armenians and Syrians while Ireland was still without self-determination, and paying tribute to US President, Woodrow Wilson, in the hope that he would put pressure on the British over Ireland.[3] The day after the Armistice, it claimed British 'Junkerism' prevailed in Ireland and blasted the perceived hypocrisy of Britain when professing to fight for the freedom of small nations when so many Irishmen had enlisted and yet Ireland was denied that same freedom.[4]

That was the landscape in Tipperary as the First World War closed. The conflict was one of unprecedented scale and intensity; a conflict that was predicted to be long; a conflict in which around 3,500 Tipperary soldiers fought; and a conflict in which the county suffered around 700 casualties.[5] This was the greatest deployment of armed manpower in the county's history and was noted as a 'holocaust' of blood and destruction.[6] The vast majority were Catholics, mostly unskilled and from the urban areas. Protestants also played a notable role. The authorities, however, maintained that thousands more were available to enlist from the county. The greatest personal impact was that of the recruits who fought and died, and there was not a village, town or parish in the county unaffected by the war.

The motives of those who joined will always remain uncertain, and it seems that the total number for Tipperary materialized in spite of recruiting efforts rather than because of them. Recruiting for the British Army was one of the principal themes of the war and serves as an excellent way of measuring the political temperature. The topic features throughout this study, from the first flush of war in 1914 through to the bitter battle over conscription in 1918. A popular perception is that men waltzed off to their oblivion during the war. We tend to see these men now as intoxicated, duped or fooled (or all three) into fighting for 'king and country' by cynical governments with scant regard for the rights of small nations. But there was no conscription in Ireland during the war. The Irish were volunteers, in the sense that they did not have to go. They gave their lives willingly. Statistics in Chapter Five show that recruiting increased in Tipperary long after it became clear that the war would not simply be a picnic stroll to Berlin, which was as early as September 1914 following the retreat from Mons. In fact, the amount of recruits from the RIRegt area actually increased from January to June on the previous six months. By 1918, men and women were still enlisting. The fact that enlistments continued to flow throughout 1915 frustrates the belief that men went off as dupes in the autumn of 1914.

Many factors influenced the decision to enlist. For some, there may have been one overriding reason; for others, perhaps several. The First World War also brought a new motivation for Irish recruits: that of idealism. Much has been made of patriotism as a motivation, and the big words that surround it in recruiting rhetoric: 'freedom', 'rights', 'honour', 'self-determination', and 'Home Rule'. Military tradition, economics, martial spirit, adventure and the 'silent appeal' also attracted men into the armed forces.

The authorities' handling of recruiting is instructive, and they were far from competent. The initial efforts at recruiting were haphazard and relied on idealistic motivations to encourage men to enlist. Irish Party MPs in Tipperary supported John Redmond's call at Woodenbridge and spoke at meetings advocating enlistment into the army by employing family tradition, martial spirit, and manliness. It was also suggested that the concession of placing Home Rule on the statute book carried a responsibility to at least consider going to the front. Lurid descriptions of atrocities by German soldiers in Belgium, the emasculation of men who refused to enlist, and threats of conscription were all employed in attempts to coerce men to enlist. This, coupled with a belief that Irish soldiers had not received due recognition for their valour on the battlefield, served to alienate people and enflame local opinion. The send-offs to troops were nothing new in Tipperary — as we have seen in the examples from South Africa and the Crimea — and did not constitute 'war enthusiasm'. I have therefore found the idea that First World War recruits joined in a burst of irrational patriotism difficult to accept. The authorities then changed tack and tried to tap groups that had not previously yielded sufficient numbers of recruits — farmers' sons and the commercial classes —through the CCORI and the DRI. This involved the use of atrocity reports and particularly bitter criticisms of farmers' sons. Eventually, people in Tipperary were threatened with conscription, a tactic that went against recruiters' own guidelines. At times, meetings disintegrated into farcical toing and froing between hecklers and military officials. Senior RC Church figures in Tipperary played a central role in the recruiting campaign before the Easter Rising and this no doubt helped to offset some of the bungling and inept methods used by the recruiters.

Ultimately, the failure of the British authorities represented a failure to understand the unique political landscape that existed in Ireland and a complete inability to tackle the crisis that existed in the country from the Easter Rising to the Armistice. This was manifested most clearly in the government's decision to extend conscription to Ireland after the German offensive in March 1918. As we have seen, the fear of conscription was present from the very beginning of the conflict. The crisis built on deep-rooted fears and confirmed for many that they could expect nothing from the British government. The issue gripped Tipperary and mass protests followed with all sections of the nationalist political spectrum and the RC Church uniting to combat the threat. Political leaders, local officials and members of the clergy denounced the move across the county, claiming it was a blood tax; enough men had gone from Tipperary and any that were left were required to work the land. The subsequent recruiting scheme introduced under the Irish Recruiting Council made little impact, although about eighty joined. The Irish Recruiting Council was generally shunned, and those who had supported the war effort, like Harty and Canon Ryan, stayed away. The move to introduce conscription was a cynical one aimed at forcing through a workable conscription policy in England. It resulted in Home Rule being discredited and rendered futile the presence of Irish MPs at Westminster. This laid the groundwork for Sinn Féin's election rout of the Irish Party in December 1918.[7]

A vibrant home front emerged during the war. Where men joined the army, women trained in first aid, some as nurses, and many others played a central role in fund-raising for war charities and sending 'comforts' to troops in the field. The effect of this increased empowerment of women was reflected in the extension of the franchise in 1918.[8]

The war also brought out the good in many people, as manifested by the outpouring of sympathy for the Belgian Refugees, which brought numerous families to homes in the county. Another unique contribution by Tipperary was the buffet provided to soldiers passing through Limerick Junction. By November 1918, the free buffet for soldiers at Limerick Junction had served 339,233. Tipperary also led the way in Munster and other provinces by coming second only to Dublin in money donated to the Red Cross in the last two years of the war, and the vista of bazaars, fêtes and jumble sales for various war charities illustrated a genuine humanitarian concern for those involved and affected by the First World War.

A darker side also existed. Few people in Tipperary were untouched by the conflict. Even those who did not have a family member serving in the war were not shielded from the horrific casualties and brutality. These were reported from the beginning of the war and injured and disabled soldiers appeared in towns and villages from the start. This was given an extra edge in the county when a military hospital for wounded servicemen was established in Tipperary town in 1916 and gave the impression of a community at war. Thousands of troops were sent there to recover from their wounds. Many of these soldiers were English, and it was accepted they would not be able to return to the front because of the nature of the injuries they received.

The war also brought social problems. Notorious in this regard were 'separation women' — wives of soldiers who received generous allowances but had difficulty in adjusting to the responsibility of more money and found themselves before the courts on charges of drunkenness and of serious neglect of their children. Another tragic side of military life was revealed in Tipperary where some soldiers struggled to cope with military life and committed suicide. Others, unable to handle the stresses of life at the front, appeared before the courts on charges involving alcohol and violence.

The war brought economic gains to the county but these were concentrated in certain areas. In this respect, Tipperary mirrored the national experience. Farmers did well out of the war. Prices paid for agricultural produce such as butter, milk and bacon rose sharply. But farmers also faced calls to increase the amount of land they tilled, and eventually the government introduced the Compulsory Tillage Order in 1917. Farmers, in turn, criticized the government for its attempts to control prices and the Ministry of Munitions for luring what they perceived as vital labour to factories in mainland Britain. The boom in agriculture did not extend to other areas. The restrictions on alcohol terminally damaged Murphy's brewery in Clonmel. Concerns about the food supply were also very prevalent during the war years with Sinn Féin repeatedly warning that a famine could reoccur. These fears proved groundless, but many poorer classes in Clonmel experienced fuel shortages with the price of coal rising beyond the means of many working people. Wages also failed to keep pace with inflation.

The general election of December 1918 and the battle for independence that followed muffled the trauma and emotion the county experienced during the First World War. Thousands had joined the armed forces, women seized the chance to play their role, farmers enjoyed increased prosperity, the humanitarian response was impressive but, crucially, Tipperary emerged more radicalized and divided.

Endnotes

Introduction

1   RIC County Inspector Monthly Report, South Riding (hereafter CI Monthly Report, SR), January 1916.

2   RIC Inspector General Monthly Report (hereafter IG Monthly Report), January 1916.

3   This idea is frequently mentioned in studies on the war. For example, see C. O'Neill, *The Irish Home Front with Particular Reference to the Treatment of Belgian Refugees*. Ph.D. Thesis (Maynooth:NUIM, 2006), pp.186–187.

4   *Nenagh News*, 26 September 1914.

5   Horatio, Herbert, 1st Earl Kitchener (1850–1916): Born Ballylongford, County Kerry; educated at the Royal Military Academy in Woolwich; accompanied Viscount Garnet Wolseley in an unsuccessful attempt to relieve General Gordon at Khartoum in Sudan; Governor-General of eastern Sudan from 1886–1888; appointed sirdar or commander-in-chief of the Egyptian army in 1891; invaded Sudan in 1895 and defeated an Arab army under Abdullah et Taaisha at Omdurman in 1898 and took Khartoum; made Baron Kitchener of Khartoum in 1898; served in the Boer wars and as commander-in-chief of the British forces in India from 1902–1909; Secretary of State for War on the outbreak of the First World War in 1914; died in 1916 when the ship on which he was travelling, the *Hampshire*, struck a mine and sank.

6   *Diary of Father Michael Maher*, Tipperary Local Studies, Thurles, Co. Tipperary.

7   D.G. Marnane, 'Canon Arthur Ryan, the National Volunteers and Army Recruitment in Tipperary', *Tipperary Historical Journal* (2006), p.165.

8   J. Horne (ed.), *Our War: Ireland and the Great War* (Dublin: Royal Irish Academy, 2008), p.8.

9   C. Clear, 'Fewer Ladies, More Women', in John Horne (ed.), *Our War*, p.170.

10 D. Fitzpatrick, 'Home Front and Everyday Life', in John Horne (ed.), *Our War*, p.137.

11 Evidenced as recently as 2008, the ninetieth anniversary of the armistice, when RTÉ commissioned the Thomas Davis Lecture Series on the subject of 'Our War: Ireland and the Great War', see John Horne (ed.), *Our War*. Other books of recent interest on the subject include A. Gregory and S. Pašeta (eds.), *Ireland and the Great War: 'A War to Unite us All?'* (Manchester: Manchester University Press, 2002), N.C. Johnson, *Ireland and the Great War and the Geography of Remembrance* (Cambridge: Cambridge University Press, 2003), Y. McEwen, *It's a Long Way to Tipperary: British and Irish Nurses in the First World War* (Dunfermline: Cualann Press, 2006), and P. Orr, *Field of Bones. An Irish Division at Gallipoli* (Dublin: Lilliput Press, 2006).

12 P. Callan, *Voluntary Recruiting for the British Army in Ireland During the First World War.* Ph.D. Thesis (Dublin: UCD, 1984); M. Staunton, *The Royal Munster Fusiliers in the Great War 1914–1919.* MA Thesis (Dublin: UCD Press, 1986); D. Fitzpatrick, *Ireland and the First World War* (Dublin: Trinity History Workshop, 1986); and T. Denman, 'The Catholic Irish Soldier in the First World War: the "Racial Environment"', *Irish Historical Studies*, 27 (1991), pp.352–65.

13 This was responded to by Professor Boyce in a subsequent edition in Autumn 1994.

14 K. Jeffery, *Ireland and the Great War* (Cambridge: Cambridge University Press, 2000), p.1.

15 C. Pennell, *A Kingdom United* (Oxford: Oxford University Press, 2012).

16 For more on the press in Tipperary, see Chapter Two, pp.59–64.

Chapter 1

1 *Nenagh News and Tipperary Vindicator* (hereafter *Nenagh News*), 2 January 1915.

2 CI Monthly Report, SR, July 1914. See also D. Gwynn, *The Life of John Redmond* (London: Harrap, 1932), p.353.

3 B. MacGiolla Choille, *Intelligence Notes 1913–16* (Dublin: Stationery Office, 1966), p.81, and CI Monthly Report SR, July 1914.

4 CI Monthly Report, North Riding (NR), July 1914.

5 C. Pennell, 'Going to War', in J. Horne (ed.), *Our War: Ireland and the Great War* (Dublin, 2008), p.38.

6 For more on the Volunteer movement, see Chapter Eight.

7 Father Michael Maher Papers, Tipperary Local Studies, Thurles, Co. Tipperary.

8 Edward John Ryan, Bureau of Military History (hereafter BMH) statement, Tipperary Local Studies.

9 CI Monthly Report, NR, June 1914.

10 Ibid.

11 *Nationalist*, 5 August 1914.

12 They were abandoned owing to the army's commandeering of horses and uncertainty over trains.

13 *Nationalist*, 5 August 1914.

14 Ibid. 12 August 1914.

15 Ibid.

16 Ibid. 5 August 1914.

17 Kellet was accompanied by Captain Maling RFA, son-in-law of Dr Harvey RMS (Resident Medical Superintendent) at Clonmel Asylum. Kellet was on John French's staff. French was an Anglo-Irish officer and Commander of the British Expeditionary Force in 1914, who would go on to become the Lord Lieutenant of Ireland in 1918.

18 *Nationalist*, 8 August 1914.

19   *Nationalist*, 8 August 1914.

20   Frank Drohan: IRB organiser in Tipperary; member of Dáil Éireann 1920; and Mayor of Clonmel 1922–1924.

21   *Nationalist*, 8 August 1914; S. Geoghegan, *The Campaigns and History of the Royal Irish Regiment from 1900-1922 Vol. II* (Edinburgh: Blackwood, 1927), pp.8; and T. Johnstone, *Orange, Green and Khaki: The Story of the Irish Regiments in the Great War* (Dublin: Gill & Macmillan, 1992), pp.7.

22   *Nationalist*, 8 August 1914.

23   Ibid.

24   *Chronicle*, 8 August 1914 and *Nationalist*, 8 August 1914.

25   *Nationalist*, 8 August1914.

26   Ibid. 12 Aug. 1914. See *Nenagh Guardian*, 15 August 1914 for Killaloe departures, where a priest gave his blessing to the reservists.

27   Father Michael Maher Papers.

28   Cheering crowds were common across the whole country, and in Dublin, even the KOSB were given a 'rousing send-off'. See Pennell, 'Going to War', p.39.

29   *Chronicle*, 8 August1914.

30   *Chronicle*, 5 August 1914.

31   Ibid. 22 August 1914.

32   *Nationalist*, 22 August1914 and *Chronicle*, 22 August 1914.

33   *Nationalist*, 15 August 1914.

34   Ibid.

35   *Chronicle*, 15 August 1914.

36   Ibid. 22 August 1914.

37   *Chronicle* and *Nationalist*, 22 August 1914. Potter was shot by the IRA in 1921.

38   *Nationalist*, 5 August 1914.

39   Ibid.

40   Ibid.

41   Ibid.

42   Ibid. 8 August 1914.

43   *Nationalist*, 8 August 1914.

44   War Diary of 2nd Brigade Royal Field Artillery, 6th Division, James Clavell Library and Archive, Royal Artillery Museum, London.

45   *Chronicle*, 26 August 1914.

46   Ibid. 10 October 1914.

47   Adrian Gregory refutes this analysis. See A. Gregory, *The Last Great War* (Cambridge: Cambridge University Press, 2008).

48   'North West Tipperary and the Great War' in *Nenagh Guardian 150th Anniversary Supplement*.

49   *Chronicle*, 13 December 1899.

50   Ibid. 3 February 1855. These were men of the 13th Regiment, while those that left for the Boer and First World War campaigns were RIRegt reserves.

51   CI Monthly Report, NR, August 1914.

52   Ibid. SR, August 1914.

53   N. Kevin, *I Remember Karrigeen* (London: Burns Oates and Washbourne, 1944), p.40. Both the author and the town are pseudonyms for Don Boyne and Templemore respectively.

54   T. Hennessey, *Dividing Ireland. World War One and Partition* (London: Routledge, 1998), p.79.

55   P. Callan, *Voluntary Recruiting*.

56   For more on economic change in Tipperary during the war, see Chapter Seven.

57   *Chronicle*, 8 August 1914.

58   *Nationalist*, 12 August 1914.

59   Ibid.

60   Prices rose across England and the general cost of living for the working class rose about 10 per cent in the last five months of 1914 and by another 20 per cent in 1915. See T.P. Dooley, *Irishmen or English Soldiers? The Times and World of a Southern Catholic Irishman Enlisting in the British Army* (Liverpool: Liverpool University Press, 1995), p.112.

61   *Nationalist*, 15 August 1914.

62   Ibid. 8 August 1914. Rising food prices caused concern across Ireland. See Pennell, 'Going to War', p.40.

63   *Nationalist*, 8 August 1914.

64   Harriet Bagwell: Married to Richard Bagwell; philanthropist; founded the Clonmel Cottage Hospital in 1895; become an executive committee member of the Women's National Health Association of Ireland; played a central role in several of the aid and comfort organizations during the war.

65   *Chronicle*, 8 August 1914.

66   Ibid.

67   *Nationalist*, 12 August 1914.

68   *Nationalist*, 15 August 1914.

69   *Nationalist*, 12 August 1914.

70   *Chronicle*, 5 August 1914.

71   This sugar was supplied by Murphy's at 3*d* per lb. The supply was limited to one lb per week for each man and boy employed, but fathers of families could also obtain 'one lb each in respect of their wives and each child over two years of age'. See *Chronicle*, 22 August 1914.

72 *Nenagh News*, 15 August 1914.

73 Ibid. 1*s* 6*d* per lb.

74 Ibid. 7 November 1914.

75 *Chronicle*, 5 September 1914.

76 *Chronicle*, 16 September 1914.

77 Ibid. 9 September 1914.

78 Ibid.

79 Ibid. 30 September 1914.

80 Ibid.

81 *Nationalist*, 28 November 1914.

82 Ibid. 2 December 1914.

83 *Chronicle*, 5 December 1914.

84 *Nationalist*, 2 December 1914.

85 *Chronicle*, 2 December 1914. The relevant legislation was the Intoxicating Liquor (Temporary Restriction) Act 1914.

86 CI Monthly Report, SR, October 1914.

87 *Nationalist*, 7 November 1914 and *Nenagh Guardian*, 14 November 1914.

88 *Nationalist*, 19 December 1914.

89 *Chronicle*, 7 November 1914.

90 Ibid. 21 November 1914.

91 *Nationalist*, 23 December 1914.

92 CI Monthly Report, SR, October 1914.

93 Ibid. November 1914.

94 For more on voluntary war work and 'comfort drives', see Chapter Six.

95 See *Chronicle*, 8, 22, and 29 August 1914.

96 *Nationalist*, 12 August 1914. Richard Bagwell: Barrister and historian; married to Harriet; die-hard unionist who was a founder of the Irish Unionist Alliance; opposed the majority report of the Irish Convention 1917; and died in 1918.

97 Ibid.

98 For the full discussion, see *Nationalist*, 12 August 1914.

99 *Chronicle*, 3 October 1914.

100 Ibid. 21 October 1914.

101 Ibid. 10 October 1914.

102 Ibid. 14 October 1914. I believe this refers to the retreat from Mons.

103 For good examples of such drives, see *Chronicle*, 4, 7, 14, and 19 November 1914.

104 *Chronicle*, 23 December 1914.

105 Prominent gentry member of North Tipperary whose son was killed fighting at the front in 1914; see Chapter Six.

106 Ibid. 12 December 1914.

107 Ibid. 26 December 1914.

108 They appear in practically every edition, but see *Nationalist*, 12, 19, and 23 December 1914.

109 *Nationalist*, 23 December 1914, and *Nenagh Guardian* on the same date.

110 *Nenagh News*, 15 August 1914.

111 *Nenagh News*, 3 October 1914.

112 Ibid. 5 September 1914.

113 Ibid. 7 November 1914.

114 Ibid. 19 December 1914.

115 D. Breen, *My Fight for Irish Freedom* (Tralee: Talbot Press, 1964), p. 23.

116 For instructive examples of subscription lists in Tipperary, see *Nationalist*, 23 December 1914 and *Chronicle*, 14 October 1914.

117 For more on the refugees, see Chapter Six. Henry O'Callaghan Prittie: 4th Baron Dunalley of Kilboy; born 1851; graduated from Trinity College and Cambridge with a Bachelor of Arts; gained the rank of Lieutenant in the service of the Rifle Brigade; was a willing participant in the recruiting campaigns in Tipperary and advocated conscription; died on 5 August 1927 at age 76. For more on Dunalley and recruiting, see Chapters Three and Four.

118 *Nenagh News*, 31 October 1914.

119 Ibid. 24 October 1914. A classic editorial. 'Educated' refugees were to receive a higher standard of accommodation and be housed in the barracks. See *Nenagh News*, 7 November 1914.

120 *Nenagh News*, 5 December 1914.

121 For more on German atrocities, see Chapter Three.

122 *Nenagh Guardian*, 31 October 1914. From a letter of a gentry friend who had written to Alexandra Palace, where Belgian refugees were kept. For the Belgian Relief Fund subscription list for Nenagh and Roscrea, see *Nenagh Guardian*, 5 December 1914.

123 Ibid. 7 November 1914.

124 Ibid.

125 Ibid.

126 Ibid. 12 December 1914.

127 *Nenagh Guardian*, 12 December 1914.

128 *Nenagh News*, 12 December 1914.

129 *Chronicle*, 24 October 1914. The LGB also advocated private hospitality for accommodating the refugees. See *Chronicle*, 28 October 1914.

130 *Nenagh News*, 12 December 1914.

131 This area is examined in Chapter Six. For examples, see *Chronicle*, 28 November and 19 December 1914. For a classic case of insulting language used towards soldiers, see *Chronicle*, 23 December 1914.

132 *Chronicle*, 4 November 1914.

133 For an incisive and engaging account of cricket in Tipperary, see P. Bracken, *Foreign and Fantastic Field Sports: Cricket in Co. Tipperary* (Thurles: Liskeveen Books, 2004).

134 This area is examined in more detail in Chapter Six.

135 *Chronicle*, 30 September 1914 and *Nationalist*, 3 October 1914.

136 *Chronicle*, 30 September 1914.

137 *Nationalist*, 9 December 1914. The attendance officer was an R. Halligan.

138 *Chronicle*, 9 December 1914.

139 Ibid. 2 December 1914.

140 Ibid. 12 December 1914.

141 Ibid. 14 November 1914.

Chapter 2

1 Captain G. Robinson, at a recruiting meeting in Dundrum (*Nationalist*, 14 July 1915).

2 Edward Grey, British Foreign Secretary from 1905 to 1916. He is most famous for his remark before the outbreak of war: 'The lamps are going out all over Europe, we shall not see them lit again in our lifetime.'

3 CI Monthly Report, SR, June 1914.

4 Ibid.

5 Ibid.

6 *Nationalist*, 8 August 1914.

7 D.G. Marnane, 'Canon Arthur Ryan', pp.150–173. Massy also wrote urging Redmond to arm the Volunteers as quickly as possible.

8 S. O'Donnell, *Clonmel 1900–1932: A History* (Clonmel: Marlfield Publications, 2009), p.266.

9 Ibid.

10 *Nationalist*, 12 August 1914.

11 T. Hennessey, *Dividing Ireland*, p.62.

12 *Nenagh Guardian*, 7 August 1914.

13 *Nenagh Guardian*, 7 August 1914. Many Irish ex-British Army men fought for the Free State army during the Civil War.

14 This is little evidence to support this.

15 *Nenagh Guardian*, 12 September 1914.

16 Ibid. 26 September 1914.

17 The People's Prize and C.J. Kickham bands.

18 *Nenagh Guardian*, 26 September 1914.

19 *Nationalist*, 19 September 1914.

20 For a good example, see Clonmel Board of Guardians, *Nationalist*, 19 September and 3 October 1914 for South Tipperary County Council.

21 *Chronicle*, 23 September 1914.

22 *Nenagh Guardian*, 26 September 1914.

23 *Freeman's Journal*, 21 September 1914.

24 P. Maume, *The Long Gestation: Irish Nationalist Life 1891–1918* (Dublin: Gill & Macmillan, 1999), pp.149–150. Redmond had already received the support of the IPP for his backing of recruiting and had issued a declaration the day the Home Rule Bill became law.

25 For interesting analyses of day-by-day developments on these events, see S. Gwynn, *John Redmond's Last Years* (London: E. Arnold, 1919) and D. Gwynn, *The Life of John Redmond (London: Harrap, 1932).*

26 T. Hennessey, *Dividing Ireland*, p.88.

27 P. Bew, *John Redmond* (Dublin: 1996), p.38.

28 J. Lee, *Ireland 1912–1985* (Cambridge: Cambridge University Press, 1990), p.21.

29 Redmond also felt a strong sense of sympathy for Belgium as his niece lived there as a nun.

30 *Nationalist*, 3 October 1914.

31 Eamon O'Duibhir, BMH statement.

32 Ibid. He says that it is one of only two centres to vote against Redmond: theirs and Upperchurch-Arnfield.

33 The one vote of dissent came from the chairman, Pierce McCan, future Sinn Féin TD. The board did pay tribute to the work of the Provisional Committee, however.

34 See *Nationalist*, 3 and 17 October 1914 for an example of those voting with the county board.

35 *Nenagh News*, 3 October 1914.

36 Liam Hoolan, BMH statement.

37 For example, 'We are only a little nation', see *Nenagh News*, 3 October 1914.

38 *Nenagh Guardian*, 17 October 1914. Pierce McCan presided at this meeting and there was one dissentient — presumably McCan. In Roscrea, one person at the meeting said to back or reject Redmond, that they had been asked to declare a traitor to Ireland every great son of Ireland. Redmond still took more then 60 per cent of the vote.

39 S. O'Donnell, *Clonmel 1900–1932*, p.267. Tom Condon: Son of Jeremiah Condon, a Clonmel victualler; IRB member in his youth; MP for Tipperary East continuously from 1885 until 1918; voted for all three Home Rule Bills; founded the *Clonmel Nationalist*; Mayor of Clonmel seven times; supported Redmond's war policy and spoke on recruiting platforms; was defeated in Tipperary East by Sinn Féin's Pierce McCan in the 1918 election; died in 1943.

40 *Nenagh News*, 14 November 1914.

41 *Nenagh Guardian*, 3 October 1914.

42 *Nenagh Guardian*, 3 October 1914.

43 Frank Drohan, BMH statement. Many of the Volunteers who agreed with Drohan were 'boys'.

44 Ibid.

45 Ibid.

46 CI Monthly Report, SR, October 1914.

47 Ibid. SR, September 1914. See King's County and Kilkenny police reports for similar assessments.

48 *Nationalist*, 3 October 1914.

49 *Chronicle*, 7 October 1914.

50 Ibid.

51 *Nationalist*, 24 March 1915.

52 *Chronicle*, 28 October 1914.

53 *Chronicle*, 16 September 1914 and *Nationalist*, 19 September 1914. Moore made similar remarks at Clanwilliam and Borrisoleigh.

54 *Nenagh News*, 26 September 1914.

55 Ibid. 3 October 1914.

56 *Nenagh Guardian*, 7 November 1914.

57 Toomevara, a village near Tipperary town.

58 *Nenagh Guardian*, 17 October 1914.

59 *Nenagh Guardian*, 31 October 1914.

60 William Meagher, BMH statement.

61 Lieutenant-Colonel Thomas Ryan, BMH statement.

62 *Nenagh News*, 28 November 1914.

63 *Nenagh Guardian*, 12 September 1914.

64 T. Hennessey, *Dividing Ireland*, pp.66–70.

65 S. O'Donnell, *Clonmel: 1900–1932*, p 267.

66 Eamon O'Duibhir, BMH statement.

67 Maurice Moore Papers (10550), National Library of Ireland. Minchin had previously offered

his resignation on 15 September 1914 as there seemed, he thought, little prospect of their being under the control of the War Office. A meeting with Redmond postponed his decision though.

68   P. Callan, *Voluntary Recruiting*, p 53.

69   *Chronicle*, 17 April 1915.

70   Ibid. 28 April 1915. The band also played in Magner's theatre in aid of the *Nationalist's* fund for POWS in Germany and at the soldiers' home.

71   Captain C.R. Jorgenson: Decorated during Boer War; political officer in Somaliland in 1905 until retirement in 1911; rejoined in 1914 and was appointed to a recruiting post.

72   *Nationalist*, 24 April 1915.

73   *Nationalist*, 24 April 1915 and J. Aan de Wiel, *The Catholic Church in Ireland 1914–1918*, (Dublin: Irish Academic Press, 2003), p.16.

74   *Chronicle*, 28 April 1915. The *Nationalist's* figure is 37, the *Chronicle's* is 36.

75   Ibid. 1 May 1915.

76   Ibid. 28 April 1915. This would be banked in his name and returned on the soldier's return. If he died, the money would go to his dependants. The brewery directors said this was in response to the press asking what firms were willing to do for their employees who joined the army (*Nationalist*, 28 April 1915). The RIRegt recruiting band also played at Magner's theatre in Clonmel in aid of the *Nationalist's* comfort drive for RIRegt prisoners in Germany.

77   Ibid. 1 May 1915.

78   *Chronicle*, 1 May 1915.

79   We should bear in mind that this was based on a huge prejudice and that these 'fighting qualities' were seen as an indication of a lower biological and political development. Fighting was an inheritance from the 'brutes', the more aggressive a race and lower in the evolutionary scale. See J. Bourke, *An Intimate History of Killing* (London: Granta, 1999), pp.116–132. Also see T. Denman, 'The Catholic Irish Soldier in the First World War', pp.352–365.

80   *Chronicle*, 1 May 1915.

81   Ibid.

82   Ibid.

83   *Chronicle*, 1 May 1915.

84   Ibid.

85   Ibid.

86   Ibid. When Piggott left for the front after the meeting, the *Chronicle* reported his speech as a fine one.

87   *Nationalist*, 19 May 1915. On the same page, it is reported that 850 men from Nenagh have enlisted.

88   Ibid. 5 June 1915. The *Lusitania* did not spike recruiting and this sort of claim cannot be verified.

89   See Figure 1 in Chapter 5 for exact figures.

90   Ministry of National Service (hereafter Nats), 1/398.

91   See Figure 1 in Chapter Five.

92   *Nationalist*, 5 May 1915.

93   CI Monthly Report, SR, April 1915.

94   Such methods were used at recruiting meetings across the country. See W. Henry, *Galway and the Great War* (Cork: Mercier Press, 2006), pp.45, 50 and 52.

95   J.C. Hayes, 'Guide to Tipperary Newspapers', *Tipperary Historical Journal* (1986), pp.1–16.

96   *Chronicle*, 28 April 1915.

97   *Nationalist*, 28 April 1915.

98   Ibid.

99   See Chapter Four.

100 *Nenagh Guardian*, 3 October 1914.

101 *Nenagh Guardian*, 3 October 1914. See 10 October for a list of Nenagh men serving at the front, but no mention of Falvey's lane. The correspondent's name is Ebag Dhu, and he lists more examples of serving soldiers on 31 October, including, for example, a Mr Maher with six sons at the front.

102 P. Callan,*Voluntary Recruiting*, p.58. This would be a recurring complaint, bubbling over into a major controversy when, in 1915, military bungling by the War Office appeared to deny Irish regiments credit for their valour at Gallipoli. See P. Maume, *The Long Gestation*, p.154, and T. Johnstone, *Orange, Green and Khaki*, p.62 and pp.148–52.

103 C. Pennell, 'Going to War', p.42. This resulted in a number of attacks on German pork butchers' shops in Dublin. See also Chapter Three for more on atrocity reports.

104 *Chronicle*, 12 September 1914.

105 *Nationalist*, 19 September 1914.

106 *Chronicle*, 28 October 1914.

107 It is a classic account from the time. See *Nationalist*, 14 November 1914.

108 For a typical example of these interviews, see *Nationalist*, 7 November 1914. Private Feehan had returned to Tipperary from India and had been immediately sent to the Western Front. A piece here also has a report on several Thurles reserve men back at home.

109 *Nationalist*, 10 October 1914. O'Dwyer was one of twenty to survive from 200 men of the Irish Guards during this engagement.

110 *Nenagh News*, 19 September 1914.

111 *Nenagh Guardian*, 28 November 1914. The letter does not state Pound Street in Nenagh, but see *Nenagh Guardian*, 10 October 1914 for lists of Nenagh men at the front, and Pound Street is included.

112 *Nationalist*, 12 August 1914.

113 C. Pennell, 'Going to War', p.44.

114 *Chronicle*, 17 March 1915.

115 *Nationalist*, 3 February 1915.

116 *Chronicle*, 20 March 1915.

117 *Nationalist*, 17 February 1915. He was headed to Chatham from Clonmel.

118 1st and 2nd Battalion ex-soldiers.

119 *Chronicle*, 2 September 1914. Both had fought with the 1st Battalion.

120 Ibid. 12 September 1914 and 4 November 1914 for a report on James Wallace and his two sons who were also fighting in France.

121 *Chronicle*, 12 September 1914.

122 *Nationalist*, 9 December 1914.

123 *Nationalist*, 16 January 1915.

124 Ibid. 13 January 1915.

125 *Irish Times*, 15 March 1915.

126 *Times*, 31 October and 24 November 1914. Lord Northcliffe, the owner of the *Times*, although born in Ireland, manifested little sympathy for Ireland during the war years. See B.P. Murphy, 'The Easter Rising in the Context of Censorship and Propaganda with Special Reference to   Major Ivon Price', in G. Doherty and D. Keogh (eds), *1916: The Long Revolution* (Cork: Mercier   Press, 2007), p144.

127 *Nationalist*, 6 February 1915. *Chronicle*, 3 February 1915.

128 *Chronicle*, 16 January 1915. Held at Ballymacarbry.

129 P. Maume, *The Long Gestation*, pp.152–153. John Lymbrick Esmonde: Elected MP for Tipperary North after his father's death in 1915 while serving in the army; served in the forces that put down the Rising; did not contest the 1918 election; subsequently became Fine Gael TD for Wexford; had been suggested as a possible candidate for Taoiseach by Seán MacBride in the inter-party government of 1948–1951 on the grounds that he had no link to either side in the Civil War.

130 CI Monthly Report, NR, March 1915.

131 Ibid. SR, March 1915. This police report also notes that there was no distress in the county and no great poverty, though fuel and provision showed a tendency to rise.

132 *Fr Michael Maher Diary*.

133 *Chronicle*, 1 May 1915. The RIC felt it was well attended. See CI Monthly Report, SR, April 1915.

134 Ibid. 1 May 1915.

135 Ibid. 5 May 1915.

136 P. Callan, *Voluntary Recruiting*, p.72.

Chapter 3

1   *Nationalist*, 14 July 1915. A military officer, Captain G. Robinson, at a recruiting meeting in Dundrum.

2   Ibid. 1 September 1915.

3   Somers was born in Belturbet, County Cavan, but his parents had moved to Tipperary some years before the war. He enlisted four years previously. Somers was also given a civic reception in Derry in early October. For more on Somers, see R. Doherty and D. Truesdale, *Irish Winners of the Victoria Cross* (Dublin: Four Courts Press, 2000), p.113.

4   *Nationalist*, 28 August and 1 September 1915. Somers' brother, Albert, had joined the Royal Irish Cadet Corps during the Jorgensen campaign in early 1915.

5   *Nenagh Guardian*, 9 October 1915.

6   *Irish Times*, 24 April 1915.

7   Henry MacLaughlin was born in Belfast and was a businessman.

8   P. Callan, *Voluntary Recruiting*, p.107.

9   B. Novick, *Conceiving Revolution* (Dublin: Four Courts Press, 2001), p.21.

10   P. Callan, *Voluntary Recruiting*, p.112.

11   Thomas Kettle: Son of Land League veteran. Thomas Kettle; MP for East Tyrone 1906–1910; Professor of National Economics at UCD; member of the nationalist intelligentsia; supported the IPP pro-war policy and was a fervent advocate of recruitment; lost much of this enthusiasm by the time of his death at the Somme in September 1916.

12   Stephen Gwynn: Grandson of William Smith O'Brien; MP for Galway City 1906–18; journalist and author; joined the army during the European war and served in the Irish Division; later career spent as a journalist and in particular was the *Observer's* Ireland correspondent during the 1920s.

13   O'Leary won the medal while a corporal with the Irish Guards. He single-handedly charged a German machine-gun position, killing eight and taking the position, see R. Doherty and D. Truesdale, *Irish Winners of the Victoria Cross*, p.107. O'Leary was the subject of much scorn from the advanced nationalist press. See B. Novick, *Conceiving Revolution*, p.112 and p.176.

14   *Chronicle, Nationalist*, 17 July 1915.

15   Ibid. Both papers vary in their reporting of the speeches. The *Nationalist* quotes Condon as saying 'if I were able to join Sergeant O'Leary and his comrades and fight in the ranks in Flanders I would be beside him there. No one ever doubted what the Irish soldiers would do when put to the test and when fighting comes to be done. It is in their blood, it is in their nature and it is written on every page of Irish history... Therefore, knowing what Sergeant O'Leary and his comrades have done in this great fight I would appeal to my fellow countrymen who are free and willing to do as they have done'.

16   *Nationalist*, 17 July 1915.

17   Ibid. He also mentioned distributing certificates of honour during this speech, but this would not take place until 1917. See Chapter Four.

18   *Chronicle, Nationalist*, 17 July 1915.

19   J.M. Wilson Papers, Public Record Office Northern Ireland (PRONI), D 989A/9/7. J.M. Wilson's Tour of the Irish Counties, 1915–1917, including notes from Tipperary detailing local feeling on the war, conscription, Redmond, Sinn Féin et cetera. One might deduce that this is Clonmel, as the tour was in the South Riding, coinciding with interviews with the depot's GOC, the editor of the *Clonmel Chronicle* and Richard Bagwell, whose seat was just outside the town at Marlfield. Thomas Condon had previously given pro-recruiting speeches. His name, however, does not appear in the Wilson's Tour file.

20   *Irish Life*, 8 October 1915.

21   *Nationalist*, 17 July 1915. This was MacLaughlin again at Clonmel. Parsons was the commander of the 16th Irish Division.

22   *Chronicle, Nationalist*, 17 July 1915.

23   This was the second meeting he spoke at in Tipperary. At Nenagh, about a week prior, he told the farmers they would lose all their land after the war as the men who were fighting it would get it. He also asked the women of Tipperary to have nothing to do with men 'behind counters doing women's work'. See *Nationalist*, 10 July 1915.

24   *Irish Life*, 8 October 1915.

25   *Nationalist*, 24 July 1914.

26   CI Monthly Report, NR, May 1915 and P. Callan, *Voluntary Recruiting*, p.116.

27   P. Callan, *Voluntary Recruiting*, p.117. There were similar reports in Wexford papers. See P. Codd, 'Recruiting and Responses to the War in Wexford,' in D. Fitzpatrick (ed.), *Ireland and the First World War* (Dublin: Trinity History Workshop, 1986), p.22.

28   British atrocity reports were the subject of much scorn by the advanced nationalist press. See B. Novick, *Conceiving Revolution*, pp.72–131. D.G. Marnane also confirms this; see 'Canon Arthur Ryan', pp.150–173.

29   A. Gregory, *The Last Great War*, p.44.

30   Ibid. p.45.

31   *Chronicle, Nationalist*, 17 July 1915.

32   *Nenagh Guardian*, 15 May 1915.

33   Ibid.

34   *Nenagh Guardian*, 15 May 1915.

35   Father Michael Maher Papers.

36   *Nenagh Guardian*, 15 May 1915.

37   Ibid. 31 July 1915.

38   Ibid. 21 August 1915.

39   A. Gregory, *The Last Great War*, p.46.

40   Ibid.

41   Ibid. p.47.

42   *Nenagh Guardian*, 15 May 1915.

43 *Nenagh Guardian*, 15 May 1915.

44 *Nationalist*, 10 July 1915. The report said he was widely cheered as he spoke.

45 Ibid.

46 Ibid. 14 July 1915. This speech was widely cheered, according to the report.

47 Ibid. 18 August 1915. This came about a week after Power rejected forming a CCORI recruiting committee.

48 *Nationalist*, 18 August 1915.

49 CI Monthly Report, NR, May 1915.

50 This had been reported in other districts. See M. Staunton, 'Kilrush, Co Clare, and the Royal Munster Fusiliers,' *Irish Sword 16* (1986), p.270.

51 CI Monthly Report, NR, June 1915.

52 *Nationalist*, 28 August 1915.

53 *Nationalist*, 11 September 1915.

54 Ibid. 10 July 1915.

55 Ibid. 8 September 1915.

56 P. Callan, *Voluntary Recruiting*, p.112.

57 Ibid. p.113.

58 Ibid.

59 *Irish Life*, 8 October 1915.

60 *Nationalist*, 14 July 1915.

61 Ibid.

62 Ibid.

63 *Irish Life*, 8 October 1915.

64 P. Callan, *Voluntary Recruiting*, p.113.

65 *Nenagh Guardian*, 26 June 1915.

66 Ibid.

67 *Nenagh Guardian*, 3 July 1915.

68 *Irish Life*, 582.

69 *Nenagh Guardian*, 18 September 1915.

70 *Nenagh Guardian*, 18 September 1915.

71 See Chapter Four for more on these certificates.

72 *Chronicle*, 7 August 1915. A week later, Power chaired a recruiting meeting in Carrick.

73 Ibid. 29 May 1915. Slattery was a councillor in Cashel, but also chairman of South Tipperary County Council.

74   *Chronicle*, 29 May 1915.

75   Ibid. 16 June 1915.

76   Ibid.

77   In newspaper reports, Prussia and the Hun were frequently used for Germany. Militarism and barbarity were common accusations against the country and this was reflected in the language, particularly at recruiting meetings and during discussions at some local authority meetings.

78   CI Monthly Report, SR, July 1915.

79   *Nationalist*, 15 May 1915.

80   *Chronicle*, 25 August 1915.

81   *Chronicle*, 25 August 1915 and *Irish Times*, 26 August 1915.

82   *Chronicle*, 25 August 1915.

83   P. Callan, *Voluntary Recruiting*, p.127.

84   See *Irish Life*, 8 October 1915 for a list of CCORI committees by county and areas where it held meetings.

85   *Irish Life*, 8 October 1915.

86   D.G. Marnane, 'Canon Arthur Ryan'. Harty could be flexible. In 1917, he sanctioned action by a priest to save a job for a Sinn Féin man, who was asked to leave because of that association, until he was free to return. See Edward McGrath, BMH statement.

87   Canon Arthur Ryan: Born in Scarteen, Knocklong, Co Limerick; educated at St Mary's College Oscott near Birmingham; ordained in 1876 and president of St Patrick's College, Thurles, from 1887 to 1903; appointed parish priest at Tipperary town in 1903; one of Redmond's nominees to the Provisional Committee of the Irish Volunteers in 1914; passionate advocate of recruitment to the British Army and spent Christmas 1916 at the front.

88   Canon Edmund Kelly: Born Newtown, New Inn, 1874; ordained in Maynooth 1900 and went on a temporary mission to South Africa from 1900–11; served as CC of Mullinahone from 1911–1915 and military chaplain from 1915–1920; received the military cross in September 1917 for bravery in assisting the injured and dying at Ypres; died in 1955 after a number of posts as CC and PP in Tipperary.

89   D.G. Marnane, 'Canon Arthur Ryan', pp.150–173.

90   William Bernard Hickie: Born in Borrisokane, Tipperary: served in the Boer War; commanded a brigade of the British Expeditionary Force in 1914; highly regarded commander of the 16th Irish Division from 1915; was on sick leave during the German spring offensive in 1918 that saw the division practically wiped out; elected to the Senate in 1925; served as President of the British Legion in southern Ireland; died 1950.

91   *Chronicle*, 10 January 1917.

92   *Nationalist*, 13 October 1915.

93   *Irish Times*, 11 October 1915.

94   J. Aan de Wiel, *The Catholic Church in Ireland*, p.22.

95   *Nationalist*, 13 October 1915 and *Chronicle*, 9 October 1915.

96   *Chronicle*, 13 October 1915.

97   *Nationalist*, 13 October 1915.

98   J. Aan de Wiel, *The Catholic Church in Ireland*, p.22. Also, the advanced nationalist press shied away from attacking soldiers who enlisted in the British Army as 1915 progressed, particularly after Suvla Bay, and instead focused on recruiting sergeants. See B. Novick, *Conceiving Revolution*, p.56.

99   Father Michael Maher Papers.

100 D.G. Marnane, 'Canon Arthur Ryan', p.158.

101 Father Ryan's speeches and political ideology had not gone unnoticed. See B. MacGiolla Choille, *Intelligence Notes*, p.119.

102 D.G. Marnane, 'Canon Arthur Ryan', p.164. It is important to note, however, that until at least the Easter Rising, anti-recruiting activity was carried out by a minute proportion of the population.

103 See *Irish Times*, 6 September 1915, for a particularly graphic account of an amphibious landing.

104 P. Orr, *Field of Bones*, p.183. These were usually officers; privates just merited name and rank.

105 *Nationalist*, 7 July 1915.

106 P. Orr, *Field of Bones*, p.188.

107 Ibid.

108 T.P. Dooley, *Irishmen or English Soldiers?*, p.136.

109 *Nationalist*, 11 September 1915.

110 Ibid. 24 Nov. 1915. The piece also carries a list of Clonmel men who were at Suvla Bay.

111 Ibid. 1 September 1915.

112 *Irish Times*, 30 August 1915.

113 This had no effect. See a confidential report on recruiting, Nats 1/249, and *Nationalist*, 28 August 1915.

114 *Irish Times*, 30 August 1915. The paper reported that Sergeant Somers (then a private) was badly wounded at Mons and only returned to active service to be sent to the Dardanelles.

115 Ibid. 6 October 1915.

116 Ibid.

117 Ibid. and *Nenagh Guardian*, 9 October 1915.

118 *Nenagh Guardian*, 9 October 1915.

119 Trench thanked the press, curiously enough. *Nenagh Guardian*, 9 October 1915. Trench finished off by quoting John Redmond: 'This is a war in which every Irishman must take his part. If Irishmen stand at one side and say this war does not concern them they will go down to posterity with contempt and dishonoured.'

120 *Nenagh Guardian*, 9 October 1915.

121 *Nationalist*, 3 September 1915. The same edition also gives an account of Oscar Hennessey, King's Liverpool Regiment, who was recommended for the Distinguished Conduct Medal. This piece on Somers is about half a broadsheet page.

122 T. Hennessey, *Dividing Ireland*, p.109.

123 Ibid.

124 Ibid. For an incisive analysis of the 10th Irish Division in Gallipoli, see P. Orr, *Field of Bones*. Orr points out that some Northern Irish media refuted nationalist ownership of the 16th, claiming that not even 25 per cent were Catholic.

125 *Nationalist*, 15 December 1915.

126 Father Michael Maher Papers.

127 *Irish Life*, 8 October 1915.

Chapter 4

1 *Irish Times*, 29 October 1915 and *Nationalist*, 30 October 1915.

2 Letters of apology came from the *Clonmel Chronicle* and *Tipperary Star*.

3 Redmond did not consider the CCORI effective and wanted a new scheme. Friend also favoured reform and Kitchener agreed to support a new appeal, of which the DRI was the result.

4 *Nationalist*, 3 November 1915.

5 *Nationalist*, 3 November 1915.

6 CI Monthly Report, NR, October 1915.

7 *Irish Life*, 8 October 1915.

8 P. Callan, *Voluntary Recruiting*, p.173.

9 *Nationalist*, 17 November 1915.

10 *Chronicle*, 24 November 1915.

11 *Nationalist*, 17 November 1915. For more on the military's distaste for voluntary recruiting meetings, see P. Callan, *Voluntary Recruiting*, pp.183–184.

12 These threats were made at other locations. See M. Staunton, *The Royal Munster Fusiliers in the Great War, 1914–19*, MA Thesis (Dublin: UCD, 1986), p.62.

13 *Nationalist*, 17 November 1915.

14 Ibid. 13 November 1915.

15 *Chronicle*, 1 December 1915.

16 *Chronicle*, 1 December 1915.

17 Ibid.

18 Ibid.

19 J.M. Wilson Papers.

20 Ibid.

21 Ibid.

22 Ibid.

23 J.M. Wilson Papers,

24 *Nationalist*, 13 November 1915.

25 CI Monthly Report, SR, November 1915.

26 Ibid. NR, November 1915.

27 Father Michael Maher Papers.

28 P. Callan, *Voluntary Recruiting*, pp.167.

29 CI Monthly Report, SR, October 1915. Also see B. MacGiolla Choille, *Intelligence Notes*, p.79.

30 CI Monthly Report, SR, October 1915.

31 Ibid. NR, November 1915.

32 Ibid. SR, November 1915.

33 J.M. Wilson Papers.

34 Ibid.

35 The use of fear or scare tactics was unlikely to encourage enlisting. This was also the case in England, where people were just as likely to rebuff recruiting appeals. See B. White, 'Volunteerism and Early Recruitment Efforts in Devonshire, August 1914 to December 1915', *The Historical Journal* (September 2009).

36 CI Monthly Report, NR, May 1915; SR, July 1915; and SR, December 1915.

37 IG Monthly Report, September 1915.

38 J.M. Wilson Papers.

39 Similar efforts were made in other recruiting regions. See M. Staunton, *Royal Munster Fusiliers*, p.62.

40 *Chronicle*, 27 October 1915.

41 Ibid.

42 *Nenagh Guardian*, 13 November 1915.

43 Thomas Patrick Gill was a native of Nenagh and was the eldest son of Robert Gill, the local engineer.

44 *Nenagh Guardian*, 13 November 1915. It was reported that several recruits joined and Gill said that members of his family were at the front.

45 *Nenagh Guardian*, 13 November 1915.

46 *Chronicle*, 1 December 1915.

47 Ibid. 27 October 1915.

48 *Nenagh Guardian*, 20 November 1915.

49   *Nationalist*, 15 December 1915 and *Nenagh Guardian*, 18 December 1915.

50   *Nenagh Guardian*, 18 December 1915.

51   Ibid.

52   Father Michael Maher Papers.

53   *Nationalist*, 15 December 1915.

54   Similar appeals were made across the country. See M. Staunton, *Royal Munster Fusiliers*, p.62.

55   P. Callan, *Voluntary Recruiting*, pp.180–181.

56   *Nenagh Guardian*, 25 December 1915.

57   Sparrow was a businessman based in Dublin.

58   *Nenagh Guardian*, 25 December 1915.

59   Ibid.

60   Ibid.

61   Ibid.

62   *Nenagh Guardian*, 25 December 1915. The Chairman of this meeting was Thomas Ryan.

63   *Nationalist*, 18 December 1915.

64   Ibid.

65   Ibid.

66   The military believed that farmers' sons would not enlist in regiments 'beneath them'.See Military Intelligence Report, Southern Division, September 1916.

67   *Chronicle*, 1 December 1915.

68   Ibid.

69   Ibid.

70   Ibid. The agricultural committee remarks related to the recruiting committee identifying potential recruits or shirkers and having them enlist. Slattery replied: 'The lord lieutenant's remark made a great impression on my mind and if it cleared up tomorrow matters will be right. We are extremely thankful to Captain Loftus for his explanation today and I am sure he has got more recruits since he came here than all those that went before him put together. After all, there is something in the blarney of an Irishman.'

71   *Chronicle*, 27 November 1915

72   Ibid.

73   He is reported in the *Nenagh Guardian* as Mr Finn, but it is the same person.

74   *Nenagh Guardian*, 18 December 1915.

75   P. Callan, *Voluntary Recruiting*, p.183.

76   *Nationalist*, 18 December 1915.

77   *Nationalist*, 18 December 1915.

78   Ibid. See also J.M. Wilson Papers, which linked Sinn Féin to this refusal.

79   CI Monthly Report, NR, December 1915.

80   *Chronicle*, 24 November 1915.

81   *Nationalist*, 11 December 1915.

82   Father Michael Maher Papers.

83   Father Michael Maher Papers.

84   N. Kevin, *I Remember Karrigeen*, p.41.

85   P. Callan, *Voluntary Recruiting*, p.187.

86   Ibid. p.240.

87   Ibid. p.241.

88   *Chronicle*, 24 February 1917.

89   *Chronicle*, 4 August 1917.

90   Ibid. 22 September 1917.

91   Ibid. 19 December 1917.

Chapter 5

1   Belfast (35.9 per cent), Dublin/Naas (22.8 per cent) and Cork/Tralee (12.9 per cent) in first, second and third respectively. The RIRegt district encompassed the counties of Tipperary, Waterford, Kilkenny and Wexford.

2   M. Staunton, *Royal Munster Fusiliers*, pp.54–55.

3   Again, Belfast (32.8 per cent), Dublin/Naas (30.1 per cent) and Cork/Tralee (13.4 per cent).

4   See *Chronicle, 2 June, 4 August,* and *19 December;* and *Irish Times,* 13 September1917.

5   This is a conservative figure, which could be as high as 5,000. This is based on police and military reports, Ministry of National Service papers and newspaper reports.

6   S.J. Watson, *A Dinner of Herbs: the History of Old St Mary's Church, Clonmel (Clonmel:* Watson Books, 1988), pp.170.

7   Ministry of National Service (Nats), L, 1–85.

8   Cabinet Papers 37–157, National Archives, Kew.

9   W.E. Vaughan and A.J. Fitzpatrick (eds.), *Irish Historical Statistics* (Dublin: Royal Irish Academy, 1978).

10   D.G. Marnane, 'Canon Arthur Ryan', p.163.

11   T.P. Dooley, *Irishmen or English Soldiers,* p.2.

12   Ibid. p.4.

13   Ibid. p.124.

14   M. Staunton, *Royal Munster Fusiliers,* p.75

15   T.P. Dooley, *Irishmen or English Soldiers?,* p.124.

16   K. Moloughney, *Roscrea Me Darlin'* (*Roscrea*: 1987), p.89.

17   Seamus Babington, BMH statement.

18   P.C. Power, *Carrick-on-Suir and its People (Dublin*: Anna Livia Books in association with the Carrick Society, 1976), p.144.

19   *Nenagh Guardian, 9* January 1915.

20   J.M. Wilson Papers.

21   D.G. Marnane, 'Canon Arthur Ryan', p.164.

22   Seamus Babington, BMH statement.

23   See Chapter Six for more on this.

24   *Nenagh News, 2* October 1915.

25   *Chronicle, 18* September 1916.

26   K. Moloughney, *Roscrea Me Darlin'*, p.89.

27   This was the offer to Sergeant James Somers. See Nats 1/249.

28   P. Callan, *Voluntary Recruiting*, p.57.

29   D. Fitzpatrick, 'Militarism in Ireland, 1900–1922', in T. Bartlett and K. Jeffery, *A Military History of Ireland* (Cambridge: Cambridge University Press, 1996), p.389.

30   T.P. Dooley, *Irishmen or English Soldiers?'*, p.124.

31   Seamus Babington, BMH statement.

32   *Nenagh Guardian, 24* April 1915.

33   Ibid.

34   *Nenagh Guardian, 29 May 1915.*

35   *Nenagh Guardian, 18* September 1915.

36   *Nationalist*, 24 March 1915.

37   *Chronicle, 24* March 1915.

38   P. Cranly, *Just Standing Idly By (Tipperary*: Patrick Cranly, 1993), p.6.

39   D. Grace, *Portrait of a Parish: Monsea and Killodiernan Co Tipperary (Nenagh*: Relay, in association with Stair-Monsea-Killodiernan Publication Committee, 1996), p.276. Peter Karsten gives the example of a military funeral in Dublin, after which it was claimed nearly 'every able-bodied man in the area had enlisted within a fortnight'. See P. Karsten, 'Irish Soldiers in the British Army, 1792–1922: Suborned or Subordinate?', *Journal of Social History (XVII, 1983)*, pp.31–64.

40   W.S. O'Shea, *A Short History of Tipperary Military Barracks 1874–1922 (Tipperary*: Phoenix Publishing,1998), pp.17–21. Also see G.A. Cooper Walker, *The Book of the Seventh Service Battalion The Royal Inniskilling Fusiliers from Tipperary to Ypres (Dublin*: Naval & Military Press, 2002).

41   *Chronicle, 10* November 1917.

42   *Irish Times, 13* September 1917.

43   B. MacGiolla Choille, *Intelligence Notes*, p.175.

44   *Irish Life, 8* October 1915.

45   The advanced nationalist press claimed British recruiters played on Irish 'traditional' courage.

46   Seamus Babington, BMH statement.

47   P.C. Power, *Carrick-on-Suir and its People*, p.144.

48   P.C. Power, *History of South Tipperary* (Cork: Mercier Press, 1989), p.203.

49   *Nenagh Guardian, 1838–1988* 150th Centenary Supplement. and K. Moloughney, *Roscrea Me Darlin'*, p.95.

50   M. Staunton, *Royal Munster Fusiliers*, p.78.

51   P. Karsten, 'Irish Soldiers in the British Army', p.39.

52   Ibid.

53   *Nenagh Guardian,* 11 September 1915.

54   There were a number of other Tipperary winners of the VC during the war, but they remain outside the scope of this study. For more, see R. Doherty and D. Truesdale, *Irish Winners of the Victoria Cross.*

55   *Nenagh Guardian, 6* November 1915.

56   P.C. Power, *Carrick-on-Suir and its People*, p.142.

57   Nats 1/398.

58   *Nenagh Guardian,* 29 May 1915.

59   *Clonmel Chronicle,* 29 September 1917.

60   Ex-soldiers were offered a protection scheme in Tipperary during the War of Independence by the 52nd Regt (Oxford and Bucks LI). They were allowed to enlist in regiments stationed in Ireland for a period of six months to be used as fatigue men. The regimental diary of the Oxford and Bucks claims that the 'local ex-soldiers (if they escaped being shot) were so bullied and boycotted that they had either to starve or go over to the rebels'.

61   M. Staunton, *Royal Munster Fusiliers*, p.81. Ex-army or reserve men were more often than not Irish Volunteer instructors.

62   A regimental commander in the Tralee garrison noted in 1892 that the more 'desirable' men — the men of the 'small farming class' rarely enlisted. See P. Karsten, 'Irish Soldiers in the British Army'.

63   T.P. Dooley, *Irishmen or English Soldiers*, p.7.

64   *Irish Times,* 11 September 1915.

65   D. Fitzpatrick, 'Militarism in Ireland', p.389. This is a source from M. Staunton, who sampled a number of RMF fatalities.

66   M. Staunton, *Royal Munster Fusiliers*, p.86.

67   P. Karsten, 'Irish Soldiers in the British Army', p.40.

68 P. Callan, *Voluntary Recruiting*, p.68.

69 Ibid. p.127.

70 *Chronicle*, 1 December 1915.

71 *Chronicle*, 1 December 1915.

72 Ibid. 1915.

73 S. Gwynn, *John Redmond's Last Years*, pp.167–168. Stephen Gwynn: MP for Galway city, 1906–18; joined the British Army during the First World War and served in the Irish Brigade; supported a compromise with unionists during the 1918 Convention; became the *Observer's* Irish correspondent in the 1920s.

74 *Nenagh Guardian*, 26 June 1915.

75 Ibid. 21 Aug. 1915.

76 *Nenagh Guardian*, 21 Aug. 1915.

77 J.M. Wilson Papers.

78 William Myles, BMH statement.

79 *Chronicle*, 3 October 1914, and IG Monthly Report, October 1914.

80 *Nenagh News*, 7 November 1914. Elected officials were Thomas Dawson (Town Clerk, Tipperary town), R.P. Gill (Vice-President, County Engineer, Nenagh), R.M. Hanrahan (Fethard, Treasurer) and John Barry (Golden, honorary Secretary).

81 *Chronicle*, 2 December 1914. The circular was also mentioned in the House of Commons.

82 CI Monthly Report, NR, October 1914.

83 *Nationalist, 19 May* 1915.

84 Ibid. 14 April 1915.

85 Seamus Babington, BMH statement

86 Eamon O'Duibhir, BMH statement. The meeting he refers to here could be at Tipperary town in 1915, where Canon Ryan was threatened. In the Bureau statement, however, O'Duibhir states it is 1914. Elements sound too similar to be a different meeting, so perhaps he got the dates mixed up.

87 CI Monthly Report, SR, November 1914.

88 Ibid. NR, November 1915.

89 P. Callan, *Voluntary Recruiting*, p.186.

90 Ibid. p.6.

91 Private letter regarding a job appointment in my care, courtesy of Rita Larkin. The man was applying for a job in Tipperary and the Board of Guardians had the power to appoint. Two members of the Meagher family were on that board.

Chapter 6

1   *Chronicle*, 16 December 1914 and *Nenagh News*, 26 December 1914. A further press cutting sent to his mother in Cashel detailed the arrival of O'Brien amid a contingent of wounded soldiers at Huddersfield in Britain. O'Brien said he didn't want anything put in the papers about the award as he was only doing his duty but remarked he was 'an Irishman and I am proud of it'. O'Brien's brother, Christopher, died a number of weeks later. He had been a RIRegt soldier but had retired a year previously due to ill-health. Christopher O'Brien had also been one of the founders of the Cashel Volunteers, see *Nenagh News*, 2 January 1914.

2   *Nationalist*, 22 December 1915. This gives an account of the battle. During the summer, he spoke at recruiting meetings in Kingstown.

3   *Nationalist*, 2 and 30 December 1914.

4   S. O'Donnell, *Clonmel 1900–1932*, p.293.

5   Ibid.

6   Lt Col Thomas Halpin, BMH statement.

7   *Diary of Father Michael Maher*

8   *Nationalist*, 20 October 1915.

9   Ibid. 3 November 1915.

10   *Diary of Father Michael Maher*.

11   Ibid.

12   For a classic example, see *Nationalist*, 7 November 1914.

13   One hundred views of Belgium were to have been screened, see *Nationalist*, 23 December 1914.

14   *Nenagh Guardian*, 27 November 1915. The lecture was given by a Miss Vengerova, a writer in Russia who had translated English plays such as Shaw and Rosetti. Proceeds were donated to Nenagh prisoners of war.

15   D. Fitzpatrick, 'Home Front and Everyday Life', p.135.

16   *Nationalist*, 13 November 1915.

17   *Chronicle*, 1 March 1916.

18   Ibid. 1 March 1916.

19   *Chronicle*, 8 April 1916.

20   *Chronicle*, 14 October 1916.

21   Ibid. 14 October 1916.

22   Ibid. 19 December 1917.

23   D.G. Marnane, 'Canon Arthur Ryan', p.167.

24   *Chronicle*, 5 May 1917.

25   Interview with Horace Ham, Imperial War Museum, London.

26   Interview with Charles Ward, Imperial War Museum, London.

27   M. Meades Letters, Imperial War Museum, London. Meades also writes of how he will miss some of the meetings at the Soldiers' Home at the town and he sends some shamrock to his wife and family.

28   *Nationalist*, 15 September 1915.

29   *Nenagh Guardian*, 20 November 1915.

30   *Chronicle*, 19 May 1915.

31   Ibid. 7 April 1915.

32   *Nationalist*, 10 February 1915.

33   Ibid.

34   *Chronicle*, 10 February 1915.

35   Ibid. 14 November 1917.

36   *Nationalist*, 15 September 1915.

37   *Nenagh Guardian*,11 September 1915.

38   Ibid. 18 September 1915.

39   P. Callan, *Voluntary Recruiting*, 185.

40   *Nenagh Guardian*, 4 September 1915.

41   Ibid. 11 December 1915.

42   Ibid. 11 December 1915.

43   *Nationalist*, 2 March 1918. These rulings were quite common across the county at the time. See P. Callan, *Voluntary Recruiting*, p.185.

44   *Nationalist*, 13 February 1915.

45   *Nationalist*, 24 February 1915.

46   K. Jeffery, *Ireland and the Great War*, p.30.

47   *Nationalist*, 21 July 1915.

48   Ibid. 13 October 1915.

49   *Nationalist*, 20 October 1915.

50   *Nationalist*, 20 October 1915.

51   *Chronicle*, 1 March 1916. Father Crotty's letter was sent to Kathleen Phelan, who wrote to Crotty with subscription lists. Mrs J. Phelan had been working for the prisoners since the outbreak of hostilities and had been despatching comforts and parcels of food to the prisoners of war in Germany every week.

52   *Chronicle*, 10 July 1918.

53   *Nationalist*, 11 September 1915.

54   *Chronicle*, 23 February 1916.

55   Ibid.

56   *Chronicle*, 12 February 1916.

57   *Nationalist*, 13 November 1918.

58   *Chronicle*, 30 January 1918.

59   *Nationalist*, 14 July 1915.

60   *Chronicle*, 14 June 1916.

61   Ibid. 19 February 1916.

62   Ibid. 1 April 1916.

63   Ibid. 4 March 1916.

64   *Nationalist*, 11 December 1915.

65   M. Downes, 'The Civilian Voluntary Aid Effort', in D. Fitzpatrick (ed.), *Ireland and the First World War*, p.32. Tipperary raised considerably more money than the other counties in the RIRegt area, with Kilkenny and Wexford actually decreasing. Note that Ulster remained aloof from the networks in the rest of Ireland and its statistics have not been included.

66   M. Downes, 'The Civilian Voluntary Aid Effort', pp.27–28.

67   *Chronicle*, 16 May 1917.

68   N. Kevin, *I Remember Karrigeen*, p.41.

69   *Nationalist*, 20 October 1915.

70   *Chronicle*, 12 December 1917.

71   E.Reilly, 'Women and Voluntary Work', in *Ireland and the Great War: 'A War to Unite us all?'* (Manchester, 2002), p.66.

72   M. Downes, 'The Civilian Voluntary Aid Effort', p.37.

73   *Nenagh Guardian*, 29 May 1915.

74   *Nationalist*, 26 May 1915.

75   *Nationalist*, 6 January 1915. *Chronicle* reports 14 or 15 children on the same date.

76   *Nationalist*, 31 July 1915.

77   Ibid. 27 July 1918.

78   Ibid. 21 October 1914.

79   *Chronicle*, 17 October 1914.

80   P.C. Power, *History of South Tipperary*, p.203, and also see *Chronicle*, 31 October 1914.

81   *Chronicle*, 21 October 1914.

82   *Chronicle*, 24 October 1914.

83   C. O'Neill, *The Irish Home Front*, p.54.

84   Ibid.

85   *Irish Times*, 19 October 1914.

86   *Nationalist*, 28 October 1914. Archbishop Harty's fund drive for the Belgians would eventually raise more than £1,800. This prompted a reply from Monsignor Dawachter, Auxiliary Bishop of Malines, commending the collection as a 'magnificent amount'. See *Chronicle*, 16 December 1914.

87   For an interesting cross section of these events, see *Chronicle*, 21 and 24 October 1914.

88   *Chronicle*, 7 November 1914, and *Nationalist*, 7 November 1914.

89   *Chronicle*, 4 November 1914. The interview is too long to repeat in its entirety, but is littered with such bombastic description and is a classic example of this style of atrocity propaganda.

90   This was fair day in Clonmel.

91   *Nationalist*, 7 November 1914.

92   *Chronicle*, 2 December 1914.

93   Ibid. 12 December 1914. One of the stalls offered items made by the wives of soldiers of the 43rd Battery RFA stationed in Fethard during the summer, and by residents of Fethard. Another sold toys made in the Fethard and Cashel convent workrooms. The newspaper report suggested that Tipperary could 'capture locally some of the big trade in this (toy) line that for so long was a German monopoly'. Also see 12 December 1914.

94   *Chronicle*, 2 December 1914.

95   *Nenagh Guardian*, 31 October 1914. They were accommodated in the Sacred Heart Convent, and Mount St Joseph's, Roscrea.

96   *Nationalist*, 9 December 1914. This group was housed in the military barracks.

97   *Nenagh Guardian*, 12 December 1914. Some reports claimed that the non-appearance of Belgians in some towns led to doubts that the war was actually taking place. See C. O'Neill, *The Irish Home Front*, p.62.

98   *Nationalist*, 9 January 1915. See also *Nationalist*, 3 February 1915.

99   Ibid. 20 February 1915. Clonmel won.

100 *Nenagh Guardian*, 2 January 1915.

101 Something similar took place in Galway. See W. Henry, *Galway and the Great War*, p.117.

102 *Chronicle*, 8 November 1916.

103 Civilian prisoners were also detained at Templemore, but moved to Oldcastle Workhouse in County Meath. See C. O'Neill, *The Irish Home Front*, p.94.

104 P.P. Walsh, *A History of Templemore and its Environs* (Roscrea: Paul P. Walsh,1991), pp.96.

105 C. O'Neill,*The Irish Home Front*, p.94.

106 Ibid. p.104.

107 P.P. Walsh, *A History of Templemore*, pp.98–99.

108 C. O'Neill, *The Irish Home Front*, p.159.

109 Ibid. p.104.

110 Ibid.

111 P.P. Walsh, *A History of Templemore*, p.102.

112 *Nationalist*, 27 January 1915. Both bodies were reinterred in the German national cemetery in Glencree, Co Wicklow, after the Second World War. A local man asked the German Graves Commission to keep the headstone at Tipperary, which was agreed to.

113 P.P. Walsh, *A History of Templemore*, p.100.

114 Ibid. p.103.

115 C. O'Neill, *The Irish Home Front*, p.105.

116 *Nationalist*, 23 January 1915.

117 *Nenagh Guardian*, 6 February 1915.

118 P.P. Walsh, *A History of Templemore*, p.106.

119 See C. O'Neill, *The Irish Home Front*, and P.P. Walsh, *A History of Templemore*, for more on this.

120 See W.S. O'Shea, *A Short History of Tipperary Military Barracks*, p.20.

121 For an incisive piece in this, see E. Reilly, 'Women and Voluntary War Work', pp.49–72.

Chapter 7

1   N. Puirséil, 'War, Work and Labour', in *Our War: Ireland and the Great War* (Dublin: 2008), p.185.

2   A.J.P. Taylor, *The First World War* (London: Penguin, 1966), p.83.

3   D. Johnson, *The Interwar Economy of Ireland* (Dundalgan: Dundalgan Press for The Economic and Social History Society of Ireland, 1985), pp.4–5.

4   N. Puirséil, 'War, Work and Labour', p.185.

5   S. O'Donnell, *Clonmel 1900–1932*, p.6.

6   Several reports appeared in the newspapers that a shell factory was to be established at Nenagh, but I cannot find any evidence that it actually made any shells.

7   *Nationalist*, 24 November 1915.

8   Ibid. 24 November 1915.

9   For an incisive study in this area, see G.D. Kelleher, *Gunpowder to Guided Missiles: Ireland's War Industries* (Cork: John F. Kelleher, 1993). The President was the Lord Mayor of Dublin and the other vice-presidents were the Lord Mayor of Cork and Mayors of Londonderry, Sligo, Waterford, Limerick, Drogheda and Wexford.

10   N. Puirséil, 'War, Work and Labour', p.184.

11   *Nationalist*, 9 October 1915.

12   Ibid. The same concerns were expressed in Waterford when recruits left there in April 1915. See T.P. Dooley, *Irishmen or English Soldiers?*, p.121.

13   *Chronicle*, 28 October 1916.

14   *Chronicle*, 11 November 1916. Copies were sent to the County Council, Corporation and the MPs.

15   *Irish Times*, 11 January 1917.

16   *Chronicle*, 28 February 1917.

17   Ibid. 3 March 1917. In Kerry, it was claimed the purchasing power of £1 was 9s 11d. See T.F. Martin, *The Kingdom in the Empire: A Portrait of Kerry During World War One* (Dublin: Nonsuch, 2006), p.72.

18   *Chronicle*, 28 April 1917.

19   *Chronicle*, 19 December 1917.

20   Clonmel Corporation Minute Book, Town Hall, Clonmel.

21   E. Lonergan, *St Luke's Hospital 1834-1984 (Clonmel: Eamonn Lonergan, 1985)*, p.53. A bonus was granted to asylum workers the following year.

22   Tipperary Urban District Council Minute Book, Dan Breen House, Tipperary town, Co. Tipperary.

23   Tipperary Urban District Council Minute Book.

24   Clonmel Board of Guardians Minute Book, 13 March 1915, Tipperary Local Studies, Thurles. Securing sugar became increasingly difficult, as noted by the Guardians later that year. See entry for 25 November 1916. Some contractors told the Board they could no longer supply amounts at previous levels. This was as low as 65 per cent of previous supplies. See 8 December 1916. These prices cover 1914 to 1915.

25   Clonmel Board of Guardians Minute Book, 3 November 1916.

26   Clonmel Board of Guardians Minute Book, 3 November 1916.

27   *Nationalist*, 20 November 1915.

28   Similar concerns were expressed in Waterford. See T.P. Dooley, *Irishmen or English Soldiers?*, p.114.

29   *Nationalist*, 6 October 1915.

30   T.P. Dooley, *Irishmen or English Soldiers?*, p.115.

31   *Nationalist*, 26 January 1918.

32   *Nationalist*, 31 July 1918.

33   Ibid.

34   Ibid. 21 Aug. 1918.

35   Ibid. 5 October 1918.

36   Ibid.

37   Ibid.

38   *Nationalist*, 16 October 1918.

39   Tipperary South Riding County Council Minute Book, Tipperary County Museum, South Riding (1984.223.8).

40   *Nationalist*, 9 February 1918.

41   Ibid.

42   Tipperary Urban District Council Minute Book. Cleeve also denied charges that he was secretly sending butter to England in condensed milk tins.

43   *Nationalist*, 20 February 1918.

44   *Chronicle*, 7 February 1917.

45   Ibid. 3 March 1917. Married people got preference. Also, as a consequence of the restrictions on malting, eleven men employed in Clonmel brewery were told that their jobs were lost.

46   *Nationalist*, 9 January 1918.

47   Ibid. 20 February 1918.

48   S. O'Donnell, *Clonmel 1900–1932*, p.8.

49   Ibid. p.9.

50   E. Hall, *Drangan Co-Operative Creamery Society Ltd, A Century of Success 1897–1997* (Kilkenny: 1997), pp.40–41.

51   Ibid. p.42.

52   W. Jenkins, *Tipp Co-op: Origin and Development of Tipperary Co-operative Creamery Ltd* (Dublin: Drangan Centenary Committee, 2000), p.68.

53   S. O'Donnell, *Clonmel 1900–1932*, p.10.

54   *Nationalist*, 30 October 1915.

55   Ibid. 3 November 1915.

56   *Nationalist*, 20 November 1915.

57   *Chronicle*, 17 January 1917.

58   *Nenagh Guardian*, 27 November 1915.

59   Central Statistics Office (CSO), *Farming Since the Famine* (CSO: 1997), p.23 and *Irish Times*, 11 January 1915.

60   *Chronicle*, 12 September 1917.

61   *Chronicle*, 17 January 1917.

62   Ibid.

63   *Chronicle*, 24 January 1917. This was also at Tipperary Farmers Society.

64   Ibid. 22 November 1916.

65   Ibid. 27 January 1917.

66   *Nationalist*, 20 October 1918. See also *Nationalist*, 8 September 1915 for another example of people departing for the munition works.

67   *Irish Times*, 24 January 1917.

68   CI Monthly Report, SR, February 1917.

69   *Chronicle*, 30 June 1917.

70   Ibid. 24 January 1917.

71   CSO, *Farming Since the Famine*, p.141.

72   *Chronicle*, 12 September 1917.

73   Ibid. 12 September 1917.

74   Ibid. 12 September 1917.

75   Ibid. 12 September 1917.

76   Tipperary Urban District Council Minute Book.

77   N. Puirséil, 'War, Work and Labour', p.184.

78   Cormac Ó'Gráda argues that while farmers did do well, they responded 'lackadaisically' to the opportunities presented by the First World War. Though the value of farm produce, food, and drink exported rose from £41.6 million in 1914 to £80m in 1918, exports declined in real terms and failed to make good the vacuum left by the collapse of Danish and Dutch exports. Ireland also lost out relative to the USA and Canada. See C.Ó'Gráda, *Ireland: A New Economic History 1780–1939* (Oxford: Clarendon Press, 1994), p.389.

79   N. Puirséil, 'War, Work and Labour', p.194.

80   L.M. Cullen, *An Economic History of Ireland since 1660* (London: Batsford, 1972), p.172.

81   *Nationalist*, 20 October 1915.

82   T.P. Dooley, *Irishmen or English Soldiers?*, p.113.

83   C.Ó'Gráda, *Ireland: A New Economic History*, p.390.

Chapter 8

1   P. Maume, *The Long Gestation*, p.157.

2   P. Bew, 'The Politics of War', in J. Horne (ed.), *Our War Ireland and the Great War* (Dublin: 2008), p.99.

3   J. Lee, *Ireland 1912–1985*, p.23.

4   *Chronicle*, 29 May 1915.

5   Ibid. 9 June 1915. The party managed to block Campbell.

6   John Esmonde: Born in Drominagh, Tipperary; son of a Justice of the Peace and Deputy Lieutenant; educated at Clongowes, Stonyhurst and Royal College of Surgeons, Dublin; avid nationalist and Home Rule MP; Colonel of Nenagh Volunteers; supported Woodenbridge and the British war effort; gazetted as a Captain in the RAMC in 1914.

7   Lieutenant William Archer Redmond MP, son of John Redmond was training here.

8   *Nationalist*, 21 April1914. Brigadier General William Hickie wired his sympathy from the front.

9   He also served in a unit that fought insurgents during the Easter Rising.

10   *Nationalist*, 2 June 1915.

11   Ibid.

12   D.R. O'Connor Lysaght, 'County Tipperary: Class Struggle and National Struggle, 1916–24', in W. Nolan and T.G. McGrath (eds.), *Tipperary: History and Society* (Dublin: Geography Publications, 1985).

13   P. Maume, *The Long Gestation*, p.169.

14   D.G. Marnane, 'Canon Arthur Ryan', p.160.

15   Ibid.

16   Ibid. p.161.

17   *Nationalist*, 13 March 1915.

18   Ibid. 3 March 1915.

19   *Nationalist*, 17 March 1915.

20   Ibid. 20 March 1915.

21   Ibid. 7 April 1915.

22   Ibid.

23   Ibid.

24   D.G. Marnane, 'Canon Arthur Ryan', p.161.

25   Timothy Tierney, BMH statement.

26   Edward McGrath, BMH statement.

27   James Duggan, BMH statement.

28   D.G. Marnane, 'Canon Arthur Ryan', p.161.

29   *Nationalist*, 4 August 1915.

30   Ibid. 4 and 7 August 1915.

31   *Nationalist*, 7 August 1915.

32   Ibid. 21 August 1915.

33   Ibid. The report also said that a 'large' number signalled their intention to resume drilling the following week, but the report did not specify how many.

34   D.G. Marnane, 'Canon Arthur Ryan', p.162.

35   *Nationalist*, 1 September 1915.

36   Ibid.

37   Ibid. The paper estimated that about 1,000 Volunteers took part in the review and spectators numbered 5,000.

38   Ibid. 9 October 1915.

39   Ibid.

40   Ibid.

41   D.G. Marnane, 'Canon Arthur Ryan', p.162.

42   Ibid.

43   See CI Monthly Report, May and October, NR, 1914 and 1916.

44   S. O'Donnell, *Clonmel 1900–1932*, p.269.

45   Ibid.

46   CI Monthly Report, SR, April 1916. An interesting point in the same report is a police claim that the Rising actually gave a 'fillip' to recruiting.

47   P.C. Power, *History of South Tipperary*, p.204.

48   CI Monthly Report, SR, April 1916.

49   D.G. Marnane, 'Canon Arthur Ryan', p.166.

50   *Chronicle*, 14 June 1916.

51   S. O'Donnell, *Clonmel 1900–1932*, p.278.

52   Ibid.

53   Ibid. p.282.

54   J. Lee, *Ireland 1912–1985*, p.39.

55   *Nationalist*, 6 March 1918.

56   Ibid. 3 March 1918.

57   Ibid. 3 March 1918.

58   Ibid. 3 March 1918.

59   Ibid. 3 March 1918.

60   J. Lee, *Ireland 1912–1985*, p.23.

61   C. Townshend, *Ireland: The Twentieth Century* (New York: Oxford University Press, 1999), p.70.

Chapter 9

1   A.J.P. Taylor, *The First World War*, p.218.

2   N. Stone, *World War One: A Short History* (London: 2007), p.134.

3   Ibid.

4   T. Hennessey, *Dividing Ireland*, p.220.

5   The performance of the 16th was the subject of criticism, with some considering that the division, undermined by political dissatisfaction, did not perform adequately. This is refuted by Terence Denman, who argues that the division was tired, undertrained, held poor positions, and 'fought bravely but hopelessly… against a numerous, determined and skilful enemy'. See T. Denman, *Ireland's Unknown Soldiers: The 16th (Irish) Division in the Great War, 1914–1918* (Dublin, 1992), p.170.

6   A. Gregory, '"You Might as Well Recruit Germans": British Public Opinion and the Decision to Conscript the Irish in 1918', in A. Gregory and S. Pašeta (eds.), *Ireland and the Great War: 'A War to Unite us All?'* (Manchester, 2002), p.113.

7   J. Aan de Wiel, *The Catholic Church in Ireland*, p.204.

8   N. Stone, *World War One: A Short History*, p.135.

9   This heavy gun fired from captured positions near the Marne, forty miles from Paris. The gun was named 'Big Bertha', after the wife of the arms manufacturer, Krupp.

10 *Nenagh Guardian*, 30 March 1918.

11 *Chronicle*, 13 April 1918.

12 T. Hennessey, *Dividing Ireland*, p.221.

13 *Chronicle*, 10 April 1918.

14 Ibid.

15 Ibid. 13 April 1918.

16 Ibid. 10 April 1918.

17 *Chronicle*, 17 April 1918.

18 Ibid.

19 Ibid.

20 *Nenagh Guardian*, 20 April 1918.

21 Ibid.

22 *Chronicle*, 17 April 1918.

23 *Nationalist*, 20 April 1918.

24 J. Aan de Wiel, *The Catholic Church in Ireland*, p.224.

25 Ibid.

26 Ibid. p.225.

27 *Chronicle*, 24 April 1918.

28 Ibid.

29 Ibid.

30 Ibid.

31 Ibid.

32 J. Aan de Wiel, *The Catholic Church in Ireland*, p.226.

33 Ibid.

34 Ibid.

35 *Chronicle*, 24 April 1918.

36 Ibid.

37 Ibid.

38 Ibid.

39 Ibid.

40 There was a similar approach in Co. Kerry. See T.F. Martin, *The Kingdom in the Empire*, p.100.

41 *Chronicle*, 24 April 1914.

42 *Chronicle*, 24 April 1918.

43 Ibid.

44 A. Gregory, 'You Might as Well Recruit Germans', pp.127–128.

45 CI Monthly Report, SR, April 1918.

46 Ibid. May 1918.

47 See *Chronicle*, 17 April 1918. Count Plunkett seemed to advocate armed resistance but didn't say exactly how to do this. See *Chronicle*, 24 April 1918.

48 *Chronicle*, 17 April 1918.

49 M. Larkin, *Mullinahone: Its Heritage and History* (Clonmel: 2002), p.176.

50 Con Spain, BMH statement. See also the statement of John Hackett for the making of pikes.

51 Edward O'Leary, BMH statement. This was something the RIC did report in the North Riding, where O'Leary was based, but it was still speculation.

52 *Nenagh Guardian*, 20 April 1918.

53 CI Monthly Report, NR, April 1918.

54 IG Monthly Report, April 1918.

55 CI Monthly Report, NR, April 1918.

56 Ibid. SR, April 1918.

57 *Nationalist*, 20 April 1918.

58 *Nenagh Guardian*, 20 April 1918.

59 Ibid. 27 April 1918. The ellipsis here is in the news report.

60 *Nationalist*, 20 April 1918. In some reports, the pledge was termed a 'covenant'.

61 Ibid.

62 Police reports noted in January 1918 that the Sinn Féin organization was the only active one. See CI Monthly Report, NR, January 1918.

63 See CI Monthly Report, SR, January and December 1918.

64 CI Monthly Report, SR, April 1918.

65 *Chronicle*, 17 April 1918.

66 Seamus Babington, BMH statement.

67 Ibid.

68 James Duggan, BMH statement.

69 William Myles, BMH statement.

70 Edward McGrath, BMH statement.

71 S.J.Watson, *A Dinner of Herbs*, p.180.

72 P. Travers, *The Irish Conscription Crisis, 1918*, MA Thesis (Dublin: UCD, 1977), p.160.

73 *Chronicle*, 17 April 1918.

74 *Nationalist*, 20 April 1918.

75 Ibid.

76 *Chronicle*, 24 April 1918.

77 A. Gregory, 'You Might as Well Recruit Germans', p.121.

78 *Chronicle*, 17 April 1918. Reported in these meetings were various shouts from the crowd. Cries of 'We'll die before we go!' were typical.

79 Ibid.

80 *Chronicle*, 13 April 1918.

81 Ibid. 17 April 1918.

82 CI Monthly Report, SR, April 1918.

83 Military Intelligence Report, Southern Division, June 1918, National Archives, Kew.

84 P. Travers, *The Irish Conscription Crisis*, p.160.

85 Ibid.

86 CI Monthly Report, SR, May 1918.

87 Walter Long: Unionist politician; Chief Secretary for Ireland in 1905; President of the Local Government Board in the 1915 coalition Cabinet; moved to the Colonial Office when Lloyd George became Prime Minister; chaired a cabinet committee delegated to draw up a Home Rule Bill which was to be implemented simultaneously with conscription; leading advocate of conscription and principal mover in the German Plot arrests.

88 P. Callan, *Voluntary Recruiting*, p.325.

89 J. Aan de Wiel, *The Catholic Church in Ireland*, p.229.

90 J. Aan de Wiel, *The Catholic Church in Ireland*, p.230.

91 *Nationalist*, 18 May 1918.

92 Ibid. 29 May 1918.

93 Ibid. 22 May 1918.

94   P. Travers, *The Irish Conscription Crisis*, p.47.

95   Ibid. p.49.

96   P. Callan, *Voluntary Recruiting*, p.327.

97   National Archives, Kew 1/249,

98   *Nationalist*, 3 August 1918.

99   Ibid.

100 Ibid.

101 Ibid. 25 September 1918.

102 *Chronicle*, 25 September 1918.

103 Ibid.

104 There was also a meeting held at Roscrea, and at Clonmel, which is detailed below. Other attempts at recruiting included 'lectures' on the RAF.

105 Military Intelligence Report, Southern Division, June 1918.

106 *Nationalist*, 16 October 1918.

107 Ibid.

108 Ibid.

109 Ibid.

110 Advanced nationalists blamed the government for the disaster; that British soldiers on board behaved in a 'cowardly and murderous fashion', rescue efforts were delayed again due to a British decision, and the Dublin press covered it up. For more on this, see B. Novick, *Conceiving Revolution*, pp.76–79.

111 CI Monthly Report, SR, October 1918.

112 Ibid. NR, October 1918.

113 *Nationalist*, 16 October 1918.

114 Ibid.

115 Ibid.

116 Ibid.

117 CI Monthly Report, NR, October 1918.

118 Ibid. SR, September 1918.

119 Ibid. NR, September 1918.

120 This figure has been collated through police reports and records of the British Ministry of National Service. It represents an estimation.

121 *Nenagh Guardian*, 19 October 1918.

122 CI Monthly Report, NR, October 1918.

123 *Chronicle*, 21 September 1918.

124 Ibid. 16 October and *Nationalist*, 30 October 1918.

125 CI Monthly Report, SR, October 1918.

126 *Chronicle*, 3 October 1918.

127 Ibid.

128 *Chronicle*, 3 October 1918 for the full account.

129 A. Gregory, 'You Might as Well Recruit Germans', p.128.

130 The move also led to the organization of IRA battalions into the Third Tipperary Brigade. See P.C. Power, *History of South Tipperary*, p.205.

131 See for example *Chronicle*, 25 May 1918. Such reports were the exception rather than the rule.

132 S.J. Watson, A *Dinner of Herbs*, pp.180–181.

Conclusion

1   *Nenagh Guardian*, 16 November 1918. This was a Saturday paper.

2   Ibid.

3   *Nationalist*, 18 and 28 September 1918.

4   Ibid. 14 November 1918.

5   Tipperary proved to be a consistently good source of recruits post-war. In fact, from 1919–20, the best recruiting office in Ireland was Clonmel and was only bettered by Dublin and Armagh from 1920–21, underlining the fact that this was a way of life and men were not dupes for enlisting. For the figures, see K. Jeffery, *An Irish Empire?: Aspects of Ireland and the British Empire* (Manchester: 1996), p.101.

6   See the *Nenagh Guardian*, 16 November 1918 for an example of this. The word was used at the time to describe the loss of life during the war. The term was also used by the *Irish Times* on the first anniversary of the Armistice. See *Irish Times*, 12 November 1919.

7   A. Gregory, 'You Might as Well Recruit Germans', p.128.

8   D. Fitzpatrick, 'Home Front and Everyday Life', p.140.

Select Bibliography

Bourke, J. *An Intimate History of Killing* (London: 1999).

Bowman, T. *Irish Regiments in the Great War — Discipline and Morale* (Manchester: 2003).

Bracken, P. *Foreign and Fantastic Field Sports: Cricket in Co Tipperary* (Thurles: 2004).

Clear, C. *Social Change and Everyday Life in Ireland* (Manchester: 2007).

Cullen, C. (ed.), *The World Upturning: Elsie Henry's Wartime Irish Diaries, 1913-1919* (Dublin: 2012).

D'Arcy, F. *Remembering the War Dead: British Commonwealth and International War Graves in Ireland since 1914* (Dublin: 2007).

Denman, T. *Ireland's Unknown Soldiers: The 16th Irish Division in the Great War* (Dublin: 1992).

de Wiel, J. Aan *The Catholic Church in Ireland 1914–1918: War and Politics* (Dublin: 2003).

Doherty, G. and Keogh D. (eds.), *1916: The Long Revolution* (Cork: 2007).

Gregory, A. and Pašeta, S. (eds.), *Ireland and the Great War: 'A War to Unite us All?'* (Manchester: 2002).

Gregory, A. *The Last Great War* (Cambridge: 2008).

Hennessey, T. *Dividing Ireland: World War One and Partition* (London: 1998).

Henry, W. *Galway and the Great War* (Cork: 2006).

Horne, J. and Kramer, A. *German Atrocities 1914. A History of Denial.* (Yale: 2001).

Horne, J. (ed.), *Our War: Ireland and the Great War* (Dublin: 2008).

Jeffery, K. *Ireland and the Great War* (Cambridge: 2000).

Johnson, N.C. *Ireland, the Great War and the Geography of Remembrance* (Cambridge: 2003).

Magennis, E. and Ó Doibhlin, C. *World War One — Ireland and Its Impacts* (Armagh: 2005).

Marnane, D.G. *Land and Violence: A History of West Tipperary from 1660* (Tipperary: 1985).

Martin, T.F. *The Kingdom in the Empire: A Portrait of Kerry During World War One* (Dublin: 2006).

McCarthy, M. *Ireland's Heritages: Critical Perspectives on Memory and Identity* (Aldershot: 2005).

McEwen, Y. *It's a Long Way to Tipperary: British and Irish Nurses in the First World War* (Dunfermline: 2006).

McMahon, D. *The Moynihan Brothers in Peace and War, 1909–1918* (Dublin: 2004).

Moore, S. *The Irish on the Somme* (Belfast: 2005).

Novick, B. *Conceiving Revolution* (Dublin: 2001).

O'Donnell, S. *Clonmel 1900-1932: A History* (Clonmel: 2009).

Orr, P. *Field of Bones. An Irish Division at Gallipoli* (Dublin: 2006).

Pennell, C. *A Kingdom United* (Oxford: 2012).

Todman, D. *The Great War: Myth and Memory* (London: 2005).

Yeates, P. *A. City in Turmoil: Dublin 1919–21* (Dublin: 2012).

Sources

Manuscript Collections

Dublin
National Archives:
Chief Secretary's Office Registered Papers.
Manuscript Census Returns, 1911.

National Library of Ireland:
Joseph Brennan Papers.
Pierce McCan Papers.
Maurice Moore Papers.
John Redmond Papers.

Trinity College Dublin:
Donoughmore Papers.

London
Imperial War Museum:
I. Kirkpatrick, 8th Royal Inniskilling Fusiliers.
M. Meades Papers (Middlesex Regiment).
Interviews with Veterans Collection.

The National Archives, Kew.

Colonial Office:
Anti-Recruiting Activity, 1905–1919 (CO 904-161).
Anti-Recruiting Notices (CO 904-162).
Censorship Reports.
Irish Crime Records, 1911–1917(CO 904-32).
Irish Office Press Statements.
Military Intelligence Officers in Ireland (CO 904-157).
Press Censor Reports.
RIC Inspector General and County Inspector's Monthly Reports for Tipperary.
RIC Intelligence Reports (CO 903-19).
RM Précis 1914 (CO/904/227).

Ministry of National Service:
Nats 1-85/398/399/400/401.

Cabinet Office:
Cabinet Papers, 37–157.

Royal Artillery Museum:
War Diary of 2nd Brigade Royal Field Artillery.

Tipperary
Bolton Library, Cashel:
Parish Records.

Dan Breen House, Tipperary town:
Urban District Council Minutes.

St. Mary's Church, Clonmel:
Vestry Minutes.

Tipperary County Council, North Riding:
Borrisokane Board of Guardians Minute Book.

Tipperary Local Studies, Thurles
Bureau of Military History Statements:
Clonmel Board of Guardians Minute Book.
Diary of Father Michael Maher.
Poor Law Union Records: Cashel, Clonmel, Nenagh, Thurles and Tipperary.

Tipperary County Museum, South Riding:
Clonmel Unitarian Church Records.
Fethard Town Commissioners Papers.
South Tipperary County Council Minute Books (1984.223.6/223.7/223.8/223.9).

Town Hall, Clonmel:
Clonmel Corporation Minute Books.

Belfast
Public Record Office:
J.M. Wilson Papers.

Contemporary Newspapers and Periodicals
Clonmel Chronicle.
Cork Examiner.
Freeman's Journal.
Irish Life.
Irish Sword.
Irish Times.
Irish Volunteer.
Nationalist.
Nenagh Guardian.
Nenagh News.
Rockwell Annual.
The Times.
Tipperary People.
Tipperary Star.

Official Publications
www.britishparliamentarypapers.com
CSO, *Farming Since the Famine (CSO: 1997)*.
Dictionary of Irish Biography.
www.theses.com

Unpublished Theses
Burke, G. *The British Army and Fermoy 1870–1922*, MA Thesis (Cork: UCC, 1999).
Callan, P. *Voluntary Recruiting for the British Army in Ireland During the First World War*, Ph.D. Thesis (Dublin: UCD, 1984).
Hennessy, D. *Ireland and the First World War: A Cork Perspective*, M.Phil Thesis (Cork: UCC, 2004).
Kelly, A.J. *County Tipperary and National Irish Politics 1916–1997*, M.Phil Thesis (Cork: UCC, 1997).
Lucey, D.J. *Cork Public Opinion and the First World War*, MA Thesis (Cork: UCC, 1972).
Moloney, T. *The Impact of World War One on Limerick*, MA Thesis (Limerick, University of Limerick, 2003).
O'Neill, C. *The Irish Home Front 1914–18: With Particular Reference to the Treatment of Belgian Refugees*, Ph.D. Thesis (Maynooth: NUIM, 2006).
Staunton, M. *The Royal Munster Fusiliers in the Great War, 1914–19*, MA Thesis (Dublin: UCD, 1986).
Travers, P. *The Irish Conscription Crisis, 1918*, MA Thesis (Dublin: UCD, 1977).

Published Works: Tipperary
Augusteijn, J. 'The Operations of South Tipperary IRA, 1916–1921', *Tipperary Historical Journal (1996)*.
Bracken, P. *Foreign and Fantastic Field Sports: Cricket in Co Tipperary* (Thurles: 2004).
Breen, D. *My Fight for Irish Freedom* (Tralee, 1964).
Burnell, T. and R. *The Tipperary War Dead: A History of the Casualties of the First World War* (Dublin: 2008).
Cooke, H. *Rectory Days* (Waterford: 2002).
Cranly, P. *Just Standing Idly By* (Tipperary: 1993).
Cranly, P. *Moving On* (Tipperary: 1995).
Cunningham, G. *Roscrea Golf Club* (Roscrea: 1992).
Elebert, M. *Recollections of Rapla* (Nenagh: 1985).
Grace, D. *Portrait of a Parish: Monsea and Killodiernan Co Tipperary* (Nenagh:1996).
Grace, D. 'Soldiers from Nenagh and District in World War I', *Tipperary Historical Journal* (1999).
Hall, E. Drangan *Co-Operative Creamery Society Ltd, A Century of Success 1897–1997* (Kilkenny: 1997).
Hayes, J.C. 'Guide to Tipperary Newspapers', *Tipperary Historical Journal* (1986), pp. 1–16.
Jenkins, W. *Tipp Co-op: Origin and Development of Tipperary Co-operative Creamery Ltd* (Dublin: 2000).
Kevin, N. *I Remember Karrigeen* (London: 1944).
Larkin, M. *Mullinahone: Its Heritage and History* (Clonmel: 2002).
Lonergan, E. *St Luke's Hospital Clonmel 1834–1984* (Tipperary; 1984).
Lonergan, E. *A Workhouse Story: A History of St Patrick's Hospital Cashel 1842–1992* (Clonmel: 1992).
Long, B. *Tipperary South Riding Council 1899 to 1999: A Century of Local Democracy* (Tipperary: 1999).

Lynch, M. *Tipperary Golf Club* (Tipperary: 1996).

Marnane, D.G. *Land and Violence: A History of West Tipperary from 1660* (Tipperary: 1985).

Marnane, D.G. 'Canon Arthur Ryan, the National Volunteers and Army Recruitment in Tipperary', *Tipperary Historical Journal* (2006).

Meskell, J.*A Political View of Boherlahan-Dualla* (Tipperary: 1996).

Moloughney, K., *Roscrea Me Darlin'* (Roscrea: 1987).

Nolan, W. and McGrath, T.G. (eds.), *Tipperary: History and Society: Interdisciplinary Essays on the History of an Irish County* (Dublin: 1985).

O'Brien, B.*How We Were in the Parish of Kilbarron-Terryglass, Co Tipperary* (Nenagh: 1999).

O'Connor Lysaght, D.R. 'County Tipperary: Class Struggle and National Struggle, 1916–24', in Nolan, W. and McGrath, T.G. (eds.), *Tipperary: History and Society* (Dublin: 1985).

O'Donnell, S. *Clonmel 1900–1932: A History* (Clonmel: 2009).

O'Shea, W.S. *A Short History of Tipperary Military Barracks 1874–1922* (Tipperary: 1998).

Power, P.C. *Carrick-on-Suir and its People* (Dublin: 1976).

Power, P.C. *History of South Tipperary* (Cork: 1989).

Walker, G.A.C. *The Book of the Seventh Service Battalion The Royal Inniskilling Fusiliers from Tipperary to Ypres* (Dublin:1920).

Walsh, P.P. *A History of Templemore and its Environs* (Roscrea: 1991).

Watson, S.J. *A Dinner of Herbs: the History of Old St Mary's Church, Clonmel* (Clonmel: 1988).

General Published Works

Bew, P. *John Redmond* (Dublin: 1996).

Bew, P. 'The Politics of War', in Horne, J. (ed.), *Our War: Ireland and the Great War* (Dublin: 2008).

Bourke, J. *An Intimate History of Killing* (London: 1999).

Bowman, T. 'The Irish Recruiting Campaign and Anti-recruiting Campaigns 1914–1918', in Taithe, B. and Thornton, T. (eds.), *Propaganda, Political Rhetoric and Identity* (Sutton: 1999).

Bowman, T. *Irish Regiments in the Great War — Discipline and Morale* (Manchester: 2003).

Boyce, G.*'The Sure Confusing Drum': Ireland and the First World War* (Swansea: 1993).

MacGiolla Choille, B. *Intelligence Notes 1913–16* (Dublin: 1966).

Clear, C. *Social Change and Everyday Life in Ireland* (Manchester: 2007).

Clear, C. 'Fewer Ladies, More Women', in John Horne (ed.), *Our War: Ireland and the Great War* (Dublin: 2008).

Codd, P. 'Recruiting and Responses to the War in Wexford', in Fitzpatrick, D. (ed.), *Ireland and the First World War* (Dublin; 1986).

Crean, T. 'Labour and Politics in Kerry during the First World War', *Saothar*, 19 (1994).

Cullen, L.M. *An Economic History of Ireland Since 1660* (London: 1987).

D'Arcy, F. *Remembering the War Dead: British Commonwealth and International War Graves in Ireland since 1914* (Dublin: 2007).

Denman, T. 'The Catholic Irish Soldier in the First World War: the "Racial Environment"', *Irish Historical Studies*, 27 (1991).

Denman, T. *Ireland's Unknown Soldiers: The 16th (Irish) Division in the Great War, 1914-18* (Dublin: 1992).

Denman, T. *A Lonely Grave: The Life and Death of Willie Redmond* (Dublin: 1995).

de Wiel, J.Aan *The Catholic Church in Ireland 1914-1918: War and Politics* (Dublin: 2003).

Doherty, G. and Keogh, D.(eds.), *1916 The Long Revolution* (Cork: 2007).

Doherty, R. and Truesdale, D. *Irish Winners of the Victoria Cross* (Dublin, 2000).

Dooley, T.P. Irishmen or English Soldiers?: The Times and World of a Southern Catholic Irishman Enlisting in the British Army (Liverpool: 1995).

Downes, M. 'The Civilian Voluntary Aid Effort,' in Fitzpatrick, D. (ed.), *Ireland and the First World War* (Dublin: 1986).

Dungan, M. *Irish Voices From the Great War* (Dublin: 1995).

Dungan, M. *They Shall Not Grow Old: Irish Soldiers and the Great War* (Dublin: 1997).

English, R. and Walker, G. (eds.), *Unionism in Modern Ireland: New Perspectives on Politics and Culture* (Basingstoke: 1996).

Ferriter, D. *The Transformation of Ireland, 1900-2000* (London: 2004).

Fitzpatrick, D. (ed.), *Ireland and the First World War* (Dublin: Trinity History Workshop, 1986).

Fitzpatrick, D. 'Militarism in Ireland, 1900–1922', in Bartlett, T. and Jeffery, K.A *Military History of Ireland* (Cambridge: 1996).

Fitzpatrick, D. *Politics and Irish Life 1913–1921: Provincial Experience of War and Revolution* (Cork: 1998).

Fitzpatrick, D. 'Home Front and Everyday Life', in Horne J. (ed.), *Our War: Ireland and the Great War* (Dublin: 2008).

Fussell, P. *The Great War and Modern Memory* (Oxford: 1975).

Geoghegan, S. *The Campaigns and History of the Royal Irish Regiment from 1900–1922 Vol. II* (Edinburgh: 1927).

Gregory, A. '"You Might as Well Recruit Germans": British Public Opinion and the Decision to Conscript the Irish in 1918', in Gregory, A. and Pašeta, S. (eds.), *Ireland and the Great War: 'A War to Unite us All?'* (Manchester: 2002).

Gregory, A. *The Last Great War* (Cambridge: 2008).

Gregory, A. and Pašeta, S. (eds.), *Ireland and the Great War: 'A War to Unite us All?'* (Manchester: 2002).

Gwynn, D. *The Life of John Redmond* (London: 1932).

Gwynn, S. *John Redmond's Last Years* (London: 1919).

Hall, D., *The Unreturned Army: County Louth Dead in the Great War* (Dublin: 2005).

Hall, D., *World War I and Nationalist Politics in County Louth, 1914–1920* (Dublin: 2005).

Harris, H. *The Irish Regiments in the First World War* (Cork: 1968).

Hennessey, T. *Dividing Ireland: World War One and Partition* (London: 1998).

Henry, W. *Galway and the Great War* (Cork: 2006).

Horne, J. (ed) *Our War: Ireland and the Great War* (Dublin: 2008).

Horne, J. and Kramer, A. *German Atrocities 1914. A History of Denial* (Yale: 2001).

Jeffery, K. *An Irish Empire?: Aspects of Ireland and the British Empire* (Manchester: 1996).

Jeffery, K. *Ireland and the Great War* (Cambridge: 2000).

Johnson, D. *The Interwar Economy in Ireland* (Dundalgan: 1985).

Johnson, N.C. *Ireland, the Great War and the Geography of Remembrance* (Cambridge: 2003).

Johnstone, T. *Orange, Green and Khaki: The Story of the Irish Regiments in the Great War* (Dublin: 1992).

Karsten, P. 'Irish Soldiers in the British Army, 1792–1922: Suborned or Subordinate?' *Journal of Social History (XVII, 1983)*, pp.31–64.

Kelleher, G.D. *Gunpowder to Guided Missiles: Ireland's War Industries* (Cork:1993).

Lee, J., *Ireland 1912–1985: Politics and Society* (Cambridge: 1989).

Leonard, J. 'Facing the Finger of Scorn': Veterans' Memories of Ireland in the Twentieth Century in Edwards, M. and Lunn, K. (eds.), *War and Memory in the Twentieth Century* (Oxford: 1997).

Magennis, E. and Ó Doibhlin, C., *World War One — Ireland and Its Impacts* (Armagh: 2005).

Martin, F.X. '1916 — Myth, Fact and Mystery', in *Studica Hibernica* 7 (1967).

Martin, T.F. *The Kingdom in the Empire: A Portrait of Kerry During World War One* (Dublin: 2006).

Maume, P. *The Long Gestation: Irish Nationalist Life 1891–1918* (Dublin:1999).

McEwen, Y. *It's a Long Way to Tipperary: British and Irish Nurses in the First World War* (Dunfermline: 2006).

McMahon, D. *The Moynihan Brothers in Peace and War, 1909–1918* (Dublin: 2004).

Moore, S. *The Irish on the Somme* (Belfast: 2005).

Moran, D. and Waldron, A. (eds.), *The People in Arms: Military Myth and National Mobilisation Since the French Revolution* (Cambridge: 2003).

Morrissey, J. 'A Lost Heritage: The Connaught Rangers and Multivocal Irishness', in McCarthy, M. *Ireland's Heritages: Critical Perspectives on Memory and Identity* (Aldershot: 2005).

Murphy, B.P. 'The Easter Rising in the Context of Censorship and Propaganda with Special Reference to Major Ivon Price', in Doherty, G. and Keogh, D. (eds.), *1916: The Long Revolution* (Cork: 2007).

Murray, P. 'The First World War and a Dublin Distillery Workforce: Recruitment and Redundancy at John Power and Sons, 1915–1917', *Saothar*, 15 (1990).

Ní Dhonnchadha, M. and Dorgan, T. (eds.), *Revising the Rising* (Derry: 1991).

Novick, B. *Conceiving Revolution,* (Dublin: 2001).

Ó'Gráda, C. *Ireland: A New Economic History 1780–1939* (Oxford: 1994).

O'Halpin, E. *The Decline of the Union: British Government in Ireland 1892–1920* (Dublin: 1987).

O'Rahilly, A. *Martyr Priest: The Life and Death of Fr William Doyle SJ who Died in the 'Great War'* (London: 1920).

Orr, P. *The Road to the Somme: Men of the Ulster Division Tell Their Story* (Belfast: 1987).

Orr, P. *Field of Bones: An Irish Division at Gallipoli* (Dublin: 2006).

Pennell, C. 'Going to War', in Horne J. (ed.), *Our War: Ireland and the Great War* (Dublin: 2008).

Prost, A. and Winter, J. *The Great War in History. Debates and Controversies, 1914 to the Present* (Cambridge: 2005).

Puirséil, N. 'War, Work and Labour', in Horne, J. (ed.), *Our War: Ireland and the Great War* (Dublin: 2008).

Reilly, E. 'Women and Voluntary War Work', in *Ireland and the Great War: 'A War to Unite us All?'* (Manchester: 2002).

Staunton, M. 'Kilrush, Co Clare, and the Royal Munster Fusiliers: The Experience of an Irish Town in the First World War', *Irish Sword,* 16 (1986).

Stone, N. *World War One: A Short History* (London: 2007).

Taylor, A.J.P. *The First World War* (London: 1966).

Todman, D. *The Great War. Myth and Memory.* (London: 2005).

Townshend, C. *Ireland :The Twentieth Century* (New York: Oxford University Press, 1999).

Urquhart, D. *Women in Ulster Politics 1890–1940* (Dublin: 2000).

Vaughan, W.E. and Fitzpatrick A.J. (eds.), *Irish Historical Statistics* (Dublin: 1978).

Wheatley, M. *Nationalism and the Irish Party: Provincial Ireland, 1910–1916 (Oxford*: 2005).

White, B. 'Volunteerism and Early Recruitment Efforts in Devonshire, August 1914 to December 1915', *The Historical Journal* (September 2009).

Winter, J. *The Great War and the British People* (London: 1985).

Winter, J. and Sivan, E. (eds.), *War and Remembrance in the Twentieth Century* (Cambridge: 1999).

Appendix 1

Date	Recruits	Weekly Average
09/08/1914	4	
10/08/1914	11	
11/08/1914	72	
12/08/1914	18	
13/08/1914	7	
14/08/1914	15	
15/08/1914	23	21
16/08/1914	14	23
17/08/1914	10	23
18/08/1914	23	16
19/08/1914	16	15
20/08/1914	12	16
21/08/1914	5	15
22/08/1914	10	13
23/08/1914	1	11
24/08/1914	13	11
25/08/1914	21	11
26/08/1914	12	11
27/08/1914	12	11
28/08/1914	8	11
29/08/1914	7	11
30/08/1914	2	11
31/08/1914	5	10
01/09/1914	6	7
02/09/1914	11	7
03/09/1914	14	8
04/09/1914	12	8
05/09/1914	18	10
06/09/1914	10	11
07/09/1914	9	11
08/09/1914	22	14
09/09/1914	17	15
10/09/1914	20	15
11/09/1914	17	16
12/09/1914	9	15
13/09/1914	7	14
14/09/1914	11	15
15/09/1914	10	13
16/09/1914	14	13
17/09/1914	17	12
18/09/1914	7	11
19/09/1914	8	11
20/09/1914	8	11
21/09/1914	2	9
22/09/1914	34	13
23/09/1914	7	12
24/09/1914	9	11
25/09/1914	4	10
26/09/1914	14	11
27/09/1914	0	10
28/09/1914	18	12
29/09/1914	8	9
30/09/1914	9	9
01/10/1914	5	8
02/10/1914	13	10
03/10/1914	17	10
04/10/1914	3	10
05/10/1914	11	9
06/10/1914	13	10
07/10/1914	15	11
08/10/1914	7	11
09/10/1914	8	11
10/10/1914	7	9
11/10/1914	0	9
12/10/1914	3	8
13/10/1914	13	8
14/10/1914	6	6
15/10/1914	5	6
16/10/1914	1	5
17/10/1914	5	5
18/10/1914	3	5
19/10/1914	3	5

Date			Date			Date		
20/10/1914	7	4	02/12/1914	1	4			
21/10/1914	7	4	03/12/1914	5	4			
22/10/1914	2	4	04/12/1914	1	3			
23/10/1914	3	4	05/12/1914	4	3			
24/10/1914	6	4	06/12/1914	0	3			
25/10/1914	2	4	07/12/1914	3	2			
26/10/1914	7	5	08/12/1914	5	3			
27/10/1914	5	5	09/12/1914	0	3			
28/10/1914	8	5	10/12/1914	2	2			
29/10/1914	4	5	11/12/1914	3	2			
30/10/1914	1	5	12/12/1914	4	2			
31/10/1914	1	4	13/12/1914	0	2			
01/11/1914	3	4	14/12/1914	15	4			
02/11/1914	2	3	15/12/1914	1	4			
03/11/1914	2	3	16/12/1914	5	4			
04/11/1914	4	2	17/12/1914	4	5			
05/11/1914	6	3	18/12/1914	2	4			
06/11/1914	7	4	19/12/1914	1	4			
07/11/1914	3	4	20/12/1914	0	4			
08/11/1914	2	4	21/12/1914	2	2			
09/11/1914	1	4	22/12/1914	1	2			
10/11/1914	5	4	23/12/1914	2	2			
11/11/1914	5	4	24/12/1914	2	1			
12/11/1914	14	5	25/12/1914	0	1			
13/11/1914	6	5	26/12/1914	2	1			
14/11/1914	4	5	27/12/1914	0	1			
15/11/1914	0	5	28/12/1914	0	1			
16/11/1914	0	5	29/12/1914	6	2			
17/11/1914	8	5	30/12/1914	4	2			
18/11/1914	8	6	31/12/1914	0	2			
19/11/1914	6	5	01/01/1915	10	3			
20/11/1914	3	4	02/01/1915	3	3			
21/11/1914	5	4	03/01/1915	2	4			
22/11/1914	1	4	04/01/1915	8	5			
23/11/1914	5	5	05/01/1915	7	5			
24/11/1914	15	6	06/01/1915	12	6			
25/11/1914	5	6	07/01/1915	3	6			
26/11/1914	3	5	08/01/1915	4	6			
27/11/1914	6	6	09/01/1915	6	6			
28/11/1914	4	6	10/01/1915	10	7			
29/11/1914	2	6	11/01/1915	9	7			
30/11/1914	6	6	12/01/1915	6	7			
01/12/1914	3	4	13/01/1915	5	6			

Date			Date		
14/01/1915	8	7	27/02/1915	9	5
15/01/1915	5	7	28/02/1915	4	5
16/01/1915	5	7	01/03/1915	3	5
17/01/1915	2	6	02/03/1915	7	5
18/01/1915	1	5	03/03/1915	5	5
19/01/1915	7	5	04/03/1915	13	7
20/01/1915	2	4	05/03/1915	7	7
21/01/1915	6	4	06/03/1915	13	7
22/01/1915	4	4	07/03/1915	0	7
23/01/1915	3	4	08/03/1915	5	7
24/01/1915	2	4	09/03/1915	11	8
25/01/1915	4	4	10/03/1915	6	8
26/01/1915	6	4	11/03/1915	6	7
27/01/1915	2	4	12/03/1915	8	7
28/01/1915	6	4	13/03/1915	4	6
29/01/1915	6	4	14/03/1915	3	6
30/01/1915	3	4	15/03/1915	7	6
31/01/1915	0	4	16/03/1915	15	7
01/02/1915	3	4	17/03/1915	2	6
02/02/1915	1	3	18/03/1915	9	7
03/02/1915	7	4	19/03/1915	20	9
04/02/1915	23	6	20/03/1915	6	9
05/02/1915	4	6	21/03/1915	5	9
06/02/1915	3	6	22/03/1915	4	9
07/02/1915	0	6	23/03/1915	17	9
08/02/1915	2	6	24/03/1915	15	11
09/02/1915	8	7	25/03/1915	8	11
10/02/1915	3	6	26/03/1915	13	10
11/02/1915	9	4	27/03/1915	7	10
12/02/1915	5	4	28/03/1915	0	9
13/02/1915	12	6	29/03/1915	12	10
14/02/1915	3	6	30/03/1915	14	10
15/02/1915	3	6	31/03/1915	8	9
16/02/1915	2	5	01/04/1915	4	8
17/02/1915	14	7	02/04/1915	0	6
18/02/1915	4	6	03/04/1915	6	6
19/02/1915	10	7	04/04/1915	4	7
20/02/1915	3	6	05/04/1915	7	6
21/02/1915	3	6	06/04/1915	10	6
24/02/1915	3	6	07/04/1915	14	6
23/02/1915	4	6	08/04/1915	11	7
24/02/1915	4	4	09/04/1915	7	8
25/02/1915	4	4	10/04/1915	8	9
26/02/1915	6	4	11/04/1915	0	8

12/04/1915	7	8
13/04/1915	18	9
14/04/1915	13	9
15/04/1915	14	10
16/04/1915	5	9
17/04/1915	2	8
18/04/1915	6	9
19/04/1915	5	9
20/04/1915	5	7
21/04/1915	10	7
22/04/1915	3	5
23/04/1915	3	5
24/04/1915	10	6
25/04/1915	5	6
26/04/1915	3	6
27/04/1915	18	7
28/04/1915	22	9
29/04/1915	23	12
30/04/1915	26	15
01/05/1915	7	15
02/05/1915	6	15
03/05/1915	11	16
04/05/1915	12	15

Figure 1

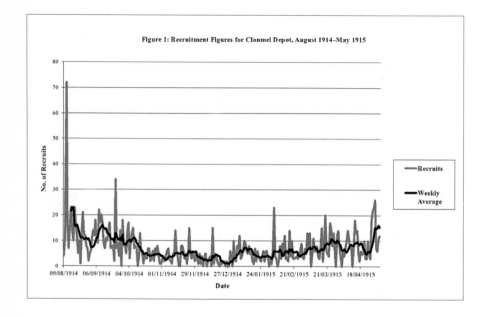

Figure 1: Recruitment Figures for Clonmel Depot, August 1914–May 1915

Index

Note: Page references in bold refer to tables and illustrations.